Framework on Academic Achievement and Leadership Qualities

Framework on Academic Achievement and Leadership Qualities

Edited by

Dr. S.K. PANNER SELVAM

Assistant Professor, Department of Education

Bharathidasan University, T.N

and

Dr. R. SUMATHI

Principal,

Cheran College of Education,

Karur, Tamil Nadu.

RANDOM

RANDOM PUBLICATIONS

NEW DELHI (INDIA)

Framework on Academic Achievement and Leadership Qualities

ISBN 978-93-5111-890-9

Published in 2016 in India by

RANDOM PUBLICATIONS

4376-A/4B, Gali Murari Lal, Ansari Road
New Delhi-110 002
Phone : +9111-43580356, 011-43142548, 011-23289044
e-mail : sales@randompublications.com
info@randompublications.com
randomexports@gmail.com

Reprinted 2026

Type Setting by : Shah Computer Graphics, Delhi-110094

Contents

Chapter-I

Failure Tolerance Among High School Students

Introduction

Education is usually understood as a course of study to acquire a body of knowledge or skills undertaken to enhance one's ability to do a particular job and be able to earn more money. The more liberal definitions of education, where it is understood as development and refinement of one's personality, without necessarily an eye to economic advantage, have been out of use for long and one finds only scattered instance of the practice of education with such aims.

Education plays an important role in molding the personality of children. Social adjustment is one of the important aims of education. In order to equip the child with necessary skills and information, concepts and attitudes and to enable him to adjust properly in his environment, our society has formulated a separate organization called school where he can develop all qualities and abilities, according to the social needs of the society.

In its broadest sense, Education can he equated with learning. Learning can be defined as change in mental process and overt behavior as a result of experience.

Education

Education is the systematic development and cultivation of the natural powers. Education includes all the processes that develop human ability and behavior. It is an organized and sustained instruction designed to communicate a combination of knowledge, skills and understanding valuable for all the activities of life.

Education is the reconstruction of events that compose the lives of individuals that new happenings and events become more powerful and more meaningful. Education is the process of initiating the child into the ways of adult life. It is the deliberate and systematic influence, exerted by the mature person upon the immature, through instruction, discipline and harmonious development of physical, intellectual, aesthetic, social and spiritual powers of the human beings.

The function of education is considered to be the adjustment of man to his environment, which means his adaptation to and reconstruction of his surroundings for his own benefit and that of society. It is a dynamic force and as such brings about the reorganization and reconstruction of human experience.

Thus, education is not a new process, it is as old as mankind, but it is receiving new interpretation. Education has been recognized by all thinkers as a manifold process of aiding the individual to come into full possession of all the desirable features of his heritage.

Scientific education is a powerful means of developing attitudes of critical enquiry, respect for truth, simplicity, adaptability and systematic work which are pre-requisites for initiating the process of social change and of national development.

Education is a dynamic force in the life of every individual, influencing the physical, mental, emotional, social and ethical development. It may be interpreted to cannot the process through which experience or information is gained or it may be used to indicate the research of such training, or the product of the learning process. Using the connotation of the term, education implies experience, insight and adjustment on the part of the learner, who is stimulated towards growth and development.

Today, education has been conceptualized as a factor that promotes economic growth and therefore, is an important area for investment. More nations are recognizing their responsibility in the area of education. In many countries, investment in education is increasingly seen as investment for economic growth and as a means to improve and create new knowledge, new technologies and new ways of managing the environment. To cope with the demands of the 21st century as rightly pointed out by Dr. Malcom Adiseshiah (1978), "Education must become more that what it is today; it should be both the reflection and the active agent of change, pushing and promoting essential or desirable changes in man and society in innovation, ranging from renovated systems of teacher training to the use of space satellites.

Meaning of Education

The act or process of education and the result of education, as determined by the knowledge, skill or discipline of character is acquired and the process is unending. The act or process or training by prescribed or customary course of study or discipline-as, an education for the bar or the pulpit-has a finishing point and we say the student has finished his education.

The Destiny of India is now being shaped in her classrooms (Kothari, 1966). Education is the most essential human value. Knowledge is developed through literacy and education.

Definition of Education

JOHN DEWEY writes the Education is the process of living through a continuous reconstruction of experience. It is the development of all these capacities in the individual, which will enable him to control his environment and fulfill his responsibilities.

Education meets the immediate needs of a child and also prepares him for his future life. It develops all his intellectual and emotional powers, so that he is able to meet the problems of life squarely and solve them successfully. It also develops the social qualities of service, tolerance, co-operation and fellow feeling. “Education is a key that open the eyes of a person towards the brightness of the world”- **Dr. Radhakrishnan.**

“The Central task of education is to implant a will and facility for learning; it should produce not learned but learning people. The “truly human society is a learning society, where grandparents, parents and children are students together”- **Eric Hoffer.**

No one has yet realized the wealth of sympathy, the kindness and generosity hidden in the soul of a child. The effort of every true education should be to unlock that treasure- **Emma Goldman**

“The only purpose of education is to teach a student how to live his life-by developing his mind and equipping him to deal with reality. The training he needs is theoretical, i.e., conceptual. He has to be taught to think understand, to integrate to provide. He has to be taught the essentials of the knowledge discovered in the past-and he has to be equipped to acquire further knowledge by his own effort”- **Ayn Rand**

The aim of education should be to teach us rather how to think, than what to think rather to improve our minds, so as to enable us to think for ourselves, than to load the memory with the thoughts of other men"- **Bill Beattie**

The Concept of Education

The word education is derived from two Latin words. They are Edure and Educere. Educere means to bring up and to nourish. Educere means to bring forth and propulsion from internal to external. Education is the modification of behavior in a controlled environment. The term education in the widest sense may be held to include the whole process of development through which a human being passes from infancy to maturity.

Education is the aggregate of all the processes by means of which a person develops abilities, attitudes and other forms of behaviour of positive value in the society in which he lives.

Gandhiji defined education in the following quote. "By Education 1 ilk all round drawing out of the, best in child and man; body, mind and spirit.

Need of Education

Across countries, education plays a vital role not only in acquiring knowledge but also inculcating social, ethical, moral and spiritual values. In our model, schooling teaches people to interact with others and raises the benefits of civic participation including voting and organizing. Education raises the benefits of civic participation. Education is able to instill in the child a sense of maturity and responsibility in bringing in him the desired changes. According to this needs and demands of ever changing society of which he is an integral part.

Importance of Education

The importance of education is quite clear. Education is the knowledge of putting one's potentials to maximum use. One can safely say that a human being is not in the proper sense complete till he is educated.

The second reason for the importance of education is that only through the attainment of education, man is enabled to receive information from the external world; to acquaint himself with past history and receive all necessary information regarding the present. Without education, main is as though in a closed room and with education he finds himself in room with all its windows open towards outside world.

Aims of Education

Life is very complex and complicated. But an aim in life can make the complex life simple and purposeful. Aims give us direction to work and without aim, destination, or objective life becomes incomplete and haphazard.

Individual has different interests, attitudes and needs. Every individual wants to achieve certain goals in life. But a clear-cut aim makes the road of life easy. Educational aims are varied. Such as knowledge aim.

Indian Education Commission (1964-66) under the chairmanship of Dr.D.S.Kothari suggested the following as the aims of education in a democratic set-up.

(i) Increasing productivity

(ii) Developing social and national integrity

(iii) Making education modernized and

(iv) Cultivating of social, moral and spiritual values.

Aims of High School Education

To Acquire Real Scientific Knowledge

The study of science consists of learning certain facts, which deals with environment, which is formulated by our natural world. The students should be taught that they may be able to use the knowledge of those things for the betterment and development of their country or in other words the teaching of science be geared to requirements of life.

To Develop in the Capacity to Solve Problem

Students should be given opportunity to know various problems related to life and to solve the same. In science we come across several problems that are created by the environment and circumstances. So, students should be taught to solve problems.

Development of Aptitude

At this stage of education we find that the students have developed psychological aptitudes and interest. The student should be encouraged to develop their aptitudes and interests by providing the opportunity for them to exercise their power of reasoning, observation, intelligence, psychological and scientific outlook.

To Develop Sense of Appreciation

Students should be trained so as to develop appreciation for the achievement of various scientists and to understand the cause and effect relationship. They should also be taught to appreciate various natural factors and natural phenomena.

To Develop Interest of Pupil in Learning Science

By the teaching of science various interests of the pupils should be developed. Psychologists have proved that students concentrate their attention on the objectives and the things that are of interest to them. If we want to success in developing their interest in certain scientific facts and principles we shall be able to help them achieve the objectives of education.

To Develop in Students the Knowledge Required For High Education

After high school level some students go for high education. This can be done only if the young pupils have thirst for knowledge. Science teaching should try to inculcate in pupils the desire to acquire further knowledge of the subject.

To Develop Practical Skill

The student is capable of doing experiments individually at this stage the student manipulate the apparatus, performs experiments, records observation and draws inferences. Making use of this, the science teacher must provide opportunity for simple experiments and practical work which may help for his future life.

Education And Society

Education is very important for an individual's success in life. Education provides pupils teaching skills that prepare them physically, mentally and socially for the world of work in later life. Education is generally seen as the foundation of society which brings economic wealth, social prosperity and political stability. High education helps in maintaining a healthy society which prepares health care professionals, educated health care consumers and maintaining healthy population. Education is major aspect of development of any modern society since if there is a deficit of educated people then society will stops its further progress. Government should pay serious attention to education and support it economically and morally all over the country.

Education is the best investment for the people because well educated people have more opportunities to get a job which gives them satisfaction. Educated individuals enjoy respect among their colleagues and they can effectively contribute to the development of their country and society by inventing new devices and discoveries. Today's ever growing numbers of people mostly are not satisfied with their basic education and try to get high education in order to meet the demands of contemporary society. Some of them enter high educational institutions and some search additional information on the internet. Good People sacrifices their time and money and sometimes even their health to raise educational level because they realize that education is their passport to the future and for tomorrow.

Main purpose of education is to educate individuals within society, to prepare and qualify them for work in economy as well as to integrate - people into society and teach them values and morals of society. Role of education is means of socializing individuals and to keep society smoothing and remain stable. Education in society prepares youngsters for adulthood so that they may form the next generation of leaders. It will yield strong families and strong 'communities. Indeed, parents taking an active role in their child education produce a willingness in children to learn Education and society provides a forum where teachers and scholars all over the world are able to evaluate problems in education and society from a balanced and comparative social and economic perspective.

Education is an important aspect of the work of society and it will raise the countryside issues and promote knowledge and understanding of rural communities. One of the education essential tasks is to enable people to understand themselves. Students must be equipped with knowledge and skills which arc needed to participate effectively as member of society and contribute towards the development of shared values and common identity. Education has a vital role to play in assisting students to understand their cultural identity. Education acts as the distribution mechanism of the cultural values such as it more layered the society and participate in society that carries the culture.

Education and society provides a forum where teachers and scholars all over the world are able to evaluate problems in education and society from a balanced and comparative social and economic perspective. Education is an important aspect of the work of society and it will raise the countryside issues and promote knowledge and understanding of rural communities. One of the education essential tasks is to enable people to understand themselves. Students must be equipped with-knowledge and skills which are needed to participate effectively as member of society and contribute towards the development of shared values and common identity.

Education has a vital role to play in assisting students to understand their cultural identity. Education acts as the distribution mechanism of the cultural values such as it more layered the society and participate in society that carries the culture. In our culture today, there is a great emphasis on high education. In a society, more educated you are, better off you are. Every society has specialized individuals that require extended education to fulfill certain main positions. These persons are normally known as professors, priests, doctors, mechanics or artists. Education has been a high part of every culture on earth and education is a systemic project. Whole society should care for and support the education patriotism, cause and socialism among the young people.

Everyone must do work hard to cultivate moral conduct. Education mainly begins at home; one does not acquire knowledge from a teacher, one can learn and get knowledge from a parent or a family member. In almost all societies, receiving education and attending school is very necessary is one wants to achieve success. Education is the key to move in the world, seek better jobs and ultimately succeed in life. Schools play a vital role in preparing our children and young people for effective participation; and responsible citizenship in society. The development of education and educational opportunities is built on creativity tempered by knowledge and wisdom gain through the experience of learning.

Investment in human capital, lifelong learning and quality education help in the development of society. Teachers are the most important factors for an innovative society because teachers' knowledge and skills not only enhance the quality and efficiency of education, but also improve the prerequisites of research and innovation. Many members of our society are not provided with a safe and secure environment in which children can develop, child abuse, violence against women and interpersonal violence cause a cancer on our society. Society plays a key role in the realization of lifelong learning. The improvement of social education facilities such as libraries and the learning opportunities are implemented by the local governments. Students today are exposed to loads of technology and information at everywhere.

Purpose of Education

The purpose of education is dependent on the form of the family and society, and the historical context and place an individual is raised within. Our American form of society is primarily a representative democracy founded on the principles in the Declaration of Independence and the Constitution as amended. The current context is one of rapid economic globalization oriented towards knowledge-based industries aimed at increasing human longevity and enhancing human capabilities.

This form of society recognizes the individual as being the source of legitimate authority and responsible for both self-conduct and the preservation of the society. Such a society is constituted of ever- expanding spheres of local autonomy, beginning with the individual and proceeding outward through the family and voluntary associations, followed by city, county, regional, national and global political jurisdictions. The importance of each sphere of local autonomy is directly proportional to the closeness to the individual, who holds ultimate responsibility, through their representatives, for the consequences of the exercise of delegated authority and power. The most important sphere of local autonomy is the individual and the immediate family and the least important are global jurisdictions.

Individuals within our form of society have a dignity that cannot be taken away from them by any power on earth because of their unique moral capacity; they are their own masters, they choose their own ends and do not have their ends chosen for them. Individuals are recognized as created beings; they did not create themselves and cannot give away the rights and responsibilities that come to them from outside themselves.

Due to this inherent dignity and as the individual source of political authority, learning self-control is vital to educational success. Students develop self-control through learning to obey authority that they accept as legitimate. It student never learn to obey others, they can hardly learn to obey their own internal restraints; they will have recurring, trouble resisting harmful vices or issuing orders while leaving people's tact.

They will, therefore, have difficulty achieving happiness or Justice. Parents and teachers are obeyed because they possess superior knowledge that students both need and desire, exhibiting a natural hierarchy.

Desiring to excel at acquiring knowledge develops the kind of character necessary for the preservation of our form of society. Developing character and achieving happiness is the terminology of secular education; within religious education, this is called the formation of the soul, both types of education are prevalent in our society. To develop character means to refine our coarse emotional states and base desires into civilized and tasteful emotional states and high desires. It also means to seek the truth, in community with others, sharing common meanings within a clear and practical language, doing good oneself and promoting good in the larger spheres of local autonomy.

Early examples of democratic local autonomy were the Ancient Greeks and Renaissance Europeans. The classical liberal arts curriculum of grammar, rhetoric, logic and arithmetic was developed because these building blocks met the needs of this form of society. These building blocks remain sound for our representative democracy and our knowledge-based global economy because they provide necessary learning within the fundamental realms of meaning, truth and purpose.

Grammar is necessary for all the social sciences broadly addressing meaning. Arithmetic and logic are necessary for all the natural sciences broadly addressing truth. Rhetoric is necessary for all the arts and humanities broadly addressing.

Once these basics have been mastered, the student has the conceptual tools necessary to go deeper into any single fundamental realm or into interdisciplinary areas between realms. Teachers guide students into studies of works proven to have permanent worth, as Matthew Arnold put it, "the best that has been thought and said." A student might choose "to learn more between the realms of meaning and purpose, such as law or anthropology, or between the realms of purpose and truth, such as medicine or engineering, or between the realms of truth and meaning, such as economic or business (see World-of-Education Map below).

The most general learning, relying equally on the tripod of the basic curriculum within all three realms, is in the areas of history, philosophy, politics and religious thought. This is the knowledge all individuals within representative democracies should attempt to achieve, at least to the degree that informed decisions are possible. Representatives themselves require this most generalized knowledge during periods of rapid technological, indeed, revolutionary changes of unknown scope duration. The purpose of education is the preservation and enhancement of knowledge and the development of character within our given form of society which will best prepare the individual for the conditions of extreme novelty the near future is bringing

Failure Tolerance

Fear of failure and failure tolerance are the tow ends of the spectrum of failure. As the Fear of Failure increases, the Failure tolerance decreases and vice versa.

Research by McClelland and his associates yield evidence suggesting that there are two recognizable aspects of achievement motivation.

(i) Hope of success and
(ii) Fear of Failure one is an approach motive involving anticipation of and the other an avoidance motive involving anticipation of punishment.

Fear of Failure was evidenced in needed achievements situations where some subjects reacted to the aroused treatments with a sense of Fear this observation was used in the development of the concept, for Fear of Failure by several researchers who conceptualized the construct, in their own way. Adkinson, concerned fear of failure as a disposition to inhibit one's achievements striving on penalty of pain, the avoidance motive inhibiting achievement orientation in order to avoid failure, the possibility of failure and the disincentive value of failure.

For Henckhansen the fare of failure surrounds that one will not be able to camp etc. with the standard of excellence, appropriate to the task in question.

Birney and others combined well both Adkinson and Hechhansen's concept of fear of failure compensating for the limitations in these concepts.

Birney is situation-oriented where as Atkinson conceives it as task-oriented. When Birney and others understand, by fear of failure in that people differ in the degree to which they fear the three possible consequence of an achievements out-come, viz devaluation of the self estimate, ego punishment and social devaluation. Three corresponding defenses develop in reaction to the three possible anticipations about the outcome of the act, defense against the loss in self-estimate defense against punishment and defense against loss in social value.

Therefore for some people the fear may be directed at the lowering of the self estimate, for others to a concern with lowering of their worth in the eyes of others and still for others to the loss of reward that is associated with non-attainment of the goal, This concept of fear of the goal. This concept of fear of failure has been made use in assessing failure tolerance of pupil, in this study.

School failure is a process where a student slips farther and farther behind his peers and gradually disconnects from the educational system. The end result of school failure is dropping out before graduation. Many cases of school failure happen among students who have the ability and intelligence to succeed but who are unable or unwilling to apply these abilities in the school setting.

Students can begin the slide into failing patterns at any time during their school career, but school failure is more likely to occur at transitional stages, such as when graduating from elementary to middle school or after a family move to a new school system. Failing grades typically are symptoms of emotional, behavioral, or learning problems.

Meaning of Failure Tolerance

The repercussions of this gap extend far beyond the schoolhouse doors. In a society as competitive as ours is today - where a person's income is so closely linked with their education - the importance of academic achievement cannot be understated. Educational success in the form of degrees and awards correlates to job prospects, and as such contributes to a student's ûlture socio-economic status (Taniguchi, 2005). According to the U.S. Bureau of Labor Statistics, as of 2013, the median weekly meanings for an individual with a bachelor's degree are $1,066, whereas the analogous earnings for an individual with only a high school diploma are $652, and $471 for less than a high school diploma. As of 2010, according to the U.S. Census, 30.9% of whites are college graduates, whereas the comparative number only amounts to 17% for African-Americans. If nonwhite students are consistently and overwhelmingly underperforming in school relative to white students, historic racial inequalities are being constantly perpetuated.

An alternative perspective of this problem is considering the idea of an "opportunity gap" rather than an "achievement gap. "Achievement" suggests a failure on the part of the student; but if the same gap is being seen nationwide, focusing on the individual student might not be so telling. Considering a gap in the opportunities the students are presented with, however, broadens the focus to underlying structural and cultural factors that may play a hand in this outcome.

Recently, disciplinary measures have been examined as another area where racial disparities exist in schools. Research indicates nonwhite students are more likely to be punished for their behavior in school than white students (Fenning, 2007). Disciplinary measures in school can take many forms, from notifying a parent or legal guardian about a- students' behavior to more severe and punitive actions, such as exclusionary discipline. Exclusionary discipline includes any corrective measure that requires the student he removed from their normal educational environment-typically, suspension and expulsion.

Exclusionary discipline has not always been a national favorite. Prior to its popularity, student behavior was treated as an in-house matter and teachers distributed punishment as they saw fit according to context, usually in a case-by-case manner. That changed however, in the late 1980s and 1990s when exclusionary discipline became hugely fashionable (Skiba, 2012). Like the culture of fear surrounding drugs in America that prevailed throughout the 1980 (which coincided with more punitive drug policy), that same time period was characterized by a culture of fear surrounding violence in schools. As such, in 1986, the Reagan Administration recommended legislation that would require schools nationally to adopt a "failure tolerance" disciplinary policy (Skiba, 2012). Although the bill was ultimately thrown out, the culture of fear "remained, and official school policies across the country began to adopt ideas of "no-nonsense" and ultimately, failure tolerance. As a result, schools increased the number and length of suspensions and expulsions and expanded the list of specific infractions that warranted such measures (e.g., sometimes including dress-code violations and failure to complete homework).

Definition of Failure Tolerance

The behavior of bothering about the failure can be termed as 'Fear (or) Failure. The act of not bothering about the failure can be termed as failure tolerance.

Reasons For Failure

Failure, just like abandoning one's studies, is never due to a single cause but to an accumulation of reasons. Singling out one can be deceptive and dangerous.

There are always interconnections between internal and external factors to the student and blaming only the student or only the institution for failure is simplistic.

Internal Factors to the Student

1. Educational project not properly thought out, hesitation between several study choices
2. lack of commitment and motivation, lack of maturity, low inclination for effort, lack of self-confidence, fear of exams
3. problems in learning how to be a student
4. insufficient intellectual skills: school baggage, prerequisites, working methods (taking notes, listening memorizing, exam preparation)
5. inadequate personal skills: time management, concentration, emotional control
6. cultural or geographical gap
7. personal or financial problems

External Factors to the Student

1. Study year, study Program me
2. Studying conditions, supervision by the professors or assistants
3. Relevance of study plans, overloaded study programmers, ambiguous requirements by the professors
4. Exam selectiveness
5. Chance
6. People who fail in school may feel "stupid," but emotional or mental health problems and "hidden" learning disorders, not low intelligence, often are the root causes of their inability to meet the standards of a school. There are several factors that can lead to school failure, among them depression, anxiety, problems in the family, and learning disabilities.

Depression

Depression is one of the most common causes of school difficulties. It is a condition that can make people feel sad for long periods of time, have low energy and lose interest in activities that normally give them pleasure. People with depression have continuing negative thoughts about themselves and the future, and they may experience changes in eating and sleeping patterns and in their ability to concentrate and make decisions. They may feel hopeless and may even think about suicide. Depression has been shown to be leading cause of school failure in young people with learning disabilities. Depression can also cause school failure in students without learning disabilities.

Anxiety

Anxiety is a feeling of excessive worry about a possible danger or an uncomfortable situation that is intense enough to interfere with a person's ability to concentrate and focus. Students can have genuine reasons to be anxious. People who have been bullied at school may worry that they will be bullied again. Students may legitimately fear personal violence on the way to or from school. They might worry about their families going through a divorce or about a parent who is ill. On the other hand, ordinary adolescent worries about looking right and fitting in can be blown so far out of proportion that a student may try to be

1. Teens with learning disabilities or who feel anxiety about school may neglect schoolwork for other distracting activities.
2. Peter Arnold Inc.
3. Absent from school just to avoid a possibly embarrassing or uncomfortable situation. This is called "school avoidance." Anxiety in any of its forms can interfere with a student's performance in school.

Problems in the Family

Students also may bring their problems at home to school with them. If a student's family is experiencing violence, unemployment, alcohol or drug use by a family member, problems with the law, or any other upsetting experience, it can be difficult to concentrate on schoolwork. Many students who are having family problems might have trouble controlling their anger and frustration at school, and they may end up* in trouble because of their behavior. Some students who are overburdened at home by circumstances that make it necessary for them to "parent" siblings, hold a job, or care for an ill or impaired parent may find it impossible to keep up. Many times students who lace overwhelming family or personal problems keep these problems to themselves. School counselors can help support a student and prevent failure if they are made aware of the problem.

Learning Disabilities

Learning disabilities are conditions that interfere with gaining specific academic skills, such as reading or writing. Learning disorders can hinder a person's ability to concentrate or to process or remember information. When these difficulties are recognized early, certain teaching strategies can help a student overcome the learning disability. Unfortunately, many learning problems may go undiagnosed or may be diagnosed incorrectly as behavior problems. The frustration and depression that can result from undetected learning disabilities is a major cause of school failure or dropping out of school.

Other Causes

Many social factors can increase the risk of school failure. These include homelessness, poverty, frequent moves from school to school, and the inability to speak English. Other circumstances such as truancy, teenage pregnancy, and chronic illness may also affect a student's ability to do his or her best in school.

The Operational Definition

(a) Failure tolerance: The behavior of bothering about the failure can be termed as "fear of failure" the cat of not bothering about the failure can be termed as failure tolerance.

Regarding the specific effects on individual students who are suspended or expelled, the research follows several paths. One of these paths focused on the effects related to the fact that students are physically removed from the classroom, and as such, barred from participating in their education because of a suspension or expulsion. In 2003, Casella prefunded an ethnographic study between the years of 1997 to 2001 in two high schools, on several students who experienced exclusionary disciplinary measures as a result of their behavior. The findings from this research denote that once a student was expelled, completing school presented significant challenges. One of the challenges these students faced had to find a new school to attend after being excluded from their "home" school, or assigned school by the county. Furthermore, this research found that a perceived stigma is placed on a student when they are suspended or expelled, which makes readmission into the educational environment difficult and uncomfortable (Casella 2003.) This research supplements the study done by the APA by showing that "failure tolerance" is largely ineffectual on school climate, but also negative in its effect on individual students who encounter its policy.

Aside from the inequality inherent in the unequal application of suspensions and expulsions, research shows that these punishments can have severe and enduring consequences on the lives of individual students. In Skiba *et al.* 2006 conducted research linking the increase in suspensions and expulsions to an increased police presence in schools. Since the advent of "failure tolerance," and a shift towards "get tough" punitive measures for students, more and more schools have been engaging law enforcement into their services. This demonstrates that student problems once handled by teachers and principals are now being handled with handcuffs in a police department. This research showed that court referrals from schools have hugely increased since the 1990s. Because of this, failure tolerance policies directly contribute to the school-to-prison pipeline (Skiba *et al.* 2006.) Unfair distribution of the exclusionary policies may not just mean an academic injustice, but also an injustice regarding who is incarcerated. At the very least, these policies in schools widen the net for who is susceptible to incarceration.

Scope of the Study

This study would stimulate the students to think positively and the capacity to solve their daily problems in life. It reduces tension, confusion, anxiety, pressure and worries. The result of this study may keep our body always fresh, good in memory and problem solving capacity. This study would develop a good atmosphere around a student and it would also avoid the wastage of time in each student. It also helps to maintain a good relationship between the teacher and the students. This study would lift every student in somewhat high level than compared to their past level.

This study would build a strange and good character and also aims at developing physical and psychological strength. This study should create more self-confidence for each student and lead this life peacefully. This study would create a meaningful growth in students and also their mind would face any kind of problem and make it successful one.

For example, the students have fear, "When the teacher called them, this creates fear." To write the exam creates the failure among students. Fear and failure are interrelated. If a student is affected by the factors such as, comparison, helplessness, restlessness, loneliness, anxiety, insecurity, it would create a variety of problem and struggles in their studies as well as their daily work. Therefore it is necessary to failure tolerance among the High School students.

Need and Significance of the Study

Study and failure tolerance will help both the teachers and students to develop their challenging future and character building. Therefore this study will help the students to adopt a better and suitable position in the changing society.

Statement of the Problem

The present investigation aims to identify the how *"A critical study on Failure Tolerance among High School Students at Pattukkottai Educational District."*

This study is limited to the students in High School level. This survey is conducted at Pattukkottai Educational District. Variables such as sex, type of schools, Parent annual income, Failure Tolerance of the students are considered. And it focuses the area on Failure Tolerance among High school Students.

Objectives of the Study

The major objective of the study is to find out the **failure tolerance** among high school student at Pattukkottai district. The specific objectives of the study are

1. To find out whether there is any significant difference on failure tolerance among High School students on the basis of their **Boys and Girls.**
2. To find out whether there is any significant difference on failure tolerance among High School students on the basis of their type of school management as Government **school and Aided school.**
3. To find out whether there is any significant difference on failure tolerance among High School students on the basis of their type of school management as **Aided school and Private school.**
4. To find out whether there is any significant difference on failure tolerance among High School students on the basis of their type of school management as Government **school and Private school.**
5. To find out whether there is any significant difference between on failure tolerance among High School students on the basis of their Locality as Rural **and Urban.**
6. To find out whether there is any significant difference between on failure tolerance among High School students on the basis of their student's locality as **Hosteller and Day Scholar.**
7. To find out whether there is any significant difference between on failure tolerance among High School students on the basis of their family nature as **Nuclear and Joint Family.**

8. To find out whether there is any significant difference between on failure tolerance among High School students on the basis of their Parents Occupation **Self Employee and Private Employee.**

9. To find out whether there is any significant difference between on failure tolerance among High School students on the basis of their Parents Occupation **Private Employee and Government Employee.**

10. To find out whether there is any significant difference between on failure tolerance among High School students on the basis of their Parents Occupation **Self Employee and Government Employee.**

Hypotheses of the Study

1. There is no significant difference in the mean scores of High School students in failure tolerance on the basis of their **Boys and Girls.**

2. There is no significant difference in the mean scores of High School students in failure tolerance on the basis of their type of school management as **Government school and Aided school.**

3. There is no significant difference in the mean scores of High School students in failure tolerance on the basis of their type of school management as **Aided school and Private school.**

4. There is no significant difference in the mean scores of High School students in failure tolerance on the basis of their type of school management as **Government school and Private school.**

5. There is no significant difference in the mean scores of High School students in failure tolerance on the basis of their locality as **Rural and Urban.**

6. There is no significant difference in the mean scores of High School students in failure tolerance on the basis of their students locality **Hosteller and Day Scholar.**

7. There is no significant difference in the mean scores of High School students in failure tolerance on the basis of their family nature as **Nuclear and Joint family**

8. There is no significant difference in the mean scores of High School students in failure tolerance on the basis of their Parent Occupation **Self employee and Private employee**

9. There is no significant difference in the mean scores of High School students in failure tolerance on the basis of their Parent Occupation **Private Employee and Government employee.**

10. There is no significant difference in the mean scores of High School students in failure tolerance on the basis of their Parent Occupation **Self employee and Government Employee.**

Limitation of the Study

The investigation on the problems how A critical study on Failure Tolerance is restricted to 300 samples of data was collected in high school students at pattukkottai educational district" The Present Educational study survey was conducted in the duration of 2014 – 2015

Conclusion

This consists of five chapters. The first chapter which has been just conducted deal with the introduction, objectives and statement of the problem. The second chapter deals with the review of related literature of the study. The third chapter describes the methods and procedures of the study. I.e. design of the study and method of investigation. The fourth chapter presents the statistical analysis, interpretations of data finally the fifth chapter gives the summary findings, suggestions, recommendations and conclusion followed by bibliography and appendices.

Chapter- II

Review of Related Literature

Introduction

Review of related literature pertaining to a problem marks the researcher familiar with the summary of previous research, the writings of recognized experts, with what is already known, what is still unknown and untested and thus provides a background for the development of the present study. A review of related literature is an important pre-requisite for the planning and efficient execution of any investigation. As Best (1978) points and "A familiarity with the literature in any problem are helps the students to discover what is already known what others have attempted to find out, what methods of attack have been promising and disappointing and what problems remain to be solved."

The study of related literature gives the investigator an idea of the quantum of work done in the field makes him scrutinize the methodology used and directs him to work along useful lines. This brings the researchers to the proximity of the solution. It is in this context, studies, on failure tolerance among the students reviewed in the following pages in view of their relevance to the present study.

Once a topic has been decided upon, it is essential to review all relevant material which has bearing on the topic. It is necessary to show how the problem under investigation related literature is one of the first steps in the research process. It is a valuable guide to defining the problem, recognizing its significance, suggesting promising data gathering devices, appropriate study design and source of data.

Aggarwal (1966) state of related literature implies locating, reading and evaluating reports of research as well as reports of casual observations and opinions that are related to the individual's have planned research report."

In the words of Best (1997) "A brief summary of previous the research and the writings of recognized experts provide evidence that the research is familiar with what is still unknown and untested. Since effective research must be based upon past knowledge, this step helps to eliminate the duplication of what has been done and provides useful hypotheses and helpful suggestion for significant investigation."

Importance of Review of Related Literature

In the words of Good, "The key to the vast store house of published literature may open doors to sources of significant problems and explanatory hypothesis and provide helpful orientation for definition of the problem, background for selection of procedure, and comparative data for interpretation of results. (Best and Khan, 1993, p.155) in order to be truly creative and original, one must read extensively .and critically, one must read extensively and critically, one must read extensively and critically as a stimulus to think. "Besides enlarging the knowledge about the topic, writing a literature review will give the investigators to gain demonstrate skills in two areas.

Information Seeking

The ability to scan the literature efficiently using manual or computerized methods, to identify a set of useful articles and books.

Critical Appraisal

The ability to apply principals of analysis to identify unbiased and valid studies.

1. It enables the researcher to define his problem. The knowledge of related literature brings the researcher up-to date on the work which others have done and thus to state the objective clearly used concisely.
2. It helps the researcher to avoid unfruitful and useless problem area.
3. It helps the researcher to avoid duplications of well established facts.

4. It helps the researcher to understand the research Methodology which refers to the way; the study is to be conducted.
5. It helps the researcher to known about tool and instruments which proved to be useful in the previous studies.
6. The final important specific reason for reviewing the relating literature is to known about the recommendations of previous researchers listed in their studies for further research.

One of the essential aspects of research process is the review of related literature. It plays a crucial role in planning of the study.

Review of the related literature. Besides, allowing the researcher to acquaint with current knowledge in the field or area in which he is going to conduct his research, serves the following specific purpose.

1. By reviewing the related literature the researcher can avoid unfruitful and useless problem areas. He can select those area in which positive finding are very, likely to result and his endeavors would be likely to add to the knowledge in a meaningful way.
2. Through the review of related literature the researcher can avoid unintentional duplication of well established findings. It is no use to replicate a study when the stability and validity of its results have been clearly established.
3. The review of related literature gives the researcher an understanding of the research methodology which refers to the way the study is to be conducted. It helps the researcher to know about the tools and instruments which proved to be useful and promising the previous studies. The advantages of the related literature are also to provide insight into the statistical methods through which validity of results is to be established.
4. The final and important specific reason for reviewing the related literature is to know about the recommendations of previous researches listed in their studies for further research.

Need of Review For Related Literature

The review of literature is essential due to the following reasons:

1. One of the early steps in planning a research work in to review research done previously in the Particular area of interest and relevant area quantitative and qualitative analysis of this the research usually gives the worker the indication of the direction.
2. It is very essential for every investigator to be up - to - date in this

information about the literature, related to his own problem already done by others. It is considered the important pre-requisite to actual planning and conducting the study.

3. It avoids the replication of the study of findings to take an advantage from similar or related literature and regards to methodology, techniques of data collection, procedure adopted and conclusion drawn. He can justify his own endeavor in the field.

4. It provides as sources of problem of study, an analogy may be drawn for identifying the selecting his own problem of research. The researcher formulates his hypotheses on the basis of review of literature. It also provides the rationale for the study. The results and findings of the study can also be discussed at length.

The review of literature indicates the clear picture of the problem to be solved. The scholarship in the field can be developed by reviewing the literature of the field.

Objectives of Review of Literature

The review of literature serves the following purpose in conducting research work:

1. It provides theories, ideas, explanations or hypotheses which may prove useful in the formulation of a new problem.

2. It indicates whether the evidence already available solves the problem adequately without requiring further investigation. It avoids the replication.

3. It provides the sources for hypotheses. The researcher can formulate research hypotheses on the basis of available studies.

4. It suggests methods, procedure, source of data and statistical techniques appropriate to the solution of the problem.

5. It locates comparative data and findings useful in the interpretation and discussion of results. The conclusions drawn in thc rclatcd studies may be significantly compared and may be used the subject for the findings of the study.

6. It helps in developing experts and general scholarship of the investigator in the area investigated.

7. In contributes towards the accurate knowledge of the evidence or the literature in one's area of activity is a good avenue towards marking oneself, this knowledge is an Institution of high learning or a research organization.

Sources of Review of Literature

There are several of literatures which may be used for this purpose. These sources can be broadly classified into these heads.

1. Books and Text - Books material
2. The Periodical Literature and ‘
3. General References.

Books and Text Books Material

The most useful lift of books published in the English language is the Cumulative Book Index and Book Review Index, Books Review Digest, Subject Guide to Books indicates that Books are in print or pres or forthcoming books. National Union Catalogue is also useful for this purpose. There are a number of publications that locate specific references that cover particular area of knowledge the cumulative book index is published in the English language.

Source of information in the social science ‘organized’ by subject area and indexed by author and title, this work contains comprehensive list or reference books and monographs.

Periodicals

A periodical is defined as a publication issued in successive parts, usually at regular intervals, and as a rule, intended to be continued indefinitely. These include Yearbook, Documents, Almanacs, Newspapers, Magazines, International index to periodicals. Periodicals are generally placed in open shelves in the Periodical room: Their effective use is predicated on the use of the index to identify the articles on subject matter under the study.

The Education Index has served as a comprehensive index of practically all publications in the area education. Education Index, New York, Published monthly. Canadian Education Index, Ottawa published by the Council of Education. Current Index of Journals in Education, New York, it is published Monthly. Index of Doctoral Dissertations International. Ann Arbor, it is published annually and consolidates all dissertations accepted ‘American, Canadian and European Universities.’

Bibliographic Index, New York, this guide indexes by subject current bibliographies of publishers of published book and educational periodicals both in English and in foreign Languages.

Abstracts

Another type of reference guide is the abstracts, review, or digest. In addition to provide a systematized list or reference sources, it includes a summary of the contents. Usually the brief summaries of research studies are given in the form of abstract - Educational Abstracts in humanities.

ERIC Educational Documents Abstracts, Washington De, this annual publication includes abstracts of all reports which appeared in Resources in education for, the year. Education Abstracts, Psychological Abstracts and Sociological Abstracts are published including research studies in these disciplines.

A wide variety of indexes and general references can be found to cover almost any area in which the modem researcher might be interested.

Purpose of Review of Literature

The Purpose of review of Literature is given below:

1. Discovering important variable.
2. Distinguishing what has been done from what needs-to be done.
3. Synthesizing the available studies to have perspective.
4. Determining meanings, Relevance of the study and relationship with the study and its deviation from the available studies.
5. The main purpose of this review is to put the hypothesis to be examined in the research report into its proper context. (Edward L. Vockell, 1983)

Secondary purpose of this part of the report are to provide readers with guidelines regarding where they can look to find more information and to establish the author's credential by letting readers know that the researcher is aware of what has been going on with regard to the current and related topics.

Principles and Procedures For the Review of Literature

The Principles and Procedures for the Review of Literature are given below:

1. It is generally advisable to get first and over all view by consulting a general source, such as a text - book which is more likely to provide the meaning and nature of the concepts and variable or theoretical framework of the field. The logical starting point is to get a clear picture of the problem to be solved. A test — book usually provides

the theoretical aspects of the problem. It is very essential to develop deep understanding about the variable and field

2. After developing the insight about the general nature of his - problem, the investigator should review the empirical researches of the area. The best reference for this phase is the handbook of research. Encyclopedia of Educational Research, the Review of Educational Research and International Abstracts for more up to-date findings.

3. The research for library material, must be systematic and thorough. The investigator generally should start by collecting his references from the educational index. When a large number of references are to be copied, they should be typed because precision is required here.

4. The researcher should take note systematically in the light of such criteria as uniformity, accuracy and ease of assembly. The notes should be taken on the card. Each entry should be made separately; references should be recorded on front side of the card and content should be taken below and reverse side of it. Each note should be recorded carefully and accurately.

5. The investigator should take as complete notes as he might need. On the other hand, taking unnecessary notes is wasteful. The useful and necessary material should be recorded precisely. It would be better that similar sources are gathered. It is necessary that a general education of source, rather than simply a summary of its content be made. Such evaluation is necessary both in presenting the study in the review of literature, and in using the study as background for the interpretation of the findings of the study.

6. The actual note-taking process is always a difficult task for the researcher. He has to spend long hours in the library taking notes by hand. It is a very tedious job and leads to importance to carelessness and illegibility. He should make use of the facilities available in the library for this purpose.

Studies Related to Failure Tolerance

The bearing of failure tolerance in academic risk taking was provided by.

Clifford (1998) to engage freely in and preserve at optimally challenging tasks, one must also have to show tolerance for failure or error-making. Such tolerance is likely to influence one's level of risk-taking as well as one's response of failure. Consistent with this speculation the theory of constructive failure (Clifford, 1984) predicts that, moderate risk-taking or a preference for optimally challenging tasks will be accompanied by relatively positive response to failure, (e.g.) identification of the causes of failure (advice-seeking, strategy-change) support for this prediction has been demonstrated with college students who asked to predict the affects behavior of students experiencing academic failure under varying levels of risk (Kim and Clifford, 1988) observed the followings:

1. Students failure tolerance has been negatively co-related with academic risk taking (i.e. difficulty level of freely chosen problems)
2. School failure tolerance has been negatively co-related with accuracy of problem solutions
3. School failure tolerance is positively co-related with academic achievement.

The above reported brief survey of research studies with regard to the variable failure tolerance and family encouragement has provided a good theoretical perspective to formulate appropriate hypotheses and design suitable experimental techniques to verify the same.

Gould (1939) has made a similar suggestion when has pointed out that individuals with strong needs, to achieve may also have an intense fear of failure. The motive to avoid failure, function activities and individual away from anxiety related activities. Because they produce a then deny avoiding or inhibiting actions which might lead to failure, failure tension has been found to have debilitating effects on the performance of the students. This failure in turn is likely to lower the aspiration.

Lantz (1945) provided the experience of success and failure in a ball game form L of stand ford Benet scale was given prior to failure of success experience and form M which was comparable to form L was given after the experience of success or failure. Verbal behavior and personality pattern of the subject were judged as graphic rating scales before and after the success and failure experimental situations in comparison to a neutral group.

McClelland and Apicella (1947) investigated the effect of false failure scores on performance the experimenter with hold the normal reward of knowledge of satisfactory performance and instead told the subject that he was failing miserably. Failure stress and tasks were found to produce significant decrement on performance.

Williams (1947) induced failure by false failure scores failure was found to have impairment of performance on the digit symbol test.

Zelber (1950) when failure experience was provided found a decrement in recall and relearning. He accounted for this decrement on the basis of repression; of the item which the subject associated with failure. Zelber comments that the subject's performance progressively, deteriorated during the accumulation of failure, while actual failure experience was provided in the above reviewed studies.

Davilson (1956), Mcelelland and Apicella (1947) that previous failure has negative effect on performance in experimental situations in comparison to a neutral group. The effect of fear of failure on aspiration behavior is also supported by studies by Dembo (1931), Hausmann (1933), and Frank (1935) Gardner (1940).

The impact of failure on performance has been studied using laboratory experimental tasks. The experience of success and failure were induced in experimental situation differently by different researches.

Birney (1969) and other combined well both Atkinson's and Heckhausaen's concepts of fear of failure compensating for the limitations in these concepts. Birney and others view fear of failure as situation oriented where as Atkinson conceives it task oriented. What Birney and others understand by fear of failure is that people differ in the degree to which they fear the three possible consequences of an achievement outcome, viz, devaluation of the self estimate, non ego punishment and social devaluation. Three corresponding defenses develop in reaction to the three possible anticipations about the outcome of the act, defense against loss in social value. Therefore for some people the fear may be directed at the lowering of self estimate, for others to a concern with covering of their worth in the eyes of the others and still for the others to the loss of rewards.

Attainment of failure in task induces fear of failure and their fear of failure is likely to have a debilitating effect on performance in a succeeding task. This attained failure is also likely to affect the aspiration behavior.

Mcelelland (1969) and his associates stressed that adequate understanding of achievement behavior would have to include failure motivation

CONCLUSION

The study of related literature has helped the investigator to have a clear perspective of the problem chosen for the present investigations. Designing the method of research, description of the variable, sample selection, selection of suitable tools, administration and scoring methods of responses have been undertaken based on the review which is discussed in the succeeding chapter.

Chapter-III

Methodology

Introduction

"Research is a power of suspending judgment with patience, of meditation with pleasures of asserting with caution of correcting with scrupulous pain" – Francis Bacon.

Webster has defined methodology as "the science of method or arrangement." Method is defined as orderliness and regularly or habitual practice of them in action. By placing stress on 'arrangement ', orderliness, regularly and habitual practice, the methodologies derive their substance essentially form the classically ideal controlled experiment which permeates in the literature of educational research. The methodology is decided with reference to research or the type of inquiry.

Research methodology involves systematic procedures starting from the initial identification of the problem to its final conclusions. Its role is to carry on the research work in a scientific and valid manner.

It provides the tools and techniques by which the research problem is analyzed. It consists of procedures and techniques and techniques for conducting a study. It is of little value unless used properly. Proper use must be learnt by the researcher.

It involves such general activates as identifying problem, review of the literature, formulating hypotheses, procedure for testing hypotheses, measurement, data collections. Thus, it all general and specific activities of research.

Mastery in it enhances understanding of the research activities. Thus research design and methodology have the identical meaning of mapping strategy of research.

The research methods must be appropriate to the objectives of the study. If you perform a case study of one commuter in order to investigate users' perceptions of the efficiency of public transport in Bangkok, your method is obviously unsuited to your objectives.

Methodology

1. "The analysis of the principles of methods, rules and postulations, employed by a discipline."
2. "The systematic study of methods that are can be, or have been applied within a discipline."

Concept

Methodology may be a description of process, or may be expanded to include a philosophically coherent collection of theories, concepts or ideas as they relate to a particular discipline or field of inquiry.

Methodology may refer to nothing more than a simple set of methods or procedures, or it may refer to the rationale and the philosophical assumptions that underline a particular study relative to the scientific method.

Research Design

This chapter presents details regarding the following.

1. Selection of Dependent variables and Categorical variables.
2. Constriction of tools to measure the students Failure Tolerance.
3. Methods of establishing the reliability and validity of the tools constructed.
4. Sampling procedure adopted in this study
5. Scheduling the survey and collecting the data.

The word survey indicated the gathering of data regarding current condition. Survey is an important type of study. It involves a clearly defined problem and defined objectives of the research. Strategy employed, tool used, sample technique employed and data collection procures followed are outlined.

Statement of the Problem

The present investigation aims to identify the how *"A critical study on Failure Tolerance among High School Students at Pattukkottai Educational District."*

This study is limited to the students in High School level. This survey is conducted at Pattukkottai Educational District. Variables such as sex, type of schools, Parent occupation, Failure Tolerance of the students are considered. And it focuses the area on Failure Tolerance among High school Students.

Objectives of the Study

The major objective of the study is to find out the failure tolerance among high school student at Pattukkottai district. The specific objectives of the study are:

1. To find out whether there is any significant difference on failure tolerance among High School students on the basis of their **Boys and Girls.**
2. To find out whether there is any significant difference on failure tolerance among High School students on the basis of their type of school management as Government **school and Aided school.**
3. To find out whether there is any significant difference on failure tolerance among High School students on the basis of their type of school management as **Aided school and Private school.**
4. To find out whether there is any significant difference on failure tolerance among High School students on the basis of their type of school management as Government **school and Private school.**
5. To find out whether there is any significant difference between on failure tolerance among High School students on the basis of their Locality as Rural **and Urban.**
6. To find out whether there is any significant difference between on failure tolerance among High School students on the basis of their student's locality as **Hosteller and Day Scholar.**
7. To find out whether there is any significant difference between on failure tolerance among High School students on the basis of their family nature as **Nuclear and Joint Family.**
8. To find out whether there is any significant difference between on failure tolerance among High School students on the basis of their Parents Occupation **Self Employee and Private Employee.**

9. To find out whether there is any significant difference between on failure tolerance among High School students on the basis of their Parents Occupation **Private Employee and Government Employee.**

10. To find out whether there is any significant difference between on failure tolerance among High School students on the basis of their Parents Occupation **Self Employee and Government Employee.**

Hypotheses of the Study

1. There is no significant difference in the mean scores of High School students in failure tolerance on the basis of their **Boys and Girls**.

2. There is no significant difference in the mean scores of High School students in failure tolerance on the basis of their type of school management as **Government school and Aided school.**

3. There is no significant difference in the mean scores of High School students in failure tolerance on the basis of their type of school management as **Aided school and Private school.**

4. There is no significant difference in the mean scores of High School students in failure tolerance on the basis of their type of school management as **Government school and Private school.**

5. There is no significant difference in the mean scores of High School students in failure tolerance on the basis of their locality as Rural **and Urban.**

6. There is no significant difference in the mean scores of High School students in failure tolerance on the basis of their students locality **Hosteller and Day Scholar.**

7. There is no significant difference in the mean scores of High School students in failure tolerance on the basis of their family nature as **Nuclear and Joint family**

8. There is no significant difference in the mean scores of High School students in failure tolerance on the basis of their Parent Occupation **Self employee and Private employee**

9. There is no significant difference in the mean scores of High School students in failure tolerance on the basis of their Parent Occupation **Private Employee and Government employee.**

10. There is no significant difference in the mean scores of High School students in failure tolerance on the basis of their Parent Occupation **Self employee and Government Employee.**

Limitation of the Study

The investigation on the problems how **Failure Tolerance** is restricted to 300 samples of data was collected in High School Students at Pattukkottai Educational District" The Present Educational study survey was conducted in the duration of 2014 – 2015.

Research Method

The investigator preferred Random- Sampling method for the present study. In this study, the investigator used Survey method to collect data and to identify the "A Critical study on Failure Tolerance among High School Students at Pattukkottai Educational District."

Research Tools

In the present study, the investigation selected questionnaire as the most important tools for collecting data because it is used increasingly to enquire into the current conditions, opinions and attitude of a groups.

The word 'tool' is defined a means to collect evidence

W. Best observes that the questionnaire is the mostly used tool in collecting both quantitative and qualitative information, for the present study questionnaire was prepared with a view to gather information in detail regarding the "Failure Tolerance among High School Students at Pattukkottai Educational District."

Construction of Research Tools

The research tool on "Failure Tolerance among High School Students at Pattukkottai Educational District" was constructed by the investigator in the present study. All the question items are closed type. The correct answers were given scores and these score were considered for data analysis.

Samples of the Study

As the entire high school students studying at Pattukkottai Educational District. Could not be taken for the present study due to time constraint. The 300 students following have been taken as sample to represent the whole population.

Description of Research Tool and Scoring Procedure

Before administering the test necessary instruction and directions were given to the students. No time limit is given to the students were asked to complete the inventory as early as possible. It is a **Five Point** of liker's types of tool.

The scale is

1. Strongly Agree (SA)
2. Moderately Agree (MA)
3. Undecided (UD)
4. Moderately Disagree (MD)
5. Strongly Disagree (SD)

Pilot Study

The pilot stage is concerned with refining the items collected. The collected items were presented before the export with a request to offer their considered opinion regarding the suitability objectively clarity and relevancy of the statement collected from different sources.

The pilot study is an initial study which is conducted by the investigator to know more about the research problem in various aspects. Based on the pilot study, the main study was conducted by the investigator while administering the research in the pilot study, some doubts were raised by their doubts and difficulties. Based on that, the investigator modified the items.

Further, the investigator obtained some ideas from the experts and modified the irrelevant. Item that is coming in the present study .After getting response from the respondents, the investigator gave frequencies for the correct response and these frequencies were converted into scores and those were used to establish reliability.

Validity of the Tool

In validation process, the investigator used two measures in order to establish validation of tools. The first measures of validation are called reliability. The second measure of validation process is called validity. The investigator established content validity.

To find out the validity of research tool, the investigator discussed each and every item of the questionnaire with the experts in the relevant field of Failure Tolerance of High School Students at Pattukkottai Educational District." Based the opinion of the expert the objectivity and worthies of the items of the questionnaire established.

In the valuation pro, the investor used two measures in order to establish addition of the tools. The first measure of validation is and reliability. The second measure of validation process is called limit. The investigator established content validity to find out the validity of research tool, the investigator discussed each and every item of the questionnaire. It he experts in the relevant field to identify the' "Failure Tolerance among High School Students at Pattukkottai Educational District." Based on the opinion of the experts, the objectivity and worthiness of the items of the questionnaire were established. The investigator also modified some of the items in the questionnaire and some item were eliminated. This kind of scientific procedure helped the investigator to established sufficient content validity.

Reliability of the Tool

The reliability of questionnaire on indentifying the "Failure Tolerance among High School Students at Pattukkottai Educational District." was established by making a rational equivalence method. The reliability of the tool refers to the internal consistency observed in measurement of reliability.

Garett (1979) Reliability is the consistency with which a tool measures what it measure. In the present study, the typical test re-test method was employed to evaluate the stability of the measurement the tools were administered to a group of High School Students and the score were computed.

The reliability of questionnaire on indentifying the "Failure Tolerance among High School Students at Pattukkottai Educational District" was established by making a rational equivalence method . The reliability of the tool refers to the internal consistency observed in measurement of reliability.

Sampling Technique Used

Random Sampling Method was adopted for this purpose. In this method of random sampling every individual in the population has an equal and independent chance of being chosen for the samples.

The sample is small proportion of a population selected for observation and analysis. In this the sample is a smaller representation of the high school students at Pattukkottai Educational District. The investigator selected 300 samples and has been collected from the study by using Random Sampling Techniques.

The sample should be selected at random from Population. The random sampling does not mean haphazard sampling i.e. sampling without and rule. Random sampling is purely based on defined principles and is a scientific technique. In this, every individual unit in the population gets a chance to be selected.

Table

Sample Distribution

S. No	Category	Group	Number	Total Sample
1.	Gender	Boys	156	300
		Girls	144	
2.	Type of School	Government	100	300
		Government Aided	100	
		Private	100	
3.	Locality	Rural	245	300
		Urban	55	
4.	Students Locality	Hosteller	49	300
		Day Scholar	251	
5.	Type of Family	Nuclear	210	300
		Joint	90	
6.	Parent Occupation	Self Employee	155	300
		Private Employee	80	
		Govt. Employee	65	

Collection of Data

The investigator himself met each and every school students who are studying in various high schools located at Pattukkottai town. Before going to administer the research tool. The investigator revealed the purpose of the present study to the school students and then asked them to give their responses for each and every item that are given in the questionnaire. The responses of the school students were recorded.

Analysis of Data

The term analysis refers to the compilation of certain measures along with searching for part ten and relationship that among groups. For the present study the investigator collected the data from high School Students using the tool developed to find out questioner of sample with problems "Failure Tolerance among High School Students at Pattukkottai Educational District." The Failure habits of high School learners with reference to Class room atmosphere.

Statistical Techniques Used

Statistics is the study of the collection, analysis, interpretation, presentation, and organization of data. In applying statistics to, e.g., a scientific, industrial, or societal problem, it is conventional to begin with a statistical population or a statistical model process to be studied. Populations can be diverse topics such as "all persons living in a country" or "every atom composing a crystal." Statistics deals with all aspects of data including the planning of data collection in terms of the design of surveys and experiments.

When census data cannot be collected, statisticians collect data by developing specific experiment designs and survey samples. Representative sampling assures that inferences and conclusions can safely extend from the sample to the population as a whole. An experimental study involves taking measurements of the system under study, manipulating the system, and then taking additional measurements using the same procedure to determine if the manipulation has modified the values of the measurements. In contrast, an observational study does not involve experimental manipulation.

Two main statistical methodologies are used in data analysis: descriptive statistics, which summarizes data from a sample using indexes such as the mean or standard deviation, and inferential statistics, which draws conclusions from data that are subject to random variation (e.g., observational errors, sampling variation). Descriptive statistics are most often concerned with two sets of properties of a *distribution* (sample or population): *central tendency* (or *location*) seeks to characterize the distribution's central or typical value, while *dispersion* (or *variability*) characterizes the extent to which members of the distribution depart from its center and each other. Inferences on mathematical statistics are made under the framework of probability theory, which deals with the analysis of random phenomena. To make an inference upon unknown quantities, one or more estimators are evaluated using the sample.

Standard statistical procedure involves the development of a null hypothesis, a general statement or default position that there is no relationship between two quantities. Rejecting or disproving the null hypothesis is a central task in the modern practice of science, and gives a precise sense in which a claim is capable of being proven false. What statisticians call an alternative hypothesis is simply a hypothesis that contradicts the null hypothesis. Working from a null hypothesis two basic forms of error is recognized: Type I errors (null hypothesis is falsely rejected giving a "false positive") and Type II errors (null hypothesis fails to be rejected and an actual difference between populations is missed giving a "false negative"). A critical region is the set of values of the estimator that leads to refuting the null hypothesis. The probability of type I error is therefore the probability that the estimator belongs to the critical region given that null hypothesis is true (statistical significance) and the probability of type II error is the probability that the estimator doesn't belong to the critical region given that the alternative hypothesis is true. The statistical power of a test is the probability that it correctly rejects the null hypothesis when the null hypothesis is false. Multiple problems have come to be associated with this framework: ranging from obtaining a sufficient sample size to specifying an adequate null hypothesis.

Measurement processes that generate statistical data are also subject to error. Many of these errors are classified as random (noise) or systematic (bias), but other important types of errors (e.g., blunder, such as when an analyst reports incorrect units) can also be important. The presence of missing data and/or censoring may result in biased estimates and specific techniques have been developed to address these problems. Confidence intervals allow statisticians to express how closely the sample estimate matches the true value in the whole population. Formally, a 95% confidence interval for a value is a range where, if the sampling and analysis were repeated under the same conditions (yielding a different dataset), the interval would include the true (population) value in 95% of all possible cases. In statistics, dependence is any statistical relationship between two random variables or two sets of data. Correlation refers to any of a broad class of statistical relationships involving dependence. If two variables are correlated, they may or may not be the cause of one another. The correlation phenomena could be caused by a third, previously unconsidered phenomenon, called a lurking variable or confounding variable.

Statistics can be said to have begun in ancient civilization, going back at least to the 5th century BC, but it was not until the 18th century that it started to draw more heavily from calculus and probability theory. Statistics continues to be an area of active research, for example on the problem of how to analyze big data.

Definition

Suppose we have a data set containing the values $a_1, ..., a_n$. the arithmetic mean is defined by the formula,

$$A = \frac{1}{n}\sum_{i=1}^{n} a_i$$

(See summation for an explanation of the summation operator, Ó). If the data set is a statistical population (i.e., consists of every possible observation and not just a subset of them), then the mean of that population is called the **population mean**. If the data set is a statistical sample (a subset of the population), we call the statistic resulting from this calculation a **sample mean**.

The arithmetic mean of a variable is often denoted by a bar, for example as in $\bar{x}$ (read "x bar"), which is the mean of the values

You can also get the mean and the standard deviation from a frequency distribution:

Arithmetic mean from a frequency distribution: $\bar{x} = \frac{\Sigma(fx^1)}{\Sigma(f)}$

Standard deviation from a frequency distribution: $\sigma = \sqrt{\frac{\Sigma(fx^1 - \bar{x})^2}{\Sigma(f)}}$

= Standard Deviation

Σfd^2 = The Squared Sum of the Scores

Σfd = The Sum of the Score of the distribution

N =Number of Scores

$$t = \frac{\bar{x}_1 - \bar{x}_2}{\sqrt{\frac{s_1^2}{n_1} + \frac{s_2^2}{n_2}}}$$

"t" Test

A ***t*-test** is any statistical hypothesis test in which the test statistic follows a Student's *t* distribution if the null hypothesis is supported. It can be used to determine if two sets of data are significantly different from each other, and is most commonly applied when the test statistic would follow a normal distribution if the value of a scaling term in the test statistic were known. When the scaling term is unknown and is replaced by an estimate based on the data, the test statistic (under certain conditions) follows a Student's *t* distribution.

The method for comparing two sample means is very similar. The only two differences are the equation used to compute the *t*-statistic, and the degrees of freedom for choosing the tabulate *t*-value. The formula is given by

X_1 - Mean of first group

X_2 - Mean of the second group

S_1 - SD of the first group

S_2 - SD of the second group

n_1 – No. of students in first group

n_2 – No. of students in second group

Conclusion

In this chapter the methodology of the study was explained clearly. Earth and every step was carefully planned and executed. The research strategies and the collection procedures have been explained. The next chapter deals with the Analysis and Interpretation of data.

Chapter - IV

Analysis and Interpretation of Data

Introduction

The most important part of the investigation is the analysis and determine of data. This is studying the tabulated material in order to determine in its meaning. It involves breaking down complex factors into simple parts together in new arrangements for the purpose of interpretation.

This serves the following functions

1. To makes raw data meaningful
2. To test the null hypothesis
3. To obtain significant results and
4. To estimate the parameters

Statistical play a vital role in the field of education. Every research is subjected to statistical analysis. Statistical techniques are used to draw inferences from the data, which are collected by the researcher. During his experiences classification, tabulation and analysis of the collected data is very much essential to draw inferences.

Statement of the Problem

The present investigation aims to identify the how *"A critical study on Failure Tolerance among High School Students at Pattukkottai Educational District."*

Objectives of the Study

The major objective of the study is to find out the **failure tolerance** among high school student at pattukkottai district. The specific objectives of the study are

1. To find out whether there is any significant difference on failure tolerance among High School students on the basis of their **Boys and Girls.**
2. To find out whether there is any significant difference on failure tolerance among High School students on the basis of their type of school management as Government **school and Aided school.**
3. To find out whether there is any significant difference on failure tolerance among High School students on the basis of their type of school management as **Aided school and Private school.**
4. To find out whether there is any significant difference on failure tolerance among High School students on the basis of their type of school management as Government **school and Private school.**
5. To find out whether there is any significant difference between on failure tolerance among High School students on the basis of their Locality as Rural **and Urban.**
6. To find out whether there is any significant difference between on failure tolerance among High School students on the basis of their student's locality as **Hosteller and Day Scholar.**
7. To find out whether there is any significant difference between on failure tolerance among High School students on the basis of their family nature as **Nuclear and Joint Family.**
8. To find out whether there is any significant difference between on failure tolerance among High School students on the basis of their Parents Occupation **Self Employee and Private Employee.**
9. To find out whether there is any significant difference between on failure tolerance among High School students on the basis of their Parents Occupation **Private Employee and Government Employee.**
10. To find out whether there is any significant difference between on failure tolerance among High School students on the basis of their Parents Occupation **Self Employee and Government Employee.**

Hypotheses of the Study

1. There is no significant difference in the mean scores of High School students in failure tolerance on the basis of their **Boys and Girls.**
2. There is no significant difference in the mean scores of High School students in failure tolerance on the basis of their type of school management as **Government school and Aided school.**
3. There is no significant difference in the mean scores of High School students in failure tolerance on the basis of their type of school management as **Aided school and Private school.**
4. There is no significant difference in the mean scores of High School students in failure tolerance on the basis of their type of school management as **Government school and Private school.**
5. There is no significant difference in the mean scores of High School students in failure tolerance on the basis of their locality as Rural **and Urban.**
6. There is no significant difference in the mean scores of High School students in failure tolerance on the basis of their students locality **Hosteller and Day Scholar.**
7. There is no significant difference in the mean scores of High School students in failure tolerance on the basis of their family nature as **Nuclear and Joint family**
8. There is no significant difference in the mean scores of High School students in failure tolerance on the basis of their Parent Occupation **Self employee and Private employee**
9. There is no significant difference in the mean scores of High School students in failure tolerance on the basis of their Parent Occupation **Private Employee and Government employee.**
10. There is no significant difference in the mean scores of High School students in failure tolerance on the basis of their Parent Occupation **Self employee and Government Employee.**

Analysis of Data

Analysis of data usually means studying the material in order to determine inherent faults or meanings it involves breaking down the existing complex factors into simple parts and putting those parts together in new arrangements for the purpose of interpretation.

The present chapter includes the analysis and interpretation of data results that emerge out of the analysis of data.

According to Burleson "Analysis is a research technique for objective, systematic and quantitative description of the manifest content of communication."

According to Wolfe "The discovery of order in the phenomena of nature, not withstanding their complexity and apparent confusion is rendered possible by the process of analysis and synthesis which are foundation stone of all scientific methods."

After collecting the data from the respondents, the investigator gave frequencies for the correct response and these frequencies were converted into scores and then the investigator calculated the percentage scores. The percentage scores were used to identify the level of Problems **failure tolerance** among high school student at Pattukkottai district. The investigator also used test of significance to find out the significant difference between the various groups of demographic variables in **failure tolerance** among high school student at Pattukkottai district.

Hypotheses

Hypothesis: 1

There is no significant difference in the mean scores of High School students in failure tolerance on the basis of their Gender.

TABLE 1
The Table shows Mean, Standard Deviation and 't' value of Failure tolerance among High School Students on the basis of their Boys and Girls

Gender	N	M	S.D	't' Value	Significance at 0.05 Level
Boys	156	102.71	20.71	0.15	No Significant
Girls	144	103.02	15.46		

df = 298 **Critical Value for 0.05 for level : 1.96**

Interpretation

Since the calculated 't' Value **(0.15)** is less than the **Table Value (1.96)** it is inferred that there is no significant difference between the mean scores of the Failure Tolerance among High School Students on the basis of their Boys and Girls.

Result

Hence the null hypothesis is **accepted.**

Hypothesis: 2

There is no significant difference in the mean scores of High School students in failure tolerance on the basis of their type of school management as Government school and Aided school.

TABLE 2
The Table shows Mean, Standard Deviation and 't' value of Failure tolerance among High School Students on the basis of their Government school and Aided School

Type of School	N	M	S.D	't'Value	Significance at 0.05 Level
Government School	100	99	15.32	1.82	No Significant
Aided School	100	95.4	12.56		

df = 198 **Critical Value for 0.05 for level : 1.96**

Interpretation

Since the calculated 't' Value **(1.82)** is less than the **Table Value (1.96)** it is inferred that there is significant difference between the mean scores of the Failure Tolerance among High School Students on the basis of their type of school management as Government school and Aided School.

Result

Hence the null hypothesis is **accepted.**

Hypothesis: 3

There is no significant difference in the mean scores of High School students in failure tolerance on the basis of their type of school management as Aided school and Private school.

TABLE 3

The Table shows Mean, Standard Deviation and 't' value of Failure tolerance among High School Students on the basis of their Aided school and Private School

Type of School	N	M	S.D	't'Value	Significance at 0.05 Level
Aided School	100	95.4	12.56	0.18	No Significant
Private School	100	95	18.42		

df = 198 **Critical Value for 0.05 for level : 1.96**

Interpretation

Since the calculated 't' Value **(0.18)** is less than the **Table Value (1.96)** it is inferred that there is no significant difference between the mean scores of the Failure Tolerance among High Scholl Students on the basis of their type of school management as Aided School and Private School.

Result

Hence the null hypothesis is **accepted.**

Hypothesis: 4

There is no significant difference in the mean scores of High School students in failure tolerance on the basis of their type of school management as Government school and Private school.

TABLE 4

The Table shows Mean, Standard Deviation and 't' value of Failure Tolerance among High School Students on the basis of their Government School and Private School

Type of School	N	M	S.D	't'Value	Significance at 0.05 Level
Government school	100	99	15.32	1.67	No Significant
Private school	100	95	18.42		

df = 198 **Critical Value for 0.05 for level : 1.96**

Interpretation

Since the calculated 't' Value **(1.67)** is less than the **Table Value (1.96)** it is inferred that there is significant difference between the mean scores of the Failure Tolerance among High School Students on the basis of their type of school management as Government School and Private School.

Result

Hence the null hypothesis is **accepted.**

Hypothesis: 5

There is no significant difference in the mean scores of High School students in failure tolerance on the basis of their locality as Rural and Urban.

TABLE 5

The Table shows Mean, Standard Deviation and 't' value of Failure Tolerance among High School Students on the basis of their Rural and Urban

Locality	N	M	S.D	't'Valuc	Significance at 0.05 Level
Rural	245	102.24	17.43	0.11	No Significant
Urban	55	102.54	18.55		

df = 298 **Critical Value for 0.05 for level : 1.96**

Interpretation

Since the calculated 't' Value **(0.11)** is less than the **Table Value (1.96)** it is inferred that there is no significant difference between the mean scores of the Failure Tolerance among High School Students on the basis of their Locality as Rural and Urban.

Result

Hence the null hypothesis is **accepted.**

Hypothesis: 6

There is no significant difference in the mean scores of High School students in failure tolerance on the basis of their students locality Hosteller and Day Scholar.

TABLE 6

The Table shows Mean, Standard Deviation and 't' value of Failure Tolerance among High School Students on the basis of their Hosteller and Day Scholar

Students Locality	N	M	S.D	't'Value	Significance at 0.05 Level
Hosteller	49	88.20	19.81	4.95	Significant
Day Scholar	251	103.45	19.33		

df = 298 **Critical Value for 0.05 for level : 1.96**

Interpretation

Since the calculated 't' Value **(4.95)** is greater than the **Table Value (1.96)** it is inferred that there is significant difference between the mean scores of the Failure Tolerance among High School Students on the basis of their Students Locality Hosteller and Day scholar.

Result

Hence the null hypothesis is **rejected.**

Hypothesis: 7

There is no significant difference in the mean scores of High School students in failure tolerance on the basis of their family nature as Nuclear and Joint family

TABLE 7

The Table shows Mean, Standard Deviation and 't' value of Failure Tolerance among High School Students on the basis of their Nuclear family and Joint family

Type of family	N	M	S.D	't'Value	Significance at 0.05 Level
Nuclear family	210	102.02	18.37	0.22	No Significant
Joint family	90	101.5	18.76		

df = 298 **Critical Value for 0.05 for level : 1.96**

Interpretation

Since the calculated 't' Value **(0.22)** is less than the **Table Value (1.96)** it is inferred that there is no significant difference between the mean scores of the Failure Tolerance among High School Students on the basis of their family nature as Nuclear family and Joint family.

Result

Hence the null hypothesis is **accepted.**

Hypothesis 8

There is no significant difference in the mean scores of High School students in failure tolerance on the basis of their Parent Occupation Self employee and Private employee

TABLE 8

The Table shows Mean, Standard Deviation and 't' value of Failure Tolerance among High School Students basis of their Self Employee and Private Employee

Parent Occupation	N	M	S.D	't'Value	Significance at 0.05 Level
Self Employee	155	98.64	21.26	0.05	No Significant
Private Employee	80	98.5	17.42		

df = 233 **Critical Value for 0.05 for level : 1.96**

Interpretation

Since the calculated 't' Value **(0.05)** is less than the **Table Value (1.96)** it is inferred that there is no significant difference between the mean scores of the Failure Tolerance among High School Students on the basis of their parent occupation Self Employee and Private Employee.

Result

Hence the null hypothesis is **accepted.**

Hypothesis: 9

There is no significant difference in the mean scores of High School students in failure tolerance on the basis of their Parent Occupation Private employee and Government employee.

TABLE 9

The Table shows Mean, Standard Deviation and 't' value of Failure Tolerance among High School Students on the basis of their Parent Occupation Private Employee and Government Employee

Parent Occupation	N	M	S.D	't'Value	Significance at 0.05 Level
Private employee	80	98.5	17.42	2.34	Significant
Government employee	65	91.84	16.75		

df = 143 **Critical Value for 0.05 for level : 1.96**

Interpretation

Since the calculated 't' Value **(2.34)** is greater than the **Table Value (1.96)** it is inferred that there is significant difference between the mean scores of the Failure Tolerance among High School Students on the basis of their parent occupation Private employee and Government Employee.

Result

Hence the null hypothesis is **rejected.**

Hypothesis: 10

There is no significant difference in the mean scores of High School students in failure tolerance on the basis of their Parent Occupation Self employee and Government Employee.

TABLE 10

The Table shows Mean, Standard Deviation and 't' value of Failure Tolerance among High School Students on the basis of their Parent Occupation Self Employee and Government Employee

Parent Occupation	N	M	S.D	't'Value	Significance at 0.05 Level
Self employee	155	98.64	21.26	2.53	Significant
Government employee	65	91.84	16.75		

df = 218 **Critical Value for 0.05 for level : 1.96**

Interpretation

Since the calculated 't' Value **(2.53)** is greater than the **Table Value (1.96)** it is inferred that there is significant difference between the mean scores of the Failure Tolerance among High School Students on the basis of their Self employee and Government Employee.

Result

Hence the null hypothesis is **rejected.**

Conclusion

A brief report of the on the result of the data analysis and the findings are liked in the chapter. Further based on the result of analysis the hypothesis verified.

Chapter V

Summary, Findings and Conclusion

Introduction

In the present Investigation and attempt has been made to study this "A critical study on Failure Tolerance among High School students at Pattukkottai Educational District." This chapter deals with the findings of the statistical analysis and Interpretation of the results. Suggestions for further research also presented in this chapter.

Need and Significance of the Study

Study a failure tolerance will help both the teachers and students to develop their challenging future and character building. Therefore this study will help the students to adopt a better and suitable position in the changing society.

Statement of the Problem

The present investigation aims to identify the how "Failure Tolerance among High school Students at Pattukkottai Educational District."

This study is limited to the students in High School level. This survey is conducted at Pattukkottai Educational District. Variables such as sex, type of schools, Parent occupation, Failure Tolerance of the students are considered. And it focuses the area on Failure Tolerance among High school Students.

Objectives of the Study

The major objective of the study is to find out the **failure tolerance** among high school student at Pattukkottai district. The specific objectives of the study are

1. To find out whether there is any significant difference on failure tolerance among High School students on the basis of their **Gender.**
2. To find out whether there is any significant difference on failure tolerance among High School students on the basis of their type of school management as Government **school and Aided school.**
3. To find out whether there is any significant difference on failure tolerance among High School students on the basis of their type of school management as **Aided school and Private school.**
4. To find out whether there is any significant difference on failure tolerance among High School students on the basis of their type of school management as Government **school and Private school.**
5. To find out whether there is any significant difference between on failure tolerance among High School students on the basis of their Locality as Rural **and Urban.**
6. To find out whether there is any significant difference between on failure tolerance among High School students on the basis of their student's locality as **Hosteller and Day Scholar.**
7. To find out whether there is any significant difference between on failure tolerance among High School students on the basis of their family nature as **Nuclear and Joint Family.**
8. To find out whether there is any significant difference between on failure tolerance among High School students on the basis of their Parents Occupation **Self Employee and Private Employee.**
9. To find out whether there is any significant difference between on failure tolerance among High School students on the basis of their Parents Occupation **Private Employee and Government Employee.**
10. To find out whether there is any significant difference between on failure tolerance among High School students on the basis of their Parents Occupation **Self Employee and Government Employee.**

Hypotheses of the Study

1. There is no significant difference in the mean scores of High School students in failure tolerance on the basis of their **Boys and Girls.**

2. There is no significant difference in the mean scores of High School students in failure tolerance on the basis of their type of school management as **Government school and Aided school.**
3. There is no significant difference in the mean scores of High School students in failure tolerance on the basis of their type of school management as **Aided school and Private school.**
4. There is no significant difference in the mean scores of High School students in failure tolerance on the basis of their type of school management as **Government school and Private school.**
5. There is no significant difference in the mean scores of High School students in failure tolerance on the basis of their locality as Rural **and Urban.**
6. There is no significant difference in the mean scores of High School students in failure tolerance on the basis of their student's locality **Hosteller and Day Scholar.**
7. There is no significant difference in the mean scores of High School students in failure tolerance on the basis of their family nature as **Nuclear and Joint family**
8. There is no significant difference in the mean scores of High School students in failure tolerance on the basis of their Parent Occupation **Self employee and Private employee**
9. There is no significant difference in the mean scores of High School students in failure tolerance on the basis of their Parent Occupation **Private Employee and Government employee.**
10. There is no significant difference in the mean scores of High School students in failure tolerance on the basis of their Parent Occupation **Self employee and Government Employee.**

Delimitations of the Study

Research studies generally may have limitation due to many factors. It is responsibility of the research to see that the study is conducted with maximum care in order to reliable. However the following limitations are inevitable in the present study.

The present study is confined to the students in the selected schools in Pattukkottai District. Academic achievement involves so many factors like intellectual factors, physical factors, etc. This study includes the Failure Tolerance management among the **Six** High School students. The sample size 300 students.

Despite the above-cited delimitations, sufficient care has been taken in selecting the sample, constructing tools, gathering suitable data and making appropriate analysis etc.

Method of Study

Normative survey method is used. The term 'survey' suggests the gathering of evidence relating to current conditions. The term normative implies the determination of normal or typical conditions. The normative study is used for the type of research that proposes to ascertain what the normal or typical condition of practice is at the present time. It brings into focus of our attention on existing educational problems and also suggests the ways of meeting them. The survey method facilitates drawing generalizations about a large population on the basis of studies of representative sample.

Findings of the Present Study

The following on the findings from this research

S. No.	Hypothesis	Result 't' Value	Findings	Status
1.	There is no significant difference in the mean scores of High School students in failure tolerance on the basis of their Gender.	0.15	No significant	Accepted
2.	There is no significant difference in the mean scores of High School students in failure tolerance on the basis of their type of school management as Government school and Aided school.	1.82	No Significant	Accepted
3.	There is no significant difference in the mean scores of High School students in failure tolerance on the basis of their basis of their type of school management as Aided school and Private school.	0.18	No significant	Accepted
4.	There is no significant difference in the mean scores of High School students in failure tolerance on the basis			

of their type of school management as Government school and Private school.	1.67	No Significant	Accepted
5. There is no significant difference in the mean scores of High School students in failure tolerance on the basis of their locality as Rural and Urban.	0.11	No Significant	Accepted
6. There is no significant difference in the mean scores of High School students in failure tolerance on the basis of their students locality Hosteller and Day Scholar.	4.95	Significant	Rejected
7. There is no significant difference in the mean scores of High School students in failure tolerance on the basis of their family nature as Nuclear and Joint family	0.22	NoSignificant	Accepted
8. There is no significant difference in the mean scores of High School students in failure tolerance on the basis of their Parent Occupation Self employee and Private employee	0.05	No significant	Accepted
9. There is no significant difference in the mean scores of High School students in failure tolerance on the basis of their Parent Occupation Private employee and Government employee.	2.34	Significant	Rejected
10. There is no significant difference in the mean scores of High School students in failure tolerance on the basis of their Parent Occupation Self employee and Government Employee.	2.53	Significant	Rejected

Recommendations

From the present study it was clearly understood that there is corresponding positive or negative Failure Tolerance High School students.

Many students are combine with problems they don't know the way to resolve their problems. These kinds of students need a proper guidance to lead a successful life. If guidance and counseling period is introduce in our educational system, the student's problem should be minimized reasonably, and also they should have the capacity to tackle any situation.

Suggestions For Further Research

1. This method is implemented to this students High School level.
2. This method may be conducted using survey method in the high school and High School students
3. Survey method may be expanded to High School students in Pattukkottai District
4. Survey may be expanded to High School Students

Conclusion

Finding of the present study has been consolidated and given in this chapter. Suggestions to come over the problems encountered by the students in Failure Tolerance have also been given this chapter. Therefore this study will certainly enhance the competence of the students as well as teachers.

Bibliography

1. Aggarwal, J.C. (1981). *Theory and Principles of Education.* New Delhi: Vikas Publishing House Private Ltd.
2. American Psychological Association (2008.) Are zero tolerance policies effective in the schools?: An evidentiary review and recommendations. (2008). *American Psychologist,* **63**(9): 852-862.
3. Best, John W. (1986). *Research in Education.* New Delhi: Prentice Hall of India (P) Ltd.
4. Best, John W. and Khan, James V. (1996). *Research in Education.* New Delhi: Prentice Hall of India.
5. Biswal, U.N. (2005). *Philosophy of Education.* New Delhi: Dominant Publishers and Distributors.
6. Caton, M. (2012). Black male perspectives on their educational experiences in high school. *Urban Education,* 47(6): 1055-1085.

7. Casella, R. (2003). Zero tolerance policy in schools: Rationale, consequences, and alternatives. *Teachers College Record,* 105(5): 872-92.
8. Fenning, P.A., Pulaski, S., Gomez, M., Morello, M., Maciel, L., Maroney, E., & Maltese, R. (2012). Call to action: A critical need for designing alternatives to suspension and expulsion. *Journal of School Violence,* 11(2): 105-117.
9. Fenning, P., & Rose, J. (2007). Overrepresentation of African American students in exclusionary discipline: The Role of School Policy. Urban Education, 42(6): 536-559.
10. Gregory, A. & Weinstein, S. R. (2008). The discipline gap and African Americans: Defiance or cooperation in the high school classroom. *Journal of School Psychology,* 46: 455-475.
11. Gupta, S.C. (1998). *Emerging Challenges in Education.* New Delhi: Arya Book Depot.
12. Gupta, S.P. (1995). *Statistical Methods.* New Delhi: Sultan Chand and Sons.
13. Kothari, C.R. (1995). *Research Methodology.* New Delhi: Wishawa Prakashan.
14. Skiba, R.J., and Rausch, M.K. (2006). School disciplinary systems: Alternatives to suspension and expulsion. In G. Bear K. Minke (Eds.), Childrens Needs III: Understanding and Addressing the Developmental Needs of Children. Washington, D. C.: National Association of School Psychologists.
15. Skiba, R.J. (2013). Reaching a critical juncture for our kids: The need to reassess school-justice practices. *Family Cowl Review,* 51(3): 380-387
16. Sullivan *et al.* (2010). Using critical policy and critical race theory to examine Texas' school disciplinary policies. *Race, Gender and Class,* 17(1/2): 72-87.
17. Symms, Kathryn (2012). A hierarchical examination of the immigrant achievement gap: The additional explanatory power of nationality and educational Selectivity over traditional explorations of race and socioeconomic status. *Journal of Advanced Academics,* 23(1):72-98.
18. Taniguchi, H. (2005). The influence of age at degree completion on college wage premiums. *Research in Higher Education,* 46(8): 861-881.
19. Teske, S.C. (2011). A Study of zero tolerance policies in schools: A multi-integrated systems approach to improve outcomes for adolescents. *Journal of Child & Adolescent Psychiatric Nursing,* 24(2): 88-97.

2. Attitude towards History among School Students

Chapter - I

Conceptual Framework

INTRODUCTION OF EDUCATION

Education in its general sense is a form of learning in which the knowledge, skills, values, beliefs and habits of a group of people are transferred from one generation to the next through storytelling, discussion, teaching, training, and or research. Education may also include informal transmission of such information from one human being to another. Education frequently takes place under the guidance of others, but learners may also educate themselves. Any experience that has a formative effect on the way one thinks, feels, or acts may be considered educational.

Education is commonly and formally divided into stages such as preschool, primary school, secondary school and then college, university or apprenticeship. The science and art of how best to teach is called pedagogy.

Education tries to develop skills understanding and confidence in the people. Though education a person is oriented in developmental activities. The trend of the status of socioeconomic development of a society.

Education is a dynamic process of advancement of knowledge in which the involvement of the teacher and taught awaits a continuous and crystallization of knowledge items and knowledge concepts in terms on human advancement in all directions that haunt the wills and aspirations of man and society. Apart from the fact that knowledge explosion is now a days a regular and challenging event in view of making a bond of comradeship with other realities encompassing social environment of an ideal and promising knowledge society is undesirably imperative.

"Education is the manifestation of the perfection that already exist in man" - **Swami Vivekananda**

DEFINITION OF EDUCATION

"The central task of education is to implant a will and facility for learning; it should produce not learned but learning people. The truly human society is a learning society, where grandparents, parents, and children are students together" -**Eric Hoffer**

"No one has yet realized the wealth of sympathy, the kindness and generosity hidden in the soul of a child. The effort of every true education should be to unlock that treasure" **- Emma Goldman**

"The only purpose of education is to teach a student how to live his life-by developing his mind and equipping him to deal with reality. The training he needs is theoretical, i.e., conceptual. He has to be taught to think, to understand, to integrate, to prove. He has to be taught the essentials of the knowledge discovered in the past-and he has to be equipped to acquire further knowledge by his own effort"**-Ayn Rand**

"The aim of education should be to teach us rather how to think, than what to think rather to improve our minds, so as to enable us to think for ourselves, than to load the memory with the thoughts of other men" **-Bill Beattie**

PRESCHOOL

Preschools provide education from ages approximately 3 to 7, depending on the country, when children enter primary education. Also known as nursery schools and as kindergarten, except in the USA, where kindergarten is a term used for primary education. Kindergarten "provide a child-centered, preschool curriculum for three to seven year old children that aim at unfolding the child's physical, intellectual, and moral nature with balanced emphasis on each of them.

PRIMARY SCHOOL

Primary (or elementary) education consists of the first 5–7 years of formal, structured education. In general, primary education consists of six to eight years of schooling starting at the age of five or six, although this varies between, and sometimes within, countries. Globally, around 89% of children aged 6–12 are enrolled in primary education and this proportion is rising. Under the Education for All programs driven by UNESCO, most countries have committed to achieving universal enrollment in primary education by 2015, and in many countries, it is compulsory. The division between primary and secondary education is somewhat arbitrary, but it generally occurs at about eleven or twelve years of age. Some education systems have separate middle schools, with the transition to the final stage of secondary education taking place at around the age of fourteen. Schools that provide primary education are mostly referred to as primary schools or elementary schools. Primary schools are often subdivided into infant schools and junior school.

In India, for example, compulsory education spans over twelve years, with eight years of elementary education, five years of primary schooling and three years of upper primary schooling. Various states in the republic of India provide 12 years of compulsory school education based on a national curriculum framework designed by the National Council of Educational Research and Training.

SECONDARY SCHOOL

In most contemporary educational systems of the world, secondary education comprises the formal education that occurs during adolescence. It is characterized by transition from the typically compulsory, comprehensive primary education for minors, to the optional, selective tertiary, "post-secondary", or "higher" education for adults. Depending on the system, schools for this period, or a part of it, may be called secondary or high schools, gymnasiums, lyceums, middle schools, colleges, or vocational schools. The exact meaning of any of these terms varies from one system to another. The exact boundary between primary and secondary education also varies from country to country and even within them, but is generally around the seventh to the tenth year of schooling. Secondary education occurs mainly during the teenage years. In the United States, Canada and Australia primary and secondary education together are sometimes referred to as K-12 education, and in New Zealand Year 1–13 is used. The purpose of secondary education can be to give common knowledge, to prepare for higher education or to train directly in a profession.

The emergence of secondary education in the United States did not happen until 1910, caused by the rise in big businesses and technological advances in factories (for instance, the emergence of electrification), that required skilled workers. In order to meet this new job demand, high schools were created, with a curriculum focused on practical job skills that would better prepare students for white collar or skilled blue collar work. This proved to be beneficial for both employers and employees, for the improvement in human capital caused employees to become more efficient, which lowered costs for the employer, and skilled employees received a higher wage than employees with just primary educational attainment.

In Europe, grammar schools or academies date from as early as the 16th century, in the form of public schools, fee-paying schools, or charitable educational foundations, which themselves have an even longer history.

Community colleges offer nonresidential junior college offering courses to people living in a particular area.

HIGH SCHOOL

A high school (also secondary school, senior school, secondary college) is a school that provides children and youth with part or all of their secondary education. It may come after primary school or middle school and be followed by higher education or vocational training

The term "high school" originated in Scotland, with the world's oldest high school being Edinburgh's Royal High School from 1505. The Royal High School was used as a model for the first public high school in the United States, the English High School founded in Boston, Massachusetts in 1821.

HIGHER EDUCATION

Higher education, also called tertiary, third stage, or post secondary education, is the non-compulsory educational level that follows the completion of a school providing a secondary education, such as a high school or secondary school. Tertiary education is normally taken to include undergraduate and postgraduate education, as well as vocational education and training. Colleges and universities are the main institutions that provide tertiary education. Collectively, these are sometimes known as tertiary institutions. Tertiary education generally results in the receipt of certificates, diplomas, or academic degrees.

Higher education generally involves work towards a degree-level or foundation degree qualification. In most developed countries a high proportion of the population (up to 50%) now enters higher education at some time in their lives. Higher education is therefore very important to national economies, both as a significant industry in its own right, and as a source of trained and educated personnel for the rest of the economy.

University education includes teaching, research, and social services activities, and it includes both the undergraduate level (sometimes referred to as tertiary education) and the graduate (or postgraduate) level (sometimes referred to as graduate school). Universities are generally composed of several colleges. In the United States, universities can be private and independent like Yale University; public and state-governed like the Pennsylvania State System of Higher Education; or independent but state-funded like the University of Virginia. A number of career specific courses are now available to students through the Internet.

A liberal arts education can be defined as a "college or university curriculum aimed at imparting broad general knowledge and developing general intellectual capacities, in contrast to a professional, vocational, or technical curriculum. Although what is known today as liberal arts education began in Europe, the term "liberal arts college" is more commonly associated with institutions in the United States.

VOCATIONAL EDUCATION

Vocational education is a form of education focused on direct and practical training for a specific trade or craft. Vocational education may come in the form of an apprenticeship or internship as well as institutions teaching courses such as carpentry, agriculture, engineering, medicine, architecture and the arts.

DEFINITION OF ATTITUDE

History (from Greek word *historic*, meaning "inquiry, knowledge acquired by investigation") is the study of the past, particularly how it relates to humans. It is an umbrella term that relates to past events as well as the memory, discovery, collection, organization, presentation, and interpretation of information about these events. Scholars who write about history are called historians. Events occurring prior to written record are considered prehistory.

1. History can also refer to the academic discipline which uses a narrative to examine and analyze a sequence of past events, and objectively determine the patterns of cause and effect that determine them. Historians sometimes debate the nature of history and its usefulness by discussing the study of the discipline as an end in itself and as a way of providing "perspective" on the problems of the present.
2. Stories common to a particular culture, but not supported by external sources (such as the tales surrounding King Arthur) are usually classified as cultural heritage or legends, because they do not support the "disinterested investigation" required of the discipline of history. Herodotus, a 5th-century BC Greek historian is considered within the Western tradition to be the "father of

history", and, along with his contemporary Thucydides, helped form the foundations for the modern study of human history. Their work continues to be read today and the divide between the culture-focused Herodotus and the military-focused Thucydides remains a point of contention or approach in modern historical writing. In the Eastern tradition, a state chronicle the Spring and Autumn Annals was known to be compiled from as early as 722 BC although only 2nd century BC texts survived.

3. Ancient influences have helped spawn variant interpretations of the nature of history which have evolved over the centuries and continue to change today. The modern study of history is wide-ranging, and includes the study of specific regions and the study of certain topical or theatrical elements of historical investigation. Often history is taught as part of primary and secondary education, and the academic study of history is a major discipline in University studies.

4. The history of the world is the memory of the past experience of Homo sapiens around the world, as that experience has been preserved, largely in written records. By "prehistory", historians mean the recovery of knowledge of the past in an area where no written records exist, or where the writing of a culture is not understood. By studying painting, drawings, carvings, and other artifacts, some information can be recovered even in the absence of a written record. Since the 20th century, the study of prehistory is considered essential to avoid history's implicit exclusion of certain civilizations, such as those of Sub-Saharan Africa and pre-Columbian America. Historians in the West have been criticized for focusing disproportionately on the Western world. In 1961, British historian E. H. Carr wrote.

5. The line of demarcation between prehistoric and historical times is crossed when people cease to live only in the present, and become consciously interested both in their past and in their future. History begins with the handing down of tradition; and tradition means the carrying of the habits and lessons of the past into the future. Records of the past begin to be kept for the benefit of future generations.[25]

6. This definition includes within the scope of history the strong interests of peoples, such as Australian Aboriginals and New Zealand Maori in the past, and the oral records maintained and transmitted to succeeding generations, even before their contact with European civilization.

7. Philosophy of history is a branch of philosophy concerning the eventual significance, if any, of human history. Furthermore, it

speculates as to a possible teleological end to its development that is, it asks if there is a design, purpose, directive principle, or finality in the processes of human history. Philosophy of history should not be confused with historiography, which is the study of history as an academic discipline, and thus concerns its methods and practices, and its development as a discipline over time. Nor should philosophy of history be confused with the history of philosophy, which is the study of the development of philosophical ideas through time.

Attitude - a complex mental state involving beliefs and feelings and values and dispositions to act in certain ways; "he had the attitude that work was fun" mental attitude cognition, knowledge, noises - the psychological result of perception and learning and reasoning acceptance, credence - the mental attitude that something is believable and should be accepted as true; "he gave credence to the gossip"; "acceptance of Newtonian mechanics was unquestioned for 200 years"

Culture - the attitudes and behavior that are characteristic of a particular social group or organization; "the developing drug culture"; "the reason that the agency is doomed to inaction has something to do with the FBI culture" defensive, defensive attitude - an attitude of defensiveness (especially in the phrase `on the defensive') hardball - a no-nonsense attitude in business or politics; "they play hardball in the Senate" high horse - an attitude of arrogant superiority; "get off your high horse and admit you are wrong"

Southernism - an attitude characteristic of Southerners (especially in the US) mentality, mindset, mind-set, outlook - a habitual or characteristic mental attitude that determines how you will interpret and respond to situations paternalism - the attitude (of a person or a government) that subordinates should be controlled in a fatherly way for their own good stance, posture, position - a rationalized mental attitude inclination, tendency, disposition - an attitude of mind especially one that favors one alternative over others; "he had an inclination to give up too easily"; "a tendency to be too strict" tolerance - willingness to recognize and respect the beliefs or practices of others intolerance - unwillingness to recognize and respect differences in opinions or beliefs esteem, respect, regard - an attitude of admiration or esteem; "she lost all respect for him"

Disrespect - a disrespectful mental attitude

Reverence - a reverent mental attitude

Irreverence - an irreverent mental attitude

Orientation - an integrated set of attitudes and beliefs

A predisposition or a tendency to respond positively or negatively towards a certain idea, object, person, or situation. Attitude influences an individual's choice of action, and responses to challenges, incentives, and rewards (together called stimuli).Major components of attitude are,

(1) Affective: emotions or feelings.

(2) Cognitive: belief or opinions held consciously.

(3) Evaluative: positive or negative response to stimuli.

The definition of an attitude is a way of feeling or acting toward a person, thing or situation. Passion for a sport, dislike for a certain actor and negativity toward life in general are each an example of an attitude. the position or posture assumed by the body in connection with an action, feeling, mood, etc. to kneel in an attitude of prayer a manner of acting, feeling, or thinking that shows one's disposition, opinion, etc. a friendly attitude one's disposition, opinion, mental set, etc.

NEED AND SIGNIFICANCE OF THE STUDY

A positive towards reading of history is important for a number of reasons. One of the most important reasons is that it enables us to appreciate the importance of institutions such as democratically elected parliaments, the rule of law, trial by jury, an independent judiciary, and the need to protect them. Another important reason is that history provides us with a frame of reference that enables us to recognize dangers to our society, both from within and externally, and it provides guidance as to how to deal with those dangers when they arise. I believe that it was the English philosopher Roger Scranton who said that denying children a solid grounding in the history of their country was calculated to produce a generation of gentle sheep that could be easily led by their political masters. I agree completely with that view.

Darwin burns as Japanese bombers attack Australia on 19 February 1942. The study of history provides us with a frame of reference that enables us to recognize dangers to our society, both from within and externally, and it provides guidance as to how to deal with those dangers when they arise.

I am sometimes asked about the apparent incongruity of a lawyer writing history. While by no means suggesting that legal experience is essential for historians, I would argue that my background in public law and politics is a valuable grounding for historical research and writing history. A Crown prosecutor spends a great deal of time assimilating facts and analyzing them impartially with a view to laying them before a judge or jury to support one or more findings of fact. Knowledge of constitutional law, legal history and the working of government is valuable equipment for an historian who wishes to understand the political as well as the social history of a country.

SCOPE OF THE STUDY

The present study will help to include an interest towards history. Due to globalization and subjects such as history are disappearing from an active since in the curriculum of high and higher secondary schools. This study will kindle the interest to inculcate a pro- atmosphere in the school to study history to develop integrated personality among high school and other students.

STATEMENT OF THE PROBLEM

"Attitude towards History among High School Students at Pudukkottai Educational District"

OPERATIONAL DEFINITION OF KEY TERMS

Definitions of Terms

Relative to this study, definitions to the following terms are provided in order to clarify each in the context of the topic;

ATTITUDE

The definition of an attitude is a way of feeling or acting toward a person, thing or situation. Passion for a sport, dislike for a certain actor and negativity toward life in general are each an example of an attitude. the position or posture assumed by the body in connection with an action, feeling, mood, etc. to kneel in an attitude of prayer a manner of acting, feeling, or thinking that shows one's disposition, opinion, etc. a friendly attitude one's disposition, opinion, mental set, etc.

HISTORY

History (from Greek word *historic*, meaning "inquiry, knowledge acquired by investigation") is the study of the past, particularly how it relates to humans. It is an umbrella term that relates to past events as well as the memory, discovery, collection, organization, presentation, and interpretation of information about these events. Scholars who write about history are called historians. Events occurring prior to written record are considered prehistory.

HIGH SCHOOL

The term "high school" originated in Scotland, with the world's oldest high school being Edinburgh's Royal High School from 1505. The Royal High School was used as a model for the first public high school in the United States, the English High School founded in Boston, Massachusetts in 1821.

The precise stage of schooling provided by a **high school** differs from country to country, and may vary within the same jurisdiction. In all of New Zealand and Malaysia along with most of Britain and parts of Australia, Bangladesh and Canada, high school is synonymous with secondary school, and encompasses the entire second stage of education. However, some remaining traditional high schools in the UK provide teaching from 12, rather than Secondary School, which starts at 11.

PUDUKKOTTAI EDUCATIONAL DISTRICT

Being the district headquarters, Pudukkottai accommodates the district administration offices, government educational institutes, colleges and schools. Pudukkottai is a part of Pudukkottai constituency and elects its member of legislative assembly every five years, and a part of the Tiruchirappalli constituency that elects its member of parliament. The city is administered by a selection-grade municipality established in 1912 as per the Municipal Corporation Act. The city covers an area of 21.25 km^2 and had a population of 143745 in 2011. Roadways are the major mode of transport to the city, while it has also got rail connectivity. The nearest airport is Tiruchirappalli International Airport, located at a distance of 45 km from the city. "Attitude towards History among High School Students at Pudukkottai Educational District".

DISTRICT

A district is a type of administrative division that, in some countries, is managed by local government. Across the world, areas known as "districts" vary greatly in size, spanning entire regions or counties, several municipalities, or subdivisions of municipalities.

EDUCATIONAL DISTRICT

School districts are quasi-municipal corporations created and organized by state legislatures and charged with the administration of public schools within the state. A quasi-municipal corporation is a political body created for the sole purpose of performing one public function. States divide up their school systems into districts because localized administration and policy making are more efficient and more responsive to community needs than one state-level bureaucracy.

A school district encompasses a specific geographical area with defined boundaries. In most areas, the head of the school district is called the superintendent. Each school district contains at least one school. Typically, a school district includes primary schools, also called grade schools, middle or junior high schools, and high schools. A school district's boundaries may be the same as the boundaries of a city. Multiple school districts may exist within larger cities, and in rural areas, a school district may encompass several towns.

Each state has numerous laws pertaining to public schools and school districts, but state statutes do not cover every educational concern. State legislatures delegate many aspects of public education to school districts. School districts have the power to fashion curricula and make rules and regulations that apply to the schools, school employees, and students within the district. School districts also have power over such matters as arranging for the construction and maintenance of educational buildings and facilities in the district. School districts may, in turn, delegate some of their powers to individual schools.

OBJECTIVES OF THE STUDY

Following are the objectives of the present study

To find out the relationship between "Attitude towards History among High School Students at Pudukkottai Educational District"

1. To find out whether any significant difference is there between **Boys and Girls** in respect of Attitude towards History among High School Students .
2. To find out whether any significant difference is there between **Government school and Private school** high school students in respect of Attitude towards History among High School Students.
3. To find out whether any significant difference is there between high school students of **Rural and Urban** areas in respect of Attitude towards History among High School Students.
4. To find out whether any significant difference is there between higher secondary students of **Hostel and Day scholar** in respect of Attitude towards History among High School Students.
5. To find out whether any significant difference is there between family in **Nuclear family and Joint family** in respect of Attitude towards History among High School Students
6. To find out whether any significant difference is there between higher secondary students with **Un Educated and Educated** of parents in respect of Attitude towards History among High School Students.

HYPOTHESES OF THE STUDY

There is no significant relationship between Attitudes towards History among High School Students.

1. There is no significant difference is there between **Boys and Girls** in respect of Attitude towards History among High School Students.
2. There is no significant difference between **Government school and Private school** in respect of Attitude towards History among High School Students.
3. There is no significant difference between high school students of Rural **and Urban** areas in their in respect of Attitude towards History among High School Students.
4. There is no significant difference between high school students of **Hostel and Day scholar** in respect of Attitude towards History among High School Students.
5. There is no significant difference between family in **Nuclear family and Joint family** in respect of Attitude towards History among High School Students.
6. There is no significant difference between high school students with **Un Educated and Educated** of parents in respect of Attitude towards History among High School Students.

LIMITATION OF THE STUDY

This study is restricted to the 300 samples high school students in Pudukkottai Educational District. As far as this study is concerned the Attitude towards History among High School Students at Pudukkottai Educational District. The present educational study survey was conducted in the duration of 2014 – 2015

CONCLUSION

The problem of present study has been discussed briefly in this chapter bringing out the need and significance, ejectives of the study etc. The term operationally defined in the study have been reviewed theoretically from the related literature available as to give a broader theoretical perspective in the light of appropriate could be framed and tested. A detailed discussion of the related literature having a bearing on the problem in heard follows in the next chapter II.

Chapter II

Review of Related Litrature

INTRODUCTION

The Review of Related Literature is the significant part of the research study. The investigator has to acquire information about what has been done in the field of study; to arrive at same meaningful conclusion for this review helps the investigator to gather up-to date information about what has been done in the particular area on which one intends to study. A familiarity with studies in the area of research and available literature is also required by the investigator for making new grants and for the proper planning and designing of the study. So a review of previous studies in relevant area of the present study is attempted and presented in this chapter.

The review of related literature involves the systematic identification, location and analysis of documents containing information related to the research problem. This knowledge provides the understanding and insights necessary for the development of a logical framework in to which a researcher's problem files. Studies that have been done will provide the rationale for the Research hypotheses, indications of what needs to be done and forms the justification of the study undertaken.

A literature review is a text of a scholarly paper, which includes the current knowledge including substantive findings, as well as theoretical and methodological contributions to a particular topic. Literature reviews use secondary sources, and do not report new or original experimental work.

Most often associated with academic-oriented literature, such as a thesis, dissertation or a peer-reviewed journal article, a literature review usually precedes the methodology and results section although this is not always the case. Literature reviews are also common in a research proposal or prospectus (the document that is approved before a student formally begins a dissertation or thesis). Its main goals are to situate the current study within the body of literature and to provide context for the particular reader. Literature reviews are a basis for research in nearly every academic field.

A systematic review is a literature review focused on a research question, trying to identify, appraise, select and synthesize all high quality research evidence and arguments relevant to that question. A Meta analysis is typically a systematic review using statistical methods to effectively combine the data used on all selected studies to produce a more reliable result.

MEANING OF THE RELATED STUDY

Study of the related literature implies locating, reading and educating reports of research as well as reports of casual observation and opinion that are related to the individual's planned research project.

NEED FOR THE REVIEW OF LITERATURE

A through survey of literature can be of great use to the investigator to understand the problem in a better way, and can help solve the problem from different dimensions, it enriches the study. It gives necessary insight to the research study by which one can think creatively.

PURPOSE OF THE REVIEW OF RELATED LITERATURE

The survey of related literature is not without purpose. The following are some of the purposes of the survey.

1. Complete survey of related literature gives the researcher necessary insight into the problem. It enables him to put forth the rationales for the study vigorously.
2. It becomes an important part of the introductory chapter of the basis.
3. A review of related literature gives the scholar an understanding of the previous work he has done.

4. It orients the reader with types of researches that have been conducted in the field previously.
5. It widens the horizon of the researches.
6. It suggests appropriate methods to take the problem under study.
7. It helps in avoiding unnecessary duplication of researches by spot lighting the solutions at the problem that the researcher desires to undertake
8. It provides basic for formulating valuable hypothesis
9. It helps to locate the data that can be used in comparative interpretation of results.
10. It helps to delimit the problem

The process of reading, analyzing, evaluating, and summarizing scholarly materials about a specific topic.

The results of a literature review may be compiled in a report or they may serve as part of a research article, thesis, or grant proposal.

Observations

"Research literature reviews can be contrasted with more subjective examinations of recorded information. When doing a research review, you systematically examine all sources and describe and justify what you have done. This enables someone else to reproduce your methods and to determine objectively whether to accept the results of the review. "In contrast, subjective reviews tend to be idiosyncratic. Subjective reviewers choose articles without justifying why they are selected, and they may give equal credence to good and poor studies. The results of subjective reviews are often based on a partial examination of the available literature, and their findings may be inaccurate or even false."Synopsis, Research Design, Analysis Implementation, Journal Papers. "There should be clear links between the aims of your research and the literature review, the choice of research designs and means used to collect data, your discussion of the issues, and your conclusions and recommendations. To summarize, we can say that the research should;

1. Focus on a specific problem, issue or debate;
2. Relate to that problem, issue or debate in terms that show a balance between the theoretical, methodological and practical aspects of the topic;
3. Include a clearly stated research methodology based on the existing literature;

4. Provide an analytical and critically evaluative stance to the existing literature on the topic.

STUDIES CONDUCTED IN INDIA

Vinod & Venugopal, (2010). Solid waste disposal has been identified as a major cause of pollution and environmental threat globally and very specially to God's own country, Kerala. In spite of the higher literacy rate and well developed educational systems and status in the state, there is lack of practicing proper waste management among Corallites, whether young or old.

Ifegbesan (2008). The findings of the present study have made it clear that they are well aware of the importance of waste management. But they are lacking in the practice of proper waste management. This study findings support the studies conducted.

Raghavan Vivek (2007) The topic of environmental protection has attained highest importance in this era globally but the practices of basic concepts waste disposal are often neglected. People around the globe are aware of the impact of improper waste disposal practices, but the negative attitude of implementation gives rise to chaotic situations. This study was conducted to obtain baseline information about waste management practices among school children in Kerala. This cross sectional study was conducted using a well designed and validated questionnaire. Out of one thousand students of a high school and higher secondary school from Thrissur City in Kerala, 300 were randomly selected. The data analyzed using student t-test showed, high school students are more aware about household waste management than the higher secondary school students. It is evident from this study that there is significant difference between awareness and practice. Our study reveals the necessity of giving mass awareness to the impact of waste disposal practices from the beginning of school education. Committed environmental education will inculcate a proper and appropriate environmental culture in the students. As the study revealed awareness of e-waste disposal is lacking there is an urgent need to rectify this gap in knowledge and practice.

Thote (2007) found that knowledge, attitude-behavior model describe that increase in knowledge will change in attitude which will in turn influence behavior. Consequently environment–knowledge and attitude have been frequently evaluated when attempting to determine the effect of outdoor education programmed on the development of environmental responsibility. Programmers' most likely to change behavior involve concrete ,environmentally positive, action oriented experiences, a relevant content and long term involvement support follow –up and reinforcement by role model.

Sharma (2003) showed that specially the behavior involved various aspects of handling hazardous and controlled wastes in a sample of 642 United States Army soldiers'. Despite the strong Army culture in which the "chain of command is highly emphasized, behavior intentions across behavior were primarily attitude driven. Furthermore, this attitude – behavioral intention link was mediated by variable levels of situational constraining .Behavior associated with high situational constrains reflected a strong attitude–intentional relation than those behavior under more volitional control.

Gyanodaya Vidya Mandir, Narsingarh(2002) Environmental Education is a process of recognized values and clarifications in order to develop skills and added tools to understand and participate, appreciate the inter-relationship among man, his culture and bio-physical surroundings. It creates an overall perspective, which acknowledges the fact that natural environment and manmade environment are inter-dependent. It should consider the environment in its totality and should be a continuous lifelong process beginning at the pre-school level and continuing through all stages. It should be inter-disciplinary and examine major environmental issues from local, national and international point of view. It should utilize various educational approaches to teach and learn about and from the environment with stress on practical activities and firsthand experience. It is through this process of education that people in the society to be aware towards protection of environment and make them skilled to solve environmental problem so as to enable them to participate in the activities undertaken for the protection of environment.

Environmental attitude is learned predisposition to respond towards a consistently given object negative or positive. Environmental behavior determines those actions which contribute towards environmental preservation and conservation is more eco-friendly awareness. The present study was conducted on the students of classes IX and X of a private co-educational school Narsingarh. In this study 100 students participated (50 boys and 50 girls). The questionnaire was used to collect the data from students about the environmental awareness and degree of awareness among students .Percentage calculation was used to find the performance of the students. Coefficient of correlation "r" was used to find out the relation hip between achievement in environmental education and environmental awareness ability. The result of the study indicated that the students are not performing well to solve the problems of population explosion, exhaustion of natural resources and pollution of environment. As a result students are not having enough awareness and skills for identifying and solving problems. No significant positive relationship was found between achievement in environmental education and environmental awareness ability. Some recommendations were made on the basis of the study. .

Kamath Saritha (2001) The topic of environmental protection has attained highest importance in this era globally but the practices of basic concepts waste disposal are often neglected. People around the globe are aware of the impact of improper waste disposal practices, but the negative attitude of implementation gives rise to chaotic situations. This study was conducted to obtain baseline information about waste management practices among school children in Kerala. This cross sectional study was conducted using a well designed and validated questionnaire. Out of one thousand students of a high school and higher secondary school from Thrissur City in Kerala, 300 were randomly selected. The data analyzed using student t-test showed, high school students are more aware about household waste management than the higher secondary school students. It is evident from this study that there is significant difference between awareness and practice. Our study reveals the necessity of giving mass awareness to the impact of waste disposal practices from the beginning of school education. Committed environmental education will inculcate a proper and appropriate environmental culture in the students. As the study revealed awareness of e-waste disposal is lacking there is an urgent need to rectify this gap in knowledge and practice.

STUDIES CONDUCTED IN ABORD

WILKINS (2010) indicated that " teachers and students attitudes can and do influence instructional practice. Understanding teachers' attitudes toward all subjects can provide additional information that could help explain differences in the instructional practices associated with the different subject areas. A review of the related literature revealed little research about social studies education and the curriculum in Jordan. Most studies focused on higher education; none focused specifically on middle and high school education.

Koballa & Glynn, (2007) Although research on students' attitudes towards learning science fueled many research projects for a long time, in the late 1980s there was a significant decline in science education researchers' interest in science-related attitudes .

Lintner, (2006).conducted a similar qualitative analysis of social studies perceptions in Jordan. The purpose of their study was to examine student's perceptions of middle and high school students in Jordan. With methodological modifications, a similar theoretical and conceptual platform was utilized in this study .In their study, targeted teachers and male students in an effort to understand social studies in Jordan. For this initial study, the scope of inquiry was narrowed to only middle and secondary female's students in Jordan (Lintner, 2006).

Monica Stefan, Florentina Ciomo° (2006) The students' interest and attitude towards history have been the object of international testing, the most recent of which is the PISA testing from 2006. The students' attitude towards sciences is considered to be a significant predictor of their school results in science, respectively of pursuing a career in areas related to Science. The present paper had in view to discover the existence of convergences or divergences among the attitudes of the students in 8th and 9th grade towards the study of history towards the teacher's role in studying for the natural sciences. The obtained results have not rendered evidently the existence of major differences but have allowed for the shaping of a profile for history as a school subject, from the interviewees' perspective. Thus, history is considered to be a difficult but pleasant and interesting subject, with use for oneself but for others as well. Our investigation has pointed out the fact that the students study too little for history at home, but that the history teacher is effective in teaching and motivating the students to learn. Although this is a pilot research project, our investigation signals a state of fact that implies reflection, mainly on the history curriculum but also on the teaching methods.

Avi Hofstein (2004) Developing positive attitudes toward an interest in science in general and learning science in particular is one of the key goals for teaching and learning the sciences. Thus, over the years, this area fuelled many research studies, these being focused on: content, pedagogical, and curricular issues. In this paper we focused on the issue of enhancing attitude and interests in the context of chemistry learning mainly at the upper secondary level of schooling. The authors of this manuscript suggest that the three key factors that should be considered for enhancing attitudes and interests are the methods used to present the content (e.g. relevance, and historical approach), instructional techniques that are implanted, and gender issues. Although throughout the years we have learned a lot regarding teaching and learning of chemistry we are unable to provide conclusive recommendations regarding how in the context of chemistry education affective constrains could be enhanced. However, based on scholarly developments and research we suggest areas (see above) that should be considered by science (chemistry) educators, curriculum developers, and chemistry teachers who believe that developing positive attitudes one of the central goals.

Alazzi and Chiodo (2004) conducted an examination of the content in social studies textbooks. Their questionnaire addressed curriculum, textbooks, teaching methods, learning objectives, and education experience. Based on his analysis of social studies textbooks, curriculum, and teaching methods, the researchers emphasized a strong need for improvement in the current social studies curriculum in Jordan's middle schools. They found that all aspects of the social studies curriculum needed significant improvement based on western standards.

Schreiner (2004), and History Education, All these initia-tives and reports include one common feature: that the con-tent of school science and its related pedagogical approaches are not aligned with the needs, motivational patterns, and in-terests of most of the students Even in countries in which the results of times and Pisa were above average, students do not view science learning as either moti-vating or relevant

Chiodo and Byford (2004) conducted a study inquiring into the attitudes students possessed regarding social studies. They interviewed eighth and eleventh grade students and found that two themes emerged. The first theme suggested that a teacher's involvement and enthusiasm led to positive images of social studies by middle and high school students. The second theme suggested that student's positive attitudes toward social studies were based on their perceived utilitarian value of the subject matter. Related to the area of student attitudes toward the social studies curriculum is student attitudes toward the teacher.

Alazzi F. KHALED (2004) The purpose of this study was to explore, in depth, the attitudes of middle school and secondary school students about social studies in Jordan's Ibid Province, with teacher and learning variables. Using a qualitative research approach, two groups of eighth and eleventh grade students was interviewed in the Ibid Province of Jordan regarding their perceptions of social studies. A total of forty-eight students were selected to participate in this qualitative study. The research revealed that the students in both middle school and secondary school valued social studies, while at the same time they did not rate social studies as their most favorite courses. Students indicated that many teachers continued to depend on textbooks and lectures as the main method for teaching.

In addition, students put a high value on teacher enthusiasm and encouragements. Generally speaking, in 2004 Alazzi and Chiodo concluded that "social studies not favorite subject for male social studies students in Jordan. Some eight years later, the same can be said regarding females social studies. The study recommended that to improve social studies education in Jordan, the Ministry of Education should abandon its role of selecting and controlling subjects included in the social studies curricula. Social studies curricula should be revised to include the most recent available information and to reflect contemporary research in social studies education in order to prepare young Jordanians for the new millennium. Schooling in all societies purports to teach students the knowledge, skills, and attitudes needed to function as responsible citizens. **Alazzi and Aldowan(2001)** conducted an evaluation of Jordan's tenth grade social studies curriculum. The researchers discussed both the status of social studies, and the problems present in the curriculum as viewed by social studies teachers. The textbooks were studied to determine their strengths and weaknesses. Their research suggested that the social studies objectives did not assist students in their development of critical thinking or critical inquiry.

Lawson, (2003) surveyed 100 tenth grade students and 100 twelfth grade students in order to determine their attitudes towards the various academic areas. In the study, History, mathematics, and reading were ranked ahead of social studies. Participants described social studies as boring and far from anything they could relate to in their life. In recent research in the United States on student's attitudes toward social studies,

Osborne et al., (2003) presented a gloomy picture regarding students' ignorance in science, the decline in their attitudes toward science in general and science learning in par-ticular, and the decline in enrollment in science-based careers.

Avi Hofstein & Rachel Mamlok-Naaman (2001) Developing positive attitudes toward an interest in science in general and learning science in particular is one of the key goals for teaching and learning the sciences. Thus, over the years, this area fuelled many research studies, these being focused on: content, pedagogical, and curricular issues. In this paper we focused on the issue of enhancing attitude and interests in the context of chemistry learning mainly at the upper secondary level of schooling. The authors of this manuscript suggest that the three key factors that should be considered for enhancing attitudes and interests are the methods used to present the content.

Dr. Samson Ondigi (2001) The purpose of this study was to investigate students' attitudes towards studying History and Government in selected secondary schools of Mosocho division, Kisii County The study was conducted in both purposively and simple random sampled private and public secondary schools in Mosocho division, Kisii County. Mosocho division was purposively chosen because it was the only division in the District that is comprised of categories chosen by the researcher. The target population was form two (2) students and their respective History and Government teachers. Data were collected using teachers and students questionnaires.

The teachers' questionnaire comprised of both open ended and closed items. The students' questionnaire used a 5 point-likert scale ranging from strongly agrees to strongly disagree. The data collected was analyzed by use of descriptive statistics and presented with the aid of tables, percentage and, graphs. From the analyzed data major discussions were made and reported. Most of the students were found to be having negative attitude towards studying History and Government and Heuristic strategies of teaching were suggested and many other more. There are other factors like negative attitudes and stereotypes that might contribute to both teachers and students claiming that the syllabus to be overloaded.

Miss. Shabina Khan (1999) The main aim of this study is to investigate the interest and attitude of higher secondary school students towards history curriculum in Khargone taluka. In the present research paper the investigator tried to compare the attitude of rural and urban students towards English curriculum. But these results are not the last truth. I hoped that in the suggestions and the results will be helpful for the development of the situation of the English curriculum in the schools in present time.

Parker, (1999). In a democratic society, schools translates these curricular goals into knowledge of the community, nation, and world. Schooling also translates to the skills required to participate competently within the larger society. It also helps promote and protect one's interests and the democratic attitudes that form the bases for decision making on one's behalf while keeping in mind the larger context of the common good In Jordan, the goal of social studies education is to prepare young people to be good citizens in a world that is becoming increasingly complex. The Jordanian Ministry of Education divides social studies objectives into four categories: knowledge, skills, values, and participation. These four categories require global perspective as an essential tool for performing successfully in a complex and rapidly changing world.

Alajaji(1999), Banjar (1984), and Al-Thuwaini (1986) conducted studies on teacher's attitudes towards social studies curricula in Saudi Arabia . The three studies concluded that social studies teachers believe all aspects of social studies curricula need to be improved and developed.

Millar & Os-borne, (1998), In addition, in many western countries, the gloomy results of the recent international comparative assessments in History education (times, since 1995 and Pisa, since 2000) also sparked a tidal wave of documents, all of which called for rethinking the goals, content, and pedagogy of History educa-tion

Rooze and Foerster, (1972) and Slater, (1995) observe that History is a unique subject in the school curriculum. This is because it is a social science without stated boundaries and it is predominantly concerned with evidence of the behavior. It is also the only social science that uses chronology to a great extent. Lastly, its content is near at hand and can be illustrated by incidence in the child's community and state. That uniqueness can influence teachers to complain about the syllabus and content. To a greater extent it influences or implants attitudes in both the teachers' and the students' minds. In Kenya there has been relatively little research into attitudes of students towards school subjects. There seems to be little interest in attitude research. One problem of this is the difficulty of constructing a reliable measure of attitudes.

Ogula, (1994). Students' attitude towards H/G has hardly been looked into. Ormerod and Duckworth (1975) point out that the attitudes of learners towards their subjects of study, their school and the teaching they receive in them cannot be ignored in any worthwhile study of reasons why learners behave as they do. This has prompted the foundation of this study. The fluctuation in H/G enrolment the emphasis put on sciences and technical oriented subjects in the current system of education. (Kamunge, 1988);the overloaded and wide H/G syllabus (Kiio, 1999, Thuo 1987, Chumba, 1986); and lack of research on students attitudes towards school subjects in Kenya (Ogula, 1994) have combined jointly to form the basis of this study. The literature reviewed formed a basis for the study. It established and made a case for the purpose and importance of the study that was filling in gaps left by the previous research. It also guided in methodology and data analysis.

Wheeler& Ryan, 1993). Mager (1978) indicated that attitude alone contributed largely to teacher success. First, how a student judged a teacher was linked to the students' potential for developing an open-minded attitude about the subject. Second, students who had a positive attitude toward the subject matter were more likely to continue being focused on that particular subject. Third, students' feelings regarding school helped to positively shape relationships with parents, teachers, and peers.

Agiro, (1990) in his study on the factors affecting teaching History in senior secondary schools in Addis Ababa, Ethiopia, found that teachers overemphasize the lecture method. He said that it should be discouraged and students should be given an opportunity to participate in classroom discussions, presenting reports and visiting historical sites.

Mwangi, (1990) in a survey on the relationship between achievement and attitudes towards mathematics among standard seven pupils in Kabazi location of Nakuru District revealed that attitudes of students towards the subject are affected generally by the class teacher's methods and challenges in the handling and operation of the subject. Magiri, (1997) in a study on the relationship between attitude and achievement in top quartile and lower quartile in physics reveals that a subject can be performed well but students have different attitudes towards it. He found out that achievement in lower quartile did not depend on attitude whereas achievement and attitude in the upper quartile was positively correlated.

Long, (1971) argues that every teacher should find out the interest of students first before he teaches. He argues that even if many methods are just introduced without finding the viewpoint of the learners the teaching is unlikely to be unsuccessful. Hence Kiio, (1999) in her study on the methods and materials used to teach History and Government in Kenya, recommended a further study into the students attitudes towards H/G; Agiro, (1990) in his study on the factors affecting the teaching of History in Senior Secondary Schools in Addis Ababa, also recommended for a study on students attitudes towards History. As shown from the above reviewed studies, performance does not reflect the students' attitudes towards a subject in the curriculum. They have also revealed that sex does not determine attitudes. The teachers' teaching styles affect the students' attitudes. The last study carried out in 1987 revealed that the students liked H/G and enjoyed it.

But from that time there have been so many changes and therefore the attitudes may have changed. It could be that the students also develop attitudes due to parental influence, Government policy and other factors. There is no serious study that has been done on secondary school students' attitudes towards H/G especially after the amalgamation of History and Government. This therefore, motivated the institution of this study in order to assess the students' attitudes towards studying H/G in selected secondary schools of Mosocho division, Kisii County.

Alkan, (1970) in his study on students' attitudes towards mathematics, established that attitudes can start early when the child enters lower primary. They either form a positive or negative attitude depending on the environment they have been exposed to. Ormerod and Duckworth (1975) quote Duckworth (1974 b) who points out that the attitudes of learners towards their subjects of study, their schools and the teaching they receive in them cannot be ignored in any worthwhile study of reasons why pupils behave as they do. Were, (1982) in a study on the examination of the problems relating to the teaching of History in secondary schools in Kenya, found that majority of head teachers feel that their students are not interested in history meaning that they have already developed attitudes. She found that 58.1% considered History a dull subject. The study revealed that History is unpopular because more emphasis is laid on science subjects.

Both Mag (1968) and Haladyna (1982) showed that the approach the teacher takes when teaching social studies had a unique influence on school curriculum. Beyond the international research cited, there have been few additional studies on the topic. Therefore, a study relating to students perceptions of social studies in Jordan is important for educational reforms in that country.

CONCLUTION

The survey of related literature has helped the investigator. The review of related literature has enabled the investigation to formulate the relevant hypothesis for the present study. Research methodology of the present study will be discussed in the next chapter III

Chapter- III

Methodology

INTRODUCTION

Research methodology is a way to systematically solve the research problem. It may be understood as a science of studying now research is done scientifically. This chapter explained the methods adopted to conduct this study. The entire chapter has been discussed under various sub-headings such as, need and significance of the study, statement of the problem, objectives framed hypotheses, formulated operationalization and measurement of variable, sampling procedure, and techniques of data collection and statically techniques.

In order that the research should be conducted successfully, a suitable methodology with specific operational steps and constructed tools are necessary. In the present study, the investigator aims at finding the relationship between the school environment and the achievement of students in their academic subjects. The details of various steps followed in the investigation are discussed in the chapter.

METHODOLOGY

1. "The analysis of the principles of methods, rules and postulations, employed by a discipline".
2. "The systematic study of methods that are can be, or have been applied within a discipline".

CONCEPT

Methodology may be a description of process, or may be expanded to include a philosophically coherent collection of theories, concepts or ideas as they relate to a particular discipline or field of inquiry.

Methodology may refer to nothing more than a simple set of methods or procedures, or it may refer to the rationale and the philosophical assumptions that underline a particular study relative to the scientific method.

RESEARCH DESIGN

This chapter presents details regarding the following.

1. Selection of Dependent variables and Categorical variables.
2. Constriction of tools to measure the students Attitude towards history.
3. Methods of establishing the reliability and validity of the tools constructed.
4. Sampling procedure adopted in this study
5. Scheduling the survey and collecting the data.

The word survey indicated the gathering of data regarding current condition. Survey is an important type of study. It involves a clearly defined problem and defined objectives of the research. Strategy employed, tool used, sample technique employed and data collection procures followed are outlined.

STATEMENT OF THE PROBLEM

This study is limited to the students in High School level. This survey is conducted at Pudukkottai Educational District. Variables such as sex, type of schools, Parent annual income, *"Attitude towards History among High School Students at Pudukkottai Educational District"*

OBJECTIVES OF THE STUDY

Following are the objectives of the present study to find out the relationship between "Attitudes towards History among High School Students at Pudukkottai Educational District"

1. To find out whether any significant difference is there between **Boys and Girls** in respect of Attitude towards History among High School Students .

2. To find out whether any significant difference is there between **Government school and Private school** high school students in respect of Attitude towards History among High School Students.

3. To find out whether any significant difference is there between high school students of **Rural and Urban** areas in respect of Attitude towards History among High School Students.

4. To find out whether any significant difference is there between higher secondary students of **Hostel and Days color** in respect of Attitude towards History among High School Students.

5. To find out whether any significant difference is there between family in **Nuclear family and Joint family** in respect of Attitude towards History among High School Students.

6. To find out whether any significant difference is there between higher secondary students with **Un Educated and Educated** of parents in respect of Attitude towards History among High School Students.

HYPOTHESES OF THE STUDY

There is no significant relationship between Attitudes towards History among High School Students.

1. There is no significant difference is there between **Boys and Girls** in respect of Attitude towards History among High School Students.

2. There is no significant difference between **Government school and Private school** in respect of Attitude towards History among High School Students.

3. There is no significant difference between high school students of Rural **and Urban** areas in their in respect of Attitude towards History among High School Students.

4. There is no significant difference between high school students of **Hostel and Days color** in respect of Attitude towards History among High School Students.

5. There is no significant difference between family in **Nuclear family and Joint family** in respect of Attitude towards History among High School Students.

6. There is no significant difference between high school students with **Un Educated and Educated** of parents in respect of Attitude towards History among High School Students

LIMITATION OF THE STUDY

This study is restricted to the 300 samples high school students in Pudukkottai Educational District. As far as this study is concerned the Attitude towards History among High School Students at Pudukkottai Educational District. The present educational study survey was conducted in the duration of 2014 – 2015.

RESEARCH METHOD

The investigator preferred Random- Sampling method for the present study. In this study, the investigator used **Survey method** to collect data and to identify the *"Attitude towards History among High School Students at Pudukkottai Educational District"*

RESEARCH TOOLS

In the present study, the investigation selected questionnaire as the most important tool for collecting data because it is used increasingly to enquire into the current conditions, opinions and attitude of a groups.

The word 'tool' is defined a means to collect evidence.

W. Best observes that the questionnaire is the mostly used tool in collecting both quantitative and qualitative information, for the present study questionnaire was prepared with a view to gather information in detail regarding the "Attitude towards History among High School Students at Pudukkottai Educational District"

CONSTRUCTION OF RESEARCH TOOLS

The research tool on "Attitude towards History among High School Students at Pudukkottai Educational District" was constructed by the investigator in the present study. All the question items are closed type. The correct answers were given scores and these score were considered for data analysis.

SAMPLES OF THE STUDY

As the entire high school students studying at Pudukkottai **Educational District** could not be taken for the present study due to time constraint. The 300 students following have been taken as sample to represent the whole population.

DESCRIPTION OF RESEARCH TOOL AND SCORING PROCEDURE

Before administering the test necessary instruction and directions were given to the students. No time limit is given to the students were asked to complete the inventory as early as possible. It is a **Five Point** of liker's types of tool.

The scale is

1. Strongly Agree (**SCALE IS** SA)
2. Moderately Agree (MA)
3. Undecided (UD)
4. Moderately Disagree (MD)
5. Strongly Disagree (SD)

Scale Options	Procedure Scoring	
	Positives Question Marks	Negative Question Marks
Strongly Agree (SA)	**5**	**1**
Moderately Agree (MA)	**4**	**2**
Undecided (UD)	**3**	**3**
Moderately Disagree (MD)	**2**	**4**
Strongly Disagree (SD)	**1**	**5**

PILOT STUDY

The pilot stage is concerned with refining the items collected. The collected items were presented before the export with a request to offer their considered opinion regarding the suitability objectively clarity and relevancy of the statement collected from different sources.

The pilot study is an initial study which is conducted by the investigator to know more about the research problem in various aspects. Based on the pilot study, The main study was conducted by the investigator while administering the research in the pilot study, some doubts were raised by their doubts and difficulties. Based on that, the investigator modified the items.

Further, the investigator obtained some ideas from the experts and modified the irrelevant. Item that is coming in the present study .After getting response from the respondents, the investigator gave frequencies for the correct response and these frequencies were converted into scores and those were used to establish reliability.

VALIDITY OF THE TOOL

In validation process, the investigator used two measures in order to establish validation of tools. The first measures of validation are called reliability. The second measure of validation process is called validity. The investigator established content validity.

To find out the validity of research tool, the investigator discussed each and every item of the questionnaire with the experts in the relevant field of "Attitude towards History among High School Students at Pudukkottai Educational District" Based the opinion of the expert the objectivity and worthies of the items of the questionnaire established.

In the valuation pro, the investor used two measures in order to establish addition of the tools. The first measure of validation is and reliability. The second measure of validation process is called limit. The investigator established content validity To find out the validity of research tool, the investigator discussed each and every item of the questionnaire. It he experts in the relevant field to identify the" "Attitude towards History among High School Students at Pudukkottai Educational District" Based on the opinion of the experts, the objectivity and worthiness of the items of the questionnaire were established. The investigator also modified some of the items in the questionnaire and some item were eliminated. This kind of scientific procedure helped the investigator to established sufficient content validity.

RELIABLITY OF THE TOOL

The reliability of questionnaire on indentifying the *"Attitude towards History among High School Students at Pudukkottai Educational District"* was established by making a rational equivalence method. The reliability of the tool refers to the internal consistency observed in measurement of reliability.

Garett (1979) Reliability is the consistency with which a tool measures what it measure. In the present study, the typical test re-test method was employed to evaluate the stability of the measurement the tools were administered to a group of Higher Secondary School Students and the score were computed.

The reliability of questionnaire on indentifying the *"Attitude towards History among High School Students at Pudukkottai Educational District"* was established by making a rational equivalence method. The reliability of the tool refers to the internal consistency observed in measurement of reliability.

SAMPLING TECHNIQUE USED

Random Sampling Method was adopted for this purpose. In this method of random sampling every individual in the population has an equal and independent chance of being chosen for the samples.

The sample is small proportion of a population selected for observation and analysis. In this the sample is a smaller representation of the high school students at Pudukkottai Educational District. The investigator selected 300 samples and has been collected from the study by using Random Sampling Techniques.

The sample should be selected at random from population. The random sampling does not mean haphazard sampling i.e. sampling without and rule. Random sampling is purely based on defined principles and is a scientific technique. In this, every individual unit in the population gets a chance to be selected.

SAMPLING PROCEDURE

The main objective of this research is to find out whether there exists a significant relationship between the *"Attitudes towards History among High School Students at Pudukkottai Educational District".* A sample of Five High schools namely,

1. Govt. Boys. Hi. Sec. School -Pudukkottai
2. Govt. Girls. Hi. Sec. School - Pudukkottai
3. Govt. High School Gandarvakottai
4. Vidhya vigas Metric Hi . school, Gandarvakkottai.
5. Guthoos Metric Hi. School- Pudukkottai was selected for the research work using the stratified random sampling technique. After selecting 300 students (140 Boys students and 160 Girls students) were selected randomly from these schools in Pudukkottai Educational District. The Students were selected both from Government High schools and Metric High Schools.

TABLE 1

Table Showing The Distribution Of Samples

Sl. No	Variables	Sub Variables	No. of Students	Total
1	Gender	Boys	140	300
	Girls	160		
2	Type of School	Govt. School	148	300
		Private School	152	
3	Locality of the school	Rural	138	300
		Urban	162	

4	Students Locality	Hosteller	110	300
		Day scholar	190	
5	Type of family	Nuclear	185	300
		Joint	115	
6	Parents Qualification	Un Educated	108	300
		Educated	192	

COLLECTION OF DATA

The investigator himself met each and every school students who are studying in various high schools located at Pudukkottai town. Before going to administer the research tool, the investigator revealed the purpose of the present study to the high school students and then asked them to give their responses for each and every item that are given in the questionnaire. The responses of the school students were recorded.

ANALYSIS OF DATA

The term analysis refers to the compilation of certain measures along with searching for part ten and relationship that among groups. For the present study the investigator collected the data from high School Students using the tool developed to find out questioner of sample with problems *"Attitude towards History among High School Students at Pudukkottai Educational District"*. The environment habits of high School learners with reference to Class room atmosphere.

STATISTIC TECHNIQUES APPLIED IN DATA ANALYSIS

The following statistical techniques here applied to analysis and interpret the collected data.

THE ARITHMETIC MEAN

The Mean of the distribution is commonly under stood as the arithmetic average. The term guide-point averages familiar to student is a Mean value. $\overline{X} = \dfrac{\sum X_i}{n}$

It is computed by dividing the sum of all the scores by the number of scores. It is probably most useful of all statistical measures for in addition to the information that it provides. It is the base from which many others in important measures are computed.

Arithmetic Mean from a frequency distribution

Some times it is more convenient to desire mean from a frequency distribution. An additional column may be opened to record the products of frequency distribution. The total of this frequency distribution will be divided by the total of 'f' (i.e) N to get mean.

$$\text{Mean} = A + \frac{\Sigma fd}{N} X Ci$$

Where, A- Assumed Mean Value

ci -Class interval

N -Sum of frequency

THE STANDARD DEVIATION

Standard deviation most widely used measure of dispersion of a series and is commonly denoted by the symbol ' s' (sigma) standard deviation is defined as the square root of the average of squares of deviation when such deviations for the values of individual items in a series are obtained from the arithmetic average.

Standard deviation **(s)** = $\sqrt{\frac{\Sigma d^2}{N}}$

XC. I

In case of frequency distribution, **SD** = $\sqrt{\frac{\Sigma fd^2}{N} - \left(\frac{\Sigma fd}{N}\right)^2}$

This is known as the shortcut method of finding

"t" TEST

't' test is based on 't' distribution and is a sample Mean or judging the significance of difference between the Means of the sample in case of small samples when population variance is not known. In case of two samples paired t-test is used for judging the significance of the co-efficient of sample and partial correlation. The relevant test statistic is calculated from the sample data and then compared with its probable value based on t-distribution at a specific level of significance for concerning degree of freedom for accepting or rejecting the Null hypothesis. This test applied only in case of small samples when population variance is not known.

X_1 -Mean of first group

X_2 -Mean of the second group

S_1 -SD of the first group

S_2 -SD of the second group

n_1 -No, of students in first group

$$t = \frac{\bar{x}_1 - \bar{x}_2}{\sqrt{\frac{s_1^2}{n_1} + \frac{s_2^2}{n_2}}}$$

n_2 -No, of students in second group

CONCULSION

In a research the statistical treatment is in an important aspect. The present study aims to find out the attitude towards history among the high school students. The investigator employed the co relational study and the differential study to analyses the data collected from the sample. The detailed analysis is explained in Chapter IV.

Chapter - IV

Analysis and Interpretation of Data

INTRODUCTION

The most important part of the investigation is the analysis and determine of data. This is studying the tabulated material in order to determine in its meaning. It involves breaking down complex factors into simple parts together in new arrangements for the purpose of interpretation.

This serves the following functions

1. To makes raw data meaningful
2. To test the null hypothesis
3. To obtain significant results and
4. To estimate the parameters

Statistical play a vital role in the field of education. Every research is subjected to statistical analysis. Statistical techniques are used to draw inferences from the data, which are collected by the researcher. During his experiences classification, tabulation and analysis of the collected data is very much essential to draw inferences

INTERPRETATION OF THE RESULTS

The purpose of this chapter is to analyze the data that were collected and presented in such a way that meaningful interpretation and discussion.

ANALYSIS OF DATA

Analysis of data usually means studying the material in order to determine inherent faults or meanings it involves breaking down the existing complex factors into simple parts and putting those parts together in new arrangements for the purpose of interpretation.

The present chapter includes the analysis and interpretation of data results that emerge out of the analysis of data.

OBJECTIVES OF THE STUDY

Following are the objectives of the present study

To find out the relationship between "Attitude towards History among High School Students at Pudukkottai Educational District"

1. To find out whether any significant difference is there between **Boys and Girls** in respect of Attitude towards History among High School Students .
2. To find out whether any significant difference is there between **Government school and Private school** high school students in respect of Attitude towards History among High School Students.
3. To find out whether any significant difference is there between high school students of **Rural and Urban** areas in respect of Attitude towards History among High School Students.
4. To find out whether any significant difference is there between higher secondary students of **Hostel and Day scholar** in respect of Attitude towards History among High School Students.
5. To find out whether any significant difference is there between family in **Nuclear family and Joint family** in respect of Attitude towards History among High School Students
6. To find out whether any significant difference is there between higher secondary students with **Un Educated and Educated** of parents in respect of Attitude towards History among High School Students

HYPOTHESES OF THE STUDY

There is no significant relationship between Attitudes towards History among High School Students.

1. There is no significant difference is there between **Boys and Girls** in respect of Attitude towards History among High School Students.

2. There is no significant difference between **Government school and Private school** in respect of Attitude towards History among High School Students.
3. There is no significant difference between high school students of Rural **and Urban** areas in their in respect of Attitude towards History among High School Students.
4. There is no significant difference between high school students of **Hostel and Day scholar** in respect of Attitude towards History among High School Students.
5. There is no significant difference between family in **Nuclear family and Joint family** in respect of Attitude towards History among High School Students.
6. There is no significant difference between high school students with **Un Educated and Educated** of parents in respect of Attitude towards History among High School Students.

HYPOTHESES DESIGN

HYPOTHESES-1

There is no significant difference is there between **Boys and Girls** in respect of Attitude towards History among High School Students.

TABLE 1

The Table shows Mean, Standard Deviation and 't' Value of Problems Attitude towards History among High School Students.

Gender	N	M	S.D	't'Value	Significanceat 0.05 Level
Boys	140	64.78	11.06	2.22	Significant
Girls	160	67.44	9.52		

df = 298 **Critical Value for 0.05 for level : 1.96**

INTERPRETATION

Since the calculated 't' Value **(2.22)** is greater than the **Table Value (1.96**) it is inferred that there is no significant difference between the mean scores of the attitude towards History among High School Students with respect to Boys and Girls.

RESULT

Hence the null hypothesis is **rejected.**

HYPOTHESES - 2

There is no significant difference is there between **Government School and Private School** in respect of Attitude towards History among High School Students.

TABLE 2

The Table shows Mean, Standard Deviation and 't' Value of Problems Attitude towards History among High School Students.

Type of Schools	N	M	S.D	't'Value	Significanceat 0.05 Level
Govt. School	148	65.03	10.28	3.21	Significant
Private School	152	68.66	9.33		
df = 298			**Critical Value for 0.05 for level : 1.96**		

INTERPRETATION

Since the calculated 't' Value **(3.21)** is greater than the **Table Value (1.96)** it is inferred that there is significant difference between the mean scores of the Attitude towards History among High School Students with respect to Government School and Private School.

RESULT

Hence the null hypothesis is **rejected.**

HYPOTHESES - 3

There is no significant difference is there between **Rural and Urban** in respect of Attitude towards History among High School Students.

TABLE 3

The Table shows Mean, Standard Deviation and 't' Value of Problems Attitude towards History among High School Students.

Locality	N	M	S.D	't'Value	Significanceat 0.05 Level
Rural	138	64.05	10.68	3.33	Significant
Urban	162	68.03	9.89		

df = 298 **Critical Value for 0.05 for level : 1.96**

INTERPRETATION

Since the calculated 't' Value **(3.33)** is greater than the **Table Value (1.96)** it is inferred that there is significant difference between the mean scores of the Attitude towards History among High School Students with respect to Rural and Urban.

RESULT

Hence the null hypothesis is **Rejected.**

HYPOTHESES - 4

There is no significant difference is there between **Hostel and Day scholar** in respect of Attitude towards History among High School Students.

TABLE 4

The Table shows Mean, Standard Deviation and 't' Value of Problems Attitude towards History among High School Students.

Students Locality	N	M	S.D	't'Value	Significanceat 0.05 Level
Hostel	110	69.41	11.76	3.91	Significant
Day scholar	190	64.34	8.9		

df = 298 **Critical Value for 0.05 for level : 1.96**

INTERPRETATION

Since the calculated 't' Value **(3.91)** is greater than the **Table Value (1.96)** it is inferred that there is significant difference between the mean scores of the Attitude towards History among High School Students with respect to Hostel and Day scholar.

RESULT

Hence the null hypothesis is **rejected.**

HYPOTHESES - 5

There is no significant difference is there between **Nuclear Family and Joint Family** in respect of Attitude towards History among High School Students.

TABLE 5

The Table shows Mean, Standard Deviation and 't' Value of Problems Attitude towards History among High School Students.

Type of Family	N	M	S.D	't'Value	Significanceat 0.05 Level
Nuclear Family	185	65.88	6.32	0.77	No Significant
Joint Family	115	66.72	10.65		

df = 298 **Critical Value for 0.05 for level : 1.96**

INTERPRETATION

Since the calculated 't' Value **(0.77)** is less than the **Table Value (1.96)** it is inferred that there is no significant difference between the mean scores of the Attitude towards History among High School Students with respect to Nuclear Family and Joint Family.

RESULT

Hence the null hypothesis is **accepted.**

HYPOTHESES - 6

There is no significant difference is there between **Un Educated and Educated Parents** in respect of Attitude towards History among High School Students.

TABLE 6

The Table shows Mean, Standard Deviation and 't' Value of Problems Attitude towards History among High School Students.

Parents Qualification	N	M	S.D	't'Value	Significanceat 0.05 Level
Un Educated	108	63.46	10.86	3.56	Significant
Educated	192	67.74	8.27		

df = 298 **Critical Value for 0.05 for level : 1.96**

INTERPRETATION

Since the calculated't' Value **(3.56)** is greater than the **Table Value (1.96)** it is inferred that there is significant difference between the mean scores of the Attitude towards History among High School Students with respect to Un Educated and Educated Parents.

RESULT

Hence the null hypothesis is **rejected.**

CONCLUSION

A brief report of the on the result of the data analysis and the findings are liked in the chapter. Further based on the result of analysis the hypothesis verified.

Chapter V

Summary, Findings and Conclusion

INTRODUCTION

The definition of an attitude is a way of feeling or acting toward a person, thing or situation. Passion for a sport, dislike for a certain actor and negativity toward life in general are each an example of an attitude. the position or posture assumed by the body in connection with an action, feeling, mood, etc. to kneel in an attitude of prayer a manner of acting, feeling, or thinking that shows one's disposition, opinion, etc. a friendly attitude one's disposition, opinion, mental set, etc.

NEED AND SIGNIFICANCE OF THE STUDY

A positive towards reading of history is important for a number of reasons. One of the most important reasons is that it enables us to appreciate the importance of institutions such as democratically elected parliaments, the rule of law, trial by jury, an independent judiciary, and the need to protect them. Another important reason is that history provides us with a frame of reference that enables us to recognize dangers to our society, both from within and externally, and it provides guidance as to how to deal with those dangers when they arise. I believe that it was the English philosopher Roger Scranton who said that denying children a solid grounding in the history of their country was calculated to produce a generation of gentle sheep that could be easily led by their political masters. I agree completely with that view.

Darwin burns as Japanese bombers attack Australia on 19 February 1942. The study of history provides us with a frame of reference that enables us to recognize dangers to our society, both from within and externally, and it provides guidance as to how to deal with those dangers when they arise.

I am sometimes asked about the apparent incongruity of a lawyer writing history. While by no means suggesting that legal experience is essential for historians, I would argue that my background in public law and politics is a valuable grounding for historical research and writing history. A Crown prosecutor spends a great deal of time assimilating facts and analyzing them impartially with a view to laying them before a judge or jury to support one or more findings of fact. Knowledge of constitutional law, legal history and the working of government is valuable equipment for an historian who wishes to understand the political as well as the social history of a country.

STATEMENT OF THE PROBLEM

"Attitude towards History among High School Students at Pudukkottai Educational District".

OBJECTIVES OF THE STUDY

Following are the objectives of the present study

To find out the relationship between "Attitude towards History among High School Students at Pudukkottai Educational District"

1. To find out whether any significant difference is there between **Boys and Girls** in respect of Attitude towards History among High School Students .
2. To find out whether any significant difference is there between **Government school and Private school** high school students in respect of Attitude towards History among High School Students.
3. To find out whether any significant difference is there between high school students of **Rural and Urban** areas in respect of Attitude towards History among High School Students.
4. To find out whether any significant difference is there between higher secondary students of **Hostel and Day scholar** in respect of Attitude towards History among High School Students.
5. To find out whether any significant difference is there between family in **Nuclear family and Joint family** in respect of Attitude towards History among High School Students.

6. To find out whether any significant difference is there between higher secondary students with **Un Educated and Educated** of parents in respect of Attitude towards History among High School Students .

HYPOTHESES OF THE STUDY

There is no significant relationship between Attitudes towards History among High School Students.

1. There is no significant difference is there between **Boys and Girls** in respect of Attitude towards History among High School Students.
2. There is no significant difference between **Government school and Private school** in respect of Attitude towards History among High School Students.
3. There is no significant difference between high school students of **Rural and Urban** areas in their in respect of Attitude towards History among High School Students.
4. There is no significant difference between high school students of **Hostel and Day scholar** in respect of Attitude towards History among High School Students.
5. There is no significant difference between family in **Nuclear family and Joint family** in respect of Attitude towards History among High School Students.
6. There is no significant difference between high school students with **Un Educated and Educated** of parents in respect of Attitude towards History among High School Students.

CONSTRUCTION OF RESEARCH TOOLS

The research tool on *"Attitude towards History among High School Students at Pudukkottai Educational District"* Was constructed by the investigator in the present study. All the question items are tick type. The correct answers were given scores and these score were considered for data analysis.

DESCRIPTION OF RESEARCH TOOL AND SCORING PROCEDURE

Before administering the test necessary instruction and directions were given to the students. No time limit is given to the students were asked to complete the inventory as early as possible. It is a **Five Point** of liker's types of tool.

The scale is

1. Strongly Agree (**SCALE IS** SA)
2. Moderately Agree (MA)
3. Undecided (UD)
4. Moderately Disagree (MD)
5. Strongly Disagree (SD)

SAMPLING TECHNIQUE USED

Random Sampling Method was adopted for this purpose. In this method of random sampling every individual in the population has an equal and independent chance of being chosen for the samples.

The sample is small proportion of a population selected for observation and analysis. In this the sample is a smaller representation of the high School students at Pudukkottai Educational District. The investigator selected 300 samples and has been collected from the study by using Random Sampling Techniques. The sample should be selected at random from population. The random sampling does not mean haphazard sampling i.e. sampling without and rule. Random sampling is purely based on defined principles and is a scientific technique. In this, every individual unit in the population gets a chance to be selected.

COLLECTION OF DATA

The investigator himself met each and every school students who are studying in various high schools located at Pudukkottai Educational District. Before going to administer the research tool, the investigator revealed the purpose of the present study to the school students and then asked them to give their responses for each and every item that are given in the questionnaire. The responses of the school students were recorded.

LIMITATION OF THE PRESENT STUDY

1. The study is confirmed to the area of in Pudukkottai Educational District in Tamil Nadu were chosen for the study.
2. The study is restricted to High School Students only.
3. The study is conducted for only High School Students.
4. Only 300 samples were collected from the High School Students.
5. A sample of about 300 students of both the sex was taken for the study.

FINDINGS OF THE PRESENT STUDY

't' Valve = 1.96 (at a level of Significant 0.05)

S. No.	Hypo-thesis	Variables	Table Value	Significant at level	Status
1.	1	Type of Gender (Boys and Girls)	2.22	Significant	Rejected
2.	2	Type of School (Government School and Private School)	3.21	significant	Rejected
3.	3	Locality of Schools (Rural and Urban)	3.33	significant	Rejected
4.	4	Locality of Students (Hostel and Day scholar)	3.91	significant	Rejected
5.	5	Type of Family (Nuclear and Joint)	0.77	No Significant	Accepted
6.	6	Parents Qualification (Un Educated and Educated)	3.56	Significant	Rejected

RECOMMENDATIONS

From the present study it was clearly understood that there is corresponding positive or negative Attitude towards History among High School Students.

SUGGESTIONS FOR FURTHER RESEARCH

1. This method is implemented to this students High School level.
2. Survey method may be expanded to other Higher Secondary students in
3. Pudukkottai Educational District and other Educational district.
4. Survey may be expanded to Higher Secondary Students and College
5. Level Students.
6. Survey method may be implemented to teacher educator at various level.

CONCLUSION

Finding of the present of the study has been consolidated and given in this chapter. Suggestions to come over the Problems encountered by Attitude towards History among High School Students have also been given in this chapter. Therefore, this study will certainly enhance the competence of the students as well teachers.

Bibliography

1. N Sasikumar, M Parimala Fathima. An Overview Study on Awareness of Global Warming Among Graduate Teacher Trainees. Journal of Education and Practice. 2011;2(9):1-5.
2. Haines A, Patz JA. Health effects of climatic change. JAMA. 2004 Jan 7;291(1):99-103.
3. Patz JA, Khaliq M. MSJAMA: Global Climatic change and health: challenges for future practitioners. JAMA. 2002 May 1;287(17):2283-4.
4. Ekpoh, Uduak Imo, Ekpoh, Imo Jackson. Assessing the Level of Climate Change Awareness among Secondary School Teachers in Calabar Municipality, Nigeria: Implication for Management Effectiveness. International Journal of Humanities and Social Science. 2011 March; 1(3):106-110.
5. Pandve H. Global warming: Need to sensitize general population. Indian J Occup Environ Med. 2007 May; 11(2):86-7
6. Vandentorren S, Suzan F, Medina S, Pascal M, Maulpoix A, Cohen JC et al. Mortality in 13 French cities during the August 2003 heat wave. Am J Public Health. 2004 Sep; 94(9):1518-20.
7. Population Census 2011. Available at http://www.census2011.co.in/census/city/451 -mangalore.html.
8. Shruti SH, Tanvi P, Aparna P, Shruti B, Vani S. A pilot study on Awareness Global Warming among School Teachers (unpublished report). Department of Community Medicine, Kasturba Medical College, Mangalore, India; 2008.
9. Nagra, V. Environmental education awareness among school teachers. The Environmentalist. 2010; 30(2):153-162.
10. J.O. Ajiboye, Adeyinka Tella. In-Service Teachers' Knowledge of Significant Global Events/Issues: Implications for Teacher Preparation Programs in Developing Countries. Essays in Education. 2007; 21:35-46.
11. Aladag, E. & Ugurlu, N. B. Global climate change education in Turkey, 2009. Conference paper, Turkey. http://www. herodot. net/ conferences/ Ayvalik/ papers/educ-08.pdf. Retrieved on 15/3/ 2012.

Chapter - I

Importance of Extra-curricular Activities and Academic Achievement

INTRODUCTION

Education is a purposeful activity. By education we intend to bring certain desirable changes in the students. Education is a conscious effort and as such, it has definite aims and objectives. In the light of these aims the curriculum is determined and the academic achievements of the student are measured.

Education research is a field of inquiry aimed at advancing knowledge of education and learning processes and development of the tools and methods necessary to support this endeavor. Education researchers aim to describe, understand and explain how learning takes place throughout the life cycle and how formal and informal processes of education affect learning, attainment and the capacity to lead productive lives. The unifying purpose for education research is to build cumulative and sound knowledge about human and social process of fundamental significance to individuals, to groups and to the larger society.

According to **"Dr. Radhakrishnan".** Education according to Indian tradition is not merely a means of earning a living; nor it is only a nursery of thought or a school for citizenship. It is initiation into the life of spirit and training of human souls in the pursuit of truth and the practice of virtue.

According to **Mahathma Gandhi,** By education I mean an all-round drawing out of the best in child and man's body, mind and spirit.

Extracurricular activities, offer students a chance to improve their soft skills which in future, employers look for in their employees. These skills include decision-making, relationship building, communicating with others and organization of time, people, resources, responsibility, problem solving, teamwork, independence and maturity. These are skills, which are best learned by doing, and students who are active in extracurricular activities can demonstrate that they have a chance to practice all of these and more on a regular basis.

At present the extracurricular program acts as a positive force in preparing school students for an enriching and vital role in Indian life. Through voluntary participation, the student gives time, energy, and loyalty to the program. The student accepts the rules, regulations and responsibilities unique to this program. In short, according to modern education thinkers, curriculum is not only teaching and learning in classroom. It also includes work in library, laboratory and workshop, participation in games and sport in playground.

Numerous informal contacts happen between teacher and pupils in these places. In these informal contacts, there are many activities, one of which is extra-curricular activity. It is a part of curriculum of the institution. Indian schools are giving attention to a child's health, hygiene, sanitation and safety. In addition, recreational games and activities are being increasingly and intelligently designed and promoted for the purpose of wholesome physical development, good citizenship, character education, manners and courtesy. The development of worthy emotions and feelings, heightened inspirations and wholesome aspirations are also provided in some Indian schools. Outside school hours, classroom activities are equally as important as those inside classroom are. They supplement curricular activities, which is the true aim of the school activities.

NEED FOR EXTRA CURRICULAR ACTIVITY IN SCHOOLS

Nowadays extra-curricular activities have been accepted as an integral part of a school's programme. They provide scope for democratic living; develop social skills, a sense of cooperation, team spirit and self-discipline, which are important for a citizen to function in a democracy. All this is possible only through students participation in extra-curricular activities. Hence, the need for extra-curricular activities is increasingly felt in schools. They are an integral part of the activities of a school. As it is a part of curricular work, it therefore needs proper organization and care.

MEANING OF EXTRA - CURRICULAR ACTIVITIES

Four decades ago, it was comparatively easy to define Extra-Curricular Activities, because it was organized and promoted largely by students themselves, with relatively little assistance from teachers and administrators. Equipments were meager, little official recognition was given and no credit was allowed for participation.

Today, it is difficult to define these activities because all teachers have some definite responsibilities for their organization; many full time professional teachers are employed, school rooms, time, equipment and materials are provided; their relationships with regular curricular activities are regarded as vital; credit for participation is allowed and recognition is also given.

The term "**extracurricular activities**" refers to, any activities that take place outside of the regular (compulsory) school curriculum. "The activities are voluntary, and students do not receive grades for academic credit for them". These activities are offered outside of school hours, but within the school setting.

Extracurricular activities are offered at most schools in India, and they consist of a wide range of activities that do not form a part of the regular school curriculum. Most schools allow a free choice for student involvement in these activities, but "many schools make involvement in one or more extracurricular activities a mandatory requirement for their students; believing that such a mandate helps to create a more well-rounded student.

It has indeed been found that in Tamil Nadu, schools such as Mont Ford, Good Shepherd, Padhma Sheshathri, Vellammal, Indian Public School, Holy Angels, Holy Cross, St.Vincents etc include compulsory extracurricular activities and students are strongly motivated to participate. It is clear that the schools promote participation in these activities, due to the merits involved.

Extra-curricular activities are pursued to educate the whole person, academically, spiritually, socially, emotionally and physically. An important part of this education lies in the participation of elementary and high school students in many and varied extra-curricular activities offered by the school. At times, there is some confusion about what is an extra-curricular. The extra-curricular is an activity of equal value to the academic activity. Therefore, extra-curricular activities complement the "student's academic studies or curriculum" and make them more comprehensive and richer.

It is the school's goal that through these opportunities, the students will learn life skills such as team work, leadership, ethical, collaborative and critical thinking.

OUT DOOR PROGRAMMES

Extra- curricular activities range from indoor programmes to outdoor programmes. Many activities, like yoga and drama, are serving as a part of their school's program over a number of years. An ecology club or painting workshop is offered for a shorter time span, to reflect a community interest or involvement of faculty member or student. For many students, extra-curricular activities present an opportunity to practice social skills and to experiment in activities that may represent a career interest. For a child who is academically weak, the opportunity to excel in the arts or sports may make a big difference in his or her self-esteem.

Many extra-curricular activities, such as the school newspaper, photography, and drama, can lead to careers. Extra-curricular activities also help to form the student's profile for consideration in college admissions. A student's academic record and scores on standardized tests form the core of his or her college application profile. However, admissions officers consider other factors, such as a demonstrated talent in athletics or the arts or leadership in school or extracurricular activities.

After-school activities can also include scouting and volunteering, such as working with the Red Cross, NSS, and NCC camps. Through these diverse activities, students can have fun, build a resume for college, increase creativity, improve organizational skills, learn time management, and develop people skills. Along with good teaching, a teacher has to undertake a number of activities in a school such as administration and organization, guidance, counseling, and so on and so forth. If a teacher teaches all the time, however effectively and excellently, the atmosphere of the school will become monotonous.

Apart from this, they will not be performing other functions that they are expected to perform. The teacher should perform a variety of roles since they are essential for promoting all-round development of students. One of the roles that they perform in the organization of extra-curricular activities is, how to organize them, what principles have to be kept in mind, which objectives are to be achieved and what the role of an extra-curricular activities teacher is.

A number of activities that are organized in the Indian schools, in the name of extra-curricular activities, existed in schools even in ancient times, for e.g., music, debate, drama, athletics, etc. In-between they were somewhat ignored and neglected, with more importance being given to academics. It was soon realized that some objectives of education could not be achieved by academics alone. A pure academician develops a lop-sided personality, and all-round development remains a far off dream. All-round development means mental, physical, psychological, spiritual and vocational development.

ACADEMIC ACHIEVEMENT

The Positive Effects of Extracurricular Activities on Students Extracurricular activities are activities that students participate in that do not fall into the realm of normal curriculum of schools. They are found in all levels of our schools. There are many forms of extracurricular activities such as sports, clubs, governance, student newspaper, music, art, and drama. Extracurricular activities are totally voluntary so students that do not want to participate in them do not have to.

Lunnenburg, states in his article that "Extracurricular activities serve the same goals and functions as the required and elective courses in the curriculum. However, they provide experiences that are not included in formal courses of study. They allow students to apply the knowledge that they have learned in other classes and acquire concepts of democratic life".

Extracurricular activities have many positive effects on education. The positive effects that extracurricular activities have on students are behavior, better grades, school completion, positive aspects to become successful adults, and a social aspect. Extracurricular activities began in the United States in the 19th century. At first they were just an additional part to the normal academic schedule for the year. Extracurricular activities usually had some practical or vocational interest that was included into the activities. The first extracurricular activities that were well known in schools started at Harvard and Yale University. They were literacy clubs that consisted of different debate clubs and Greek systems such as fraternities and sororities. Students in American schools were the first to initiate athletic clubs.

NATURE OF EXTRA-CURRICULAR ACTIVITIES

Extracurricular activities are any activities that facilitate learning outside the classroom, and that is not directly relevant to the course. Therefore, for example, the students cannot count fieldwork as extracurricular because they are needed for the exam. Whereas, any groups, clubs, societies or trips that happen during or outside of school time, are counted as Extracurricular, as long as they are not directly relevant to the course. There is a wide variety of Extra-Curricular Activities. Such varieties are sports, arts and crafts, to technological designing, ICT, and computer based courses. Moreover, there are homework-based clubs, special interest clubs and peer mentoring where the senior students look after the younger students, often in their first year of school. Any student can take part in extra-curricular activities.

There are some institutions where students are split by sex or by age. Hence, such institutions may have groups like junior level and senior level, male, female and so on. But overall, any student who wants to volunteer, who feels that he wants to take part in a club or even set up a club is perfectly able to participate. Activities may be conducted before school hours, during school, after school, at weekends, and during the holidays. So, the schools, have everything starting from a basketball practice at lunch time, right through to a week-long ski trip that's about to go over the summer holidays. The vast majority of activities take place within the school, so the separate block would be used as practicing halls.

The classrooms would be used for indoor extra-curricular activities like chess and carom, etc and facilities, like basketball courts, tennis courts, and throw ball courts, are for outdoor games. Extracurricular activities are definitely not compulsory. The real key part of these activities is that the students can choose the activities of their choice. Not only do the students choose to do the activities, but also take part in organizing them and ensuring that they run smoothly they can also get out of the activities when they want.

William Aurther Ward (2013) quoted, "The mediocre teacher tells. The good teacher explains. The superior teacher demonstrates. The great teacher inspires".

An extra-curricular activity teacher is trained in a particular extra-curricular activity. In most of the schools, untrained teachers conduct the majority of the extracurricular activities. Student involvement is necessary for the success of the activities. Once, part-time teachers were appointed to carry out these activities, but now many fulltime professional teachers are employed and school rooms, time, equipment and materials are also provided to promote extra-curricular activity.

Their relationships with regular curricular activities are vital. The Government sanctions teacher postings for these activities in Government schools. The management sponsors such activities in private schools. It can take some time to find the extracurricular activity which best fits both a parent's lifestyle and a child's interests.

A student should never be pressured to join as many activities as possible for the sake of college admissions or its parent's priorities. Extracurricular can bring out the best in a child if he is the right fit for the child's interests, curiosities and abilities. As important, as the activities themselves are the relationships young people can build with the committed adults who direct the activities. Most school teachers, counselors, or Principals provide a list of activities for student participation. The lists are often posted on the school notice boards, and announcements are sometimes made in the classes, such as history teachers promoting the history club or teachers promoting the group that they advise. Information can also be found in the school's student newsletters. Some students like to join clubs, to make friends.

A student who has been declared academically ineligible due to the scholastic rule or other school practices may try out and practice for extra-curricular activities at the discretion of the school. This research paper mainly focuses on extracurricular activities in High School education.

BENEFITS OF EXTRA-CURRICULAR ACTIVITIES

Activities Support the Academic Mission of Schools; they are not a diversion but rather an extension of a good educational program. Students who participate in activity programs tend to have higher grade-point averages, better attendance records, lower dropout rates and fewer discipline problems than students generally.

Activities are inherently Educational; activity programs provide valuable lessons for practical situations teamwork, sportsmanship and hard work. Through participation in activity programs, students learn self-discipline, build Self-confidence and develop skills to handle competitive situations. These are qualities students need if they are to become responsible adults, productive citizens and skilled professionals.

Activities Foster Success in Later Life, participation in high school activities is often a predictor of later success in schools, a career and becoming a contributing healthy member of society.

Athletics, clubs, and other extracurricular activities have benefits beyond the enjoyment they provide. These pursuits assist students in developing personally, socially, and intellectually. They might even help students to advance their academic and professional goals.

INTEGRATING EXTRA-CURRICULAR ACTIVITIES IN SCHOOL CURRICULUM

The programme of extra-curricular activities should be gradual. Only when the school has a need for it and when its students are interested in it, an activity may be introduced. Activities for mere enjoyment are useless. A limitation on student's participation in activities is required because it will check the overload. It will affect their regular studies. Student should have development in both curricular and extra-curricular activities.

All extra-curricular activities are considered part and parcel of school curriculum. With regards to the educational practices, Tagore made a clear distinction between bookish knowledge, emphasizing bookish knowledge and the real intellectual attainment, because our intellect never receives genuine intellectual nourishment. He said that all these years we adorned the cage, but the parrot within remained starving.

Education should cultivate the power of acquiring ideas through independent effort, and develop the ability to learn directly from Nature and Life.

In India, extra-curricular activities of the students fall outside the realm of the normal curriculum of school or university education. Extra-curricular activities exist at all levels of education, such as elementary, middle, high school, higher secondary, college and university level. Such activities not only voluntary as opposed to mandatory, non-paying but also social, and philanthropic as opposed to scholastic. Students often organize and direct these activities under faculty supervision. Modern societies now require that everyone has a certain number of skills that can apply in daily life. As a result, schools now have a new role in introducing skills that will be helpful for the students after they graduate through many activities known as extracurricular activities. They have great varieties of options from which every student can choose the most appropriate according to his personality and interests.

Extra - curricular activities may be athletic or non-athletic. Such activities shall generally be conducted outside the regular school hours, available to pupils who voluntarily come to participate, marked by pupil participation in the processes of initiation, planning, organizing and execution and shall ordinarily include band, clubs, dramatic or musical presentations and intramural and inter-scholastic sports. Equal access to school facilities shall be granted to all activities that meet this definition. The head of the school, shall prepare procedures to implement a extra-curricular program, which shall, assess the needs and interests of the pupils of this district, ensure the provision of competent guidance and supervision by staff, guard against the exploitation of pupils, provide for a variety of experiences and a diversity of organizational models, to order the school heads to organize tournaments and cultural contests. Teacher's role in organizing extracurricular activities in schools is very important.

ROLE OF AN EXTRA-CURRICULAR ACTIVITY TEACHER

As a leader

The teacher should give the student opportunity to exhibit their leadership qualities and these opportunities should be given in rotation.

As Innovator

In order to break monotony of activities, a teacher should try to introduce some novelty new programme.

As a Director

As a director the teacher should see that the programmes selected by the students are constructive. The prgrammes or activities should be scrutinized for their educational relevance.

As an Organizer

The planned activities should be implemented through a strong organizer. The teacher should supervise activities of students for effective programme.

As a Recorder and Innovator

A teacher has to keep a record of all activities undertaken in the academic year. The record must consist of names of participants and winners. The programme should be evaluated periodically.

As a Manager

The teacher has to be an effective manager in order to plan, organize, co-operate, direct, record, evaluate and control activities.

As a Decision Maker

As far as possible a teacher should use democratic methods for taking decisions regarding organization of activities. Care should, however, be taken that style of decision –making is democratic.

As an Advisor

The role of a teacher is to advise students as and when it is required. Teacher should not impose upon and compel students to accept his/her ideas.

As a Motivator

At times, students are reluctant to participate in some co-curricular activities. In such circumstances, the teacher must motivate them to participate in such activities.

As a Commander

The teacher should be able to communicate well regarding the programme and its objectives very clearly and well in advance.

The changing scenario

Today, education is not confined to the 3R's. It is an all-round development of a person. In modern times, the knowledge of 3R's is considered incomplete education. Now anything and everything that goes on in the school campus within school hours or after school hours comes within the purview of school activities. We can hardly distinguish between a curricular activity and some other activity of the school, which was previously taken as extracurricular. Both the types of activities are now considered complementary to each other.

The better meaning of education is making a man to come out of the ignorance and lead a happy life. For some, the meaning for education is to make man earn money and lead a luxurious life. In the present day schools, the state of extra-curricular activities is very pitiable. There are some schools, which are all the time after the examinations. They do not give any importance to extra-curricular activities but they exist only in papers. There is no special care taken. Undoubtedly, the number of schools that provide these activities in a very balanced way is limited. Mostly the institutions lay stress on these activities at the time of the annual day celebrations. During the District tournaments, every school prepares for it, but otherwise they continue being busy with studies only.

Education through activity

The gentle breeze, the warm, glowing sun, the refreshing exercise: these are all part of extracurricular activities. Students cherish this time of the day and are able to release stress through their enjoyment. Whether it is athletics, dance, drama or music, extracurricular activities allow students to embark on activities that they like. Of course, not everyone agrees with the allowance of extracurricular activities, but they are overall beneficial. Although valuable time could be better-spent improving academics, school-sponsored extracurricular activities are unlimited because they keep students involved in the school and in the character building.

Naturally, some people believe that valuable time could be better-spent improving academics than participating in numerous extracurricular activities. However, enough time is already spent in school. Finally, students pick up many real-life applications, extracurricular activities. Obviously, time spent in extracurricular activities should be cherished and cannot be better spent in any other way.

IMPORTANCE OF EXTRA -CURRICULAR ACTIVITIES

Recreation is one of the new comers in the educational family. Organizcd recreation is a relative new comer in the educational arena; roots penetrate rather deep into the social, emotional and mental fiber of the students. It develops the student's moral excellence and social adjustment. Something must be done to make the school activity centered around; extra-curricular activities. Education aims at the development of the whole man, his physical fitness, his mental alertness, his moral excellence and his social adjustment. Therefore, the educational activities should not be exclusively concerned with the teaching of prescribed courses, but should reflect the other objectives of education. Care must be taken to make the school, activity centered.

Educators should take greater responsibility for the development of not only curricular but also extra - curricular activities .If a student is engaged in extra - curricular activity he gains opportunity for self-expression and self-fulfillment. A school, which organizes extra-curricular activity, hums with life and pursuits. Our libraries our laboratories, our playing fields and debating halls should be throbbing with life and intense activity throughout the year.

A prospective teacher should well arrange for extra-curricular activity for the overall development of the student. Teachers enjoy the thrill and liveliness of extra-curricular activities in and outside of the classroom. Extracurricular activities help keep students involved in their school. Many students are able to meet other students with similar interests through extracurricular activities. By meeting people with common interests, students can share their passion for something and make others feel as if they were still in their school.

Extracurricular activities can also boost school spirit. For instance, when students participate in these activities they come to school eager and excited because of their activity. This helps students feel like a part of the school and gives them a purpose for attending. Lastly, extracurricular activities extend the school day, keeping students supervised longer. This allows students to spend more time with their teachers and classmates, improving relationships. It is quite clear that participation in extracurricular activities allows students to become included in their school.

Ultimately, extracurricular activities build character in students. More specifically, they teach students life lessons. Of course, a basketball player will realize his responsibility if he is forced to run for being late to practice. Not only that, but extracurricular activities also provide supervision to help keep students out of trouble. For example, a student may have parents who work overtime. Rather than staying at home or with friends after school, where someone could get into trouble, students can stay at school participating in activities where they are watched and kept busy. Finally, extracurricular activities encourage positive leadership roles. Granted an athlete respects the opinion of their coach, he is likely to pass on positive morals instilled by his coach. Many athletes are respected by their fellow students and are able to encourage high moral standards among them. Overall, students can achieve exemplary virtues by participating in extracurricular activities.

School-sponsored extracurricular activities should not be limited because they allow students to participate in the school and encourage good morals. Students will become happier and more virtuous because of extracurricular activities. If students can handle these activities, they should not be restricted from taking part in them. After all, students enjoy extracurricular activities, while improving their overall well-being. In conclusion, this is the appropriate time to provide the students with positive direction in their lives.

THE BENEFITS OF EXTRACURRICULARS

Much of student's time outside the classroom is already spoken for. So why add extracur-ricular activities to an already busy schedule? The benefits to participants including mak-ing friends, developing skills, and improving academic and employment prospects are a strong argument in their favor.

A primary reason that students take part in an activity is personal interest. And an immediate benefit of pursuing interests through extracurricular is meeting others who share those same interests.

The opportunity to form friendships also gives students a chance to develop social skills. For some students, social interaction in extracurricular activities is their first experi-ence working with others toward a common goal. And teamwork is an important skill that most instructors and employers view favor-ably.

Teamwork often evolves into leadership in the extracurricular environment, because each club or organization has leadership posts.

CHOOSING ACTIVITIES

The number and type of extracurricular activities available is sometimes overwhelm-ing. Students should choose activities that are based on their interests and then weigh the potential conflicts those activities would have with other demands for their time includ-ing academic study. Prospective college- or graduate-level students should also consider the potential for scholarships that exist with many types of activities.

Some activities may be more prestigious than others, but genuine appeal should out-weigh ulterior motives. Students should not attempt to boost their credentials with activi-ties that do not match their interests or abili-ties. Whether they seek to improve their skills or enhance their future prospects, students should pursue an extracurricular activity for at least one other reason: to have fun.

Academic clubs. In high schools and col-leges, many academic subjects have a related club. These clubs promote their members' shared interest in the subject and supplement classroom learning. Club members may hold leadership positions and arrange to invite guest speakers, take field trips, or organize study groups.

Academic clubs provide students with an opportunity to discuss topics beyond the scope of the classroom. Language clubs, for example, allow students to watch foreign films or eat delicacies that are native to the country of origin. These cultural experiences are enjoyable and help make learning a lan-guage more meaningful.

Academic competitions. Not all competi-tion takes place on fields and in gymnasiums. Many schools offer students the chance for intellectual contests.

Academic competitions might be limited to a single subject, such as mathematics or history, or cover a broad range of subjects. Competitions may take place within a single school, or school teams might participate in State, national, or international events. To participate in these competitions, students must first qualify for their school's team. Academic competitions usually require significant preparation. It is likely that the study skills of students who are selected for the team are already well developed; however, competitions give them the chance to hone these skills further. Participants also learn to work together with other team members.

Athletics. Athletics are among the most prominent and popular of extracurricular activities in both higher secondary school and colleges. Par-ticipation in varsity athletics usually requires major commitments of time and effort. But many students take part in another popular option: intramural sports. Although intramural athletics may not require the same commitment as varsity sports, both help students develop the same kinds of skills. In team sports, for example, participants usually develop a sense of cama-raderie and learn to work together with others. And physically active students learn to appre-ciate the benefits of an active lifestyle.

Debate. Debate, sometimes called forensics, requires a wide range of skills. In debate competitions, participants present an argument they have researched, based on established topics and rules. Higher secondary school and college debate teams might compete intramural or against other schools.

Performing arts. Most high schools and colleges have performing arts organizations, such as music band, orchestra, chorus and drama clubs. Like elite athletes, student per-formers usually must make a major time com-

DIFFERENT TYPES OF EXTRA -CURRICULAR ACTIVITIES

Activities for physical development: Games, physical-exercises, wrestling, swimming, yoga, boating, skating.

Activities of subjective type: Subject associations, symposium, library organization, literary society, writing competition, poetical recitation, debates, magazine writing.

Civic training activity: Organizing student's co-operative store, student's council, visiting civic institutions municipal committee, post office, gram panchayat, zila parishad, legislative assembly, high court etc Celebrating national and religious

Activities for aesthetic and cultural development: Music and dancing, drawing and painting, fancy dress, variety programme, folk and classical song, organizing exhibitions, celebrating festivals, decorating the school and garden maintaining.

Leisure time activities: Philately, numismatics, stone-collection, photography, album making, collecting of leaves and pictures.

Craft activities: Spinning and weaving, tailoring, embroidery, clay modeling, soap making, basket making, leatherwork, toy making, book binding.

Community activities: Mass prayer, scouting, girl guide, Red Cross, NSS, village survey.

Excursion activities: Picnics, trips and tours, historical place (museum, monuments), zoo, exhibition- visit. A common problem for many students involved in extracurricular activities is that they take on too much time for it. Students should make out a schedule in advance of a semester that balances school, work, after-school activities, and home life. In addition, activities should be fun rather than stressful for students. School grades should not suffer because of time spent at work or in after-school activities.

OBJECTIVES OF EXTRA- CURRICULAR ACTIVITIES AT SCHOOL LEVEL

i) For the physical and mental development of the child,

ii) To develop academic and literary interests,

iii) To develop a sense of social service,

iv) To develop moral training for the academic development of the student,

v) To provide recreational value for the maintenance of good mental health, for the development of self-discipline, to provide leadership opportunities, for the development of community life, for developing the skill of proper planning,

vi) To develop useful new capabilities in pupils that can lead to extension of career opportunities,

vii) To develop pupil initiative and responsibility.

viii) To develop leadership capabilities and good organizational skills,

xi) To enable pupils to explore a wider range of individual interests than what is available in the regular program.

x) To aid pupils in the social skills,

ACTIVITIES-A FILLIP OF LEARNING

Activity is an overt expression of the under current urge for doing and achieving things. This dates back to the age when the child starts perceiving and discovering from his surroundings. This urge is never satisfied. The same could be adopted beneficially in the teaching-learning strategy. Activities have a wide connotation. It ranges from direct experiences, techniques and devices. Direct experiences include activities like field trips, exhibitions, museums; techniques include activities like experimentation computation, demonstration and so on; devices include activities like working with TV, VCR, Radio, Audio Cassettes and Video Cassettes. In the activity approach, the strategies pre-suppose provision of meaningful experiences that are directional. This makes learning incidental, natural and purposeful.

NEED FOR EXTRA-CURRICULAR ACTIVITIES

Extra-Curricular activities have a number of values like educational value, development of social spirit, character-training education for leadership, worthy use of leisure time or recreational value, team spirit, development of civic virtue, physical development, improved discipline, aesthetic development and development of cultural values.

Simply knowing something does not guarantee the ability to act on that knowledge. There is a profound difference between knowing and doing. Teachers may know, for example, that they should provide prompt feedback to their students on written assignments, but they are not always able to act on that knowledge. All prospective teachers need to organize extra - curricular activities for the all round development of the students. These activities ensure dynamism in the school programme. Everyone associated with teaching and learning in a school feels sense of living and thrilling atmosphere in the event of activities going on inside or outside the classroom is guaranteed.

Physical fitness is guaranteed while learning extra-curricular activities

1. Defective digestive system is rectified.
2. Student gains practical experience of sharing responsibility and exercising self-control.

3. Students lack social adjustment; extra-curricular activity develop them as effective citizens.
4. Extra-curricular activities improve student's imagination and aesthetic sense.
5. A varied cultural programme can meet the juvenile drives, needs and interests of the student.
6. Effective moral training can be given only through extra-curricular activities, which provide situations with moral programme.
7. Extra-curricular activities save students from leisure hour's boredom.
8. Extra-curricular activities provide opportunities for Leadership.
9. Extra-curricular activity is necessary to balance the indigestive system of residential students, to develop physical fitness proper growth and development of the body.

BENEFITS OF EXTRA-CURRICULAR ACTIVITIES

At a cost of only one to three percent or less in many cases of an overall school's budget, higher secondary school activity programs are one of the best bargains around. It is in these vital programs – sports, music, speech, drama, debate – where young people learn lifelong lessons as important as those taught in the classroom. Unfortunately, there appears to be a creeping indifference toward support for higher secondary school activity programs by the public. This neglect undermines the educational mission of our schools and the potential prosperity of our communities

COCURRICULAR ACTIVITIES TEACH LESSONS THAT LEAD TO BETTER CITIZENS

Extracurricular activities allow students;

To form new connections with peers and acquire social capital. Activity programs are one of the few contexts, outside of the classroom, where adolescents regularly come in contact with adults to whom they are not related. Students who spend no time in extracurricular activities are more likely to become in extracurricular activities.

PROBLEMS IN ORGANIZING EXTRA-CURRICULAR ACTIVITIES

These activities are carried after school hours in most of the Indian schools. Due to lack of transport facility, some students miss such activities after school hours though they have a lot of interest. In most of the schools, these programmes are teacher centered. Poor students cannot afford to pay for these activities in private schools. Student's funds for this purpose are sometimes misappropriated. Teacher should not develop an attitude of partiality. Some Teachers do their work for namesake because they are not properly trained in that particular activity. Particular extra-curricular period should be used to teach only that particular activity.

Some students are compelled by the teacher to participate in an activity which they have no interest. Proper records are not maintained regarding attendance during the period and no accounts maintained regarding expenditure. Financially strong fair ones, beautiful ones, studious children only are given bright opportunities. A wide variety of activities will create confusion and a lot of expenditure. In the present day schools, the position of extra-curricular activities is very pitiable. There are some schools, which are all the time after the examinations. They do not give any importance to extra-curricular activities but they exist only in the papers. There is no special care for them. Very few schools are of the type where more stress is laid on these activities only. Undoubtedly, the number of schools which provide these activities in a very balanced way is limited. Children who refuse to join any extracurricular activities yet appear unhappy or have no friends may be suffering from emotional problems such as depression or low self-esteem.

Professional help, such as counseling, may be needed. Sometimes a lack of self-esteem or other problems are too much for a student to handle alone. Parents may need to seek professional psychological help for children suffering from low self-esteem when the child is depressed or shows overly aggressive behavior. In a developing country like India with huge population, poverty, poor health care system, illiteracy, people are still unaware of the importance of extra - curricular activities.

NEED OF THE STUDY

"Participation in extracurricular activities in higher secondary school appears to be one of the few interventions that benefit low-status, disadvantaged students those less well served by traditional educational programs as much as or more than their more advantaged peers" - **Everson and Millsap (2012).**

Student's classroom engagement is related to student participation in activities, especially among students from poor families. Activities help students to build supportive relationships on academic achievement. This component in classroom engagement and aspire students. This activity programs create higher secondary school students with higher aspirations and more commitment to academic success. This programs help promote healthy physical, psychological, emotional and social health. For the above reason the present study is taken to find *"A Study on Effect of Sound and*

Light Equipments in Eradicating Errors in Pronunciation Among IXth Standard Students.

SCOPE OF THE STUDY

Students who participate in extracurricular activities generally benefit from many opportunities afforded them. Benefits of participating in extracurricular activities included having better grades, having higher standardized test scores and higher educational attainment, attending school more regularly and having a higher self-concept. Participants in out-of-school activities often learned skills such as teamwork and leadership while decreasing the likelihood of alcohol use and illicit drug use and related problem behaviors. Those who participate in out-of-school activities often have higher grade point averages, a decrease in absenteeism and an increased connectedness to the school. When balanced with academic learning, extracurricular activities may help students raise self-esteem, develop school spirit and connect with the adults in the community in a positive manner creating a good situation for all.

STATEMENT OF THE PROBLEM

Over the years the costs and effect of extracurricular activities have generated many studies and numerous relations to academic performance. It is defined that traditional extracurricular activity in class instruction that impact academic achievement. Educationists are interested in the relationship between academic achievement and participation in extracurricular activities. Implying that these activities do have some sort of influence on how students perform academically. To find the involvement of the students the present study is entitled as *"A Study on Importance of Extra-Curricular Activities and Academic Achievement among Higher Secondary School Students In Tiruchirappalli District".*

OBJECTIVES OF THE STUDY

The following are the objectives of the present study chosen

1. To find whether there is any significant difference between the mean scores on importance of extra-curricular activities and academic achievement among male higher secondary school students.
2. To find whether there is any significant difference between the mean scores on importance of extra-curricular activities and academic achievement among rural higher secondary school students.
3. To find whether there is any significant difference between the mean scores on importance of extra-curricular activities and academic achievement among government higher secondary school students.

4. To find whether there is any significant difference between the mean scores on importance of extra-curricular activities and academic achievement among nuclear family higher secondary school students.
5. To find whether there is any significant difference between the mean scores on importance of extra-curricular activities and academic achievement among higher secondary school students father educational level as schooling.
6. To find whether there is any significant difference between the mean scores on importance of extra-curricular activities and academic achievement among higher secondary school students family economy status as average.
7. To find whether there is any significant difference between the mean scores on importance of extra-curricular activities and academic achievement among female higher secondary school students.
8. To find whether there is any significant difference between the mean scores on importance of extra-curricular activities and academic achievement among urban area higher secondary school students.
9. To find whether there is any significant difference between the mean scores on importance of extra-curricular activities and academic achievement among non-government higher secondary school students.
10. To find whether there is any significant difference between the mean scores on importance of extra-curricular activities and academic achievement among joint family higher secondary school students.
11. To find whether there is any significant difference between the mean scores on importance of extra-curricular activities and academic achievement among higher secondary school students father educational level as collegiate.
12. To find whether there is any significant difference between the mean scores on importance of extra-curricular activities and academic achievement among higher secondary school students family economy status as good.

HYPOTHESES OF THE STUDY

The following are the hypotheses of the present study chosen

1. There is no significant difference between the mean scores on importance of extra-curricular activities and academic achievement among male higher secondary school students.

2. There is no significant difference between the mean scores on importance of extra-curricular activities and academic achievement among rural higher secondary school students.
3. There is no significant difference between the mean scores on importance of extra-curricular activities and academic achievement among government higher secondary school students.
4. There is no significant difference between the mean scores on importance of extra-curricular activities and academic achievement among nuclear family higher secondary school students.
5. There is no significant difference between the mean scores on importance of extra-curricular activities and academic achievement among higher secondary school students father educational level as schooling.
6. There is no significant difference between the mean scores on importance of extra-curricular activities and academic achievement among higher secondary school students family economy status as average.
7. There is no significant difference between the mean scores on importance of extra-curricular activities and academic achievement among female higher secondary school students.
8. There is no significant difference between the mean scores on importance of extra-curricular activities and academic achievement among urban area higher secondary school students.
9. There is no significant difference between the mean scores on importance of extra-curricular activities and academic achievement among non-government higher secondary school students.
10. There is no significant difference between the mean scores on importance of extra-curricular activities and academic achievement among joint family higher secondary school students.
11. There is no significant difference between the mean scores on importance of extra-curricular activities and academic achievement among higher secondary school students father educational level as collegiate.
12. There is no significant difference between the mean scores on importance of extra-curricular activities and academic achievement among higher secondary school students family economy status as good.

DEFINITION OF THE KEY TERMS USED

Extracurricular Activities - organized student activities connected with school and usually carrying no academic credit.

Curricular activities occur within the regular school day and constitute the delivery of instruction to students in the school, e.g. language, mathematics, science, history, geography etc.

Co-curricular activities are an extension of classroom instruction in which participation is by the entire class or a significant portion thereof. They relate directly to, and enhance student learning of, essential elements through participation, demonstration, illustration, and observation.

Extra-curricular activities are school-sponsored activities that are not directly related to instruction of the essential elements, but that may have an indirect relation to some areas of the curriculum. They offer worthwhile and significant contributions to a student's personal, physical, and social development. Participation in extracurricular activities is a privilege and not a right, and students must meet specific requirements in order to participate. Activities may include, but are not limited to, performances, contests, demonstrations, displays, and club activities, e.g. dance, drama, music etc.

Extra-Curricular activities are activities that education organizations in some parts of the world have created for school students. They serve to promote a variety of activities, which all school students should attend alongside the standard study curriculum. As per the Cambridge Dictionary of American English, "Extra" means added, additional, or more than expected outside or in addition to. Similarly the definition of extracurricular activities from the Cambridge Advanced Learner's Dictionary is - activities that are not part of the usual school or college hours. Extra means - in addition with. Curricular means course of study. So Extra -curricular probably mean activities or studies that are done as extra studies, in addition to the regular studies.

DELIMITATIONS OF THE STUDY

Delimitations for this study include:

1. The independent variables to be manipulated.
2. The time frame to complete this research study was limited.
3. Data was gathered solely from students of the 2014-2015 academic year since data was gathered from higher secondary student.

CONCLUSION

This chapter deals with the significance of the problem, statement of the study, operation definition of the key terms, objectives of the study, major hypotheses, limitations of the study, plan and procedure of the study. The review of related literature and research studies related with the present investigation are included in the next chapter.

Chapter - II

Review of Related Literature

INTRODUCTION

A literature review (also known as a literature survey or bibliographic essay) is a survey and discussion of the literature in a given area of study. It is a concise overview of what has been studied, argued and established about a topic and it is usually organized chronologically or thematically.

A literature review is written in essay format. It is not an annotated bibliography, because it groups related works together and discusses trends and developments rather than focusing on one item at a time. It is not a summary rather, it evaluates previous and current research in regard to how relevant and/or useful it is and how it relates to your own research.

A literature review is written to highlight specific arguments and ideas in a field of study. By highlighting these arguments, the writer attempts to show what has been studied in the field and also where the weaknesses, gaps or areas needing further study are. The review should therefore also demonstrate to the reader why the writer's research is useful, necessary, important and valid.

STRUCTURE

The length of a literature review varies depending on its purpose and audience. In a thesis or dissertation, the review is usually a full chapter, but for an assignment it may only be a few pages.

There are several ways to organize and structure a literature review. Two common ways are chronologically and thematically.

CHRONOLOGICAL

In a chronological review, group and discuss the sources in order of their appearance (usually publication), highlighting the changes in research in the field and your specific topic over time. This method is useful for papers focusing on research methodology, historic graphical papers and other writing where time becomes an important element.

THEMATIC

In a thematic review, group and discuss the sources in terms of the themes or topics they cover. This method is often a stronger one organizationally and it can help you resist the urge to summarize your sources. By grouping themes or topics of research together, it will be able to demonstrate the types of topics that are important to your research. No matter which method you choose, remember: Within each section of a literature review, it is important to discuss how the research relates to other studies (how is it similar or different, what other studies have been done, etc.) as well as to demonstrate how it relates to own work.

A summary of the writings of recognized authorities and or previous research provides evidence that the researcher is familiar with what is already known and what is still known and untested.

Review of related literature helps of eliminated the duplication of what has been done and provided useful hypotheses and helpful suggestions for significant investigation.

The related literature should have certain important elements like,

1. Report of studies of closely related problems that have been investigated.
2. Design of the study including procedure employed and data gathering instruments used.
3. Populations that were sampled and sampling methods employed.
4. Variables that were defined.
5. Extraneous variables that could have affected the findings.
6. Faults that could that have been avoided.
7. Recommendation for further research.

MEANING OF RELATED STUDY

Studying about the related literature gives proper guidelines to the investigator for identifying, reading and educating reports of research as well as reports of causal observation and opinion that are related to individual's planned observation.

NEED FOR THE REVIEW OF LITERATURE

A thorough survey of related literature gives useful information to the investigator for understanding the problem and shows a way to solve the chosen problem from different dimensions. It enriches the present study by the past findings and gives a proper insight to the research study by which any one can think creatively.

THE PURPOSE OF THE REVIEW OF LITERATURE

It helps the investigator to find was already done and what problems remain to be solved in a chosen topic.

1. It is the basis for the foundation upon which all future work will be built.
2. It helps to know the means of getting to the frontier in the field of the research.
3. It furnishes indispensable suggestions about comparative data, good procedure, likely methods and tried techniques.
4. It helps to avoid the duplication of previous researches.
5. It provides basic structure for formulating valuable hypotheses.
6. It helps to analyze and locating comparative data which is useful in the interpretation of results.

Related literature is a valuable guide to defining the problem, recognizing is significance, suggesting premising data- gathering devices appropriate study design and source of data. In this chapter an attempt is made to review the relevant previous studies on *"A Study on Effect of Sound and Light Equipments in Eradicating Errors in Pronunciation Among IXth Standard Students"*.

STUDIES CONDUCTED IN INDIA

Sultan Mohiy-ud-din (2014) says that these activities are no longer looked upon as mere „extras , but as an integral part of the school programme. The distinction between curricular and extra- curricular has been gradually disappearing in modern education practice and coordination and integration of all the experiences of the pupil-intellectual, social, moral, emotional and physical has become the object of persistent efforts of the school.

According to a study published in the **Winter (2014)** issue of Education, the benefits of teen participation in extracurricular activities go well beyond just filling up an already-busy schedule and having another line to add to the college application. Benefits include having a sense of team spirit and belonging, personal pride and an understanding of the value of fair play, an increased sense of honesty and trustworthiness, and, importantly, the prevention of drug and substance abuse – among others. The study states that repeated records of higher secondary students across the United States have shown that those students who become heavily involved in extracurricular activities tend to be model students.

Boatwright's (2014) quantitative study which compared GPA and extracurricular involvement. Data was gathered from 9th -12th graders in twenty-five Southwest schools for the year 2013-2014. This data included HSGPA and dropout rates. The dependent variable in this study was extracurricular involvement, while GPA and dropout rates were independent variables. The goal of this study was to determine a difference between the academic performance of those who do and those that do not participate in extracurricular activities. Therefore, it was causal comparative in nature. The researcher's hypotheses included:

1) There is a statistically significant higher GPA for students who participate in ECAs when compared to those who chose not to participate in any activity.

2) There is a statically lower dropout rate for students who participate in ECAs when compared to those students who do not participate in any activity. While the second research question was interesting, it did not apply to my study, therefore my focus rested on the first research question.

Chandran.K (2013) collected data from student records and state eligibility forms. Yearbooks were also used to determine which students were involved in extracurricular activities. Student names were not listed in order to maintain confidentiality. An Excel spreadsheet was used to organize data and a t test was used to correlate the information and determine whether or not the groups were statistically different. Limitations in this study included the fact that there was no discrimination, meaning that all students in 9th - 12th grade were used. Also, the population was not disaggregated by sport or activity. Boatwright concluded that there was a higher mean GPA for participants in extracurricular activities using a significance level of $p < .05$ (Boatwright, 2010).

Dick (2012) examined possible relationships between participation in extracurricular activities and student achievement, attendance, and behavior. The dependent variable being examined was participation in extracurricular activities (ECAs) and the remaining variables were independent in nature. As noted in, O'Brien and Rollefson (1995) stated that "Extracurricular activities, including fine arts, interscholastic athletics, cheerleading, and academic clubs provide students with the opportunity to develop the value of teamwork, the value of individual and group responsibility, and a sense of community" (p. 22). Regardless of the benefits of extracurricular involvement, the lingering question posed is: What influence do extracurricular activities have on academic performance? To answer this question, data from 275 high school graduates in Nebraska were gathered to test a total of ten research hypotheses (Dick, 2010). Of these ten hypotheses, I focused on one Relationship relevant hypothesis: Students who participated in extracurricular activities had higher GPAs than students who did not participate.

Delimitations addressed by the researcher included: the study was limited to one school district and also limited to students who graduated in 2007-2008.

These delimitations were comparable to those in my research study. After using a t test to analyze differences at the $p < .001$ level of significance, Dick concluded that students who participated in extracurricular activities were found to have a significantly higher GPA than those not involved in ECAs (Dick, 2010). His results concluded that those who participated in extracurricular activities had a mean GPA of 3.06 with a standard deviation of .789. However, those who did not participate in extracurricular activities held a mean GPA of 2.39 with a standard deviation of .780.

Watkins' (2012) of all of the dissertations reviewed concerning the variables of extracurricular involvement, study best related to my current research study. This descriptive study investigated the effects of participation in extracurricular activities on the mean GPA of students enrolled at Dade County High School in northwest India. Both the independent variable of GPA and the dependent variable of extracurricular involvement related to my study. The school and student population were comparable to the sample setting of my research study which was very beneficial in my examination as well.

Wilsons (2011) hypothesized the following: "Male students who participate in extracurricular activities will have higher mean GPAs than those students who participated in no activities" (p.6). His second hypothesis was identical except for the substitution of females for males being considered. The researcher delimited his study to the interscholastic athletics and co curricular activities that occurred at higher secondary School over the last five years. Similarly, my study is limited to a one year period. The remaining delimitation listed was that the extracurricular activities were divided into groups. Limitations for this study included the fact the number and types of activities participated in were unknown. The data gathered concerning extracurricular activities in my research study did not classify activities either. Watkins also limited his study to the fact that the level of participation was unknown.

Deva (2011), "for a large percentage of students, particularly those who live in rural school districts, the high school experience serves as the primary, and final forum for learning personal and professional skills in a formal public school environment" (p.13). With so much value placed on participation in extracurricular activities and the effects of involvement on our students, research regarding its advantages and disadvantages must be conducted.

Sing Prateep (2010) research was analyzed using a one-way ANOVA, followed by the Scheffe´ multiple comparison procedure. As a results of the ANOVA, he found that there was a statistically significant effect of participation on mean GPA of male students (F (31619)=86.85, p<.001. The researcher concluded that at p< .05, students who participated in ECAs had higher mean GPAs than those who did not participate.

Streb (2009) explored the issue of extracurricular involvement, HSGPA, and ACT performance. A statistical comparison was made between students who were involved in co curricular activities and their peers who were not. Whereas Streb's (2009) study distinguished between types of activities that students were involved in, the current study does not, but it is still interesting to observe the differences. The dependent variable of academic achievement measured by ACT and HSGPA was juxtaposed with participation in co-curricular activities.

Theoretical framework Studies conducted by the National Council of Educational Research and Training (1991, 1994, 1996) and by the National Institute of Educational Planning and Administration (1990) were probing into the learning achievements only. Inspite of Operation Black Board Scheme and District Institute of Education and Training, there is low learning achievement (Lockheed et al. 1997).This study says that though free education is given to the students till they reach the age of 14, nearly 40 % dropouts are there due to various reasons. Boredom is one among the major reasons. It has been found out that extra - curricular activities should be introduced at this juncture to attract students towards school and make learning enjoyable.

NCTE (1999) published a compilation of Gandhiji s works entitled "Gandhi and Education" that contains an important abstract about education of the whole child education, real education and education making the whole man. Gandhiji had amply emphasized, "True education of the intellect can only come through a proper exercise, health education and physical education but caring properly for these is as important and essential to human kind as air water and food. It adds that physical and mental health has to be maintained and strongly recommended as an integral part of education." Gandhiji expressed his views on education on 22nd and 23rd October 1937 at Wardha Educational Conference. For him, education meant the comprehensive and integral development of the individual and the child, in other words the development of the brain, body, and spirit. According to Gandhi, "Real education consists in drawing the best out of you. What better book can there be than the book of humanity?" Harijan: March 30, 1934. According to Tagore, - "The highest aim of education is that which does not merely give us information but makes our life in harmony with all existence". In accordance with the general philosophy, Tagore emphasized the physical culture, enjoyment of nature and the cultivation of arts in schools (Kripalani Krishna,1971). 'Praner aram, maner anand, atmar sant....' which means the play of life, happiness, the satisfaction of mind, is the complete, the whole man - Bagavat Geetha (Swami Sithbavanandha, 2010).

Brown (2008), student participants in extracurricular activities had better grades, had higher standardized test scores, higher educational attainment, attended school more regularly, and had higher self-concepts. In addition, young people who participate also have been found to be less likely to use substances such as drugs and alcohol, less likely to drop out of school, misbehave at school, and commit delinquent acts.

Smith Holy (2007) example of a helpful extracurricular activity is participation in athletics. Student athletes interact with peers, work for the best interest of the team, and learn to follow instructions of the team leader. This type of interaction may contribute to the student athlete's development of self-identity. A student's identification and involvement with school sports creates a social network for these student athletes that emphasizes the value of the school, academics, and continuing their education after high school. Participation in sports may also provide students with unique development opportunities that positively impact the student's social self-concept. This may lead to a higher academic expectations and therefore better academic outcomes for student athletes. Adolescent students who do not have opportunities to identify with a particular group or who are affiliated with delinquent social groups are more likely to suffer negative repercussions including: dropout, suicide, substance abuse, or discipline problems (Smith, 2005).

STUDIES CONDUCTED IN ABROAD

Streb (2015) was: "Are there differences on academic success measures (ACT and GPA) by student type (students who participate in co-curricular activities vs. students who do not participate in co-curricular activities" (p. 13). In order to answer this question, he gained permission to access archived data from the guidance office, and then imported that data into SPSS 15.0.

Streb (2014) considered several limitations. Some that were relevant to the current study include: Only data from one school was used; there was no separation by student gender; socioeconomic status and its influence on the decision to participate in activities could not be assessed. ANOVAs were conducted on both ACT and HSGPA to reveal that "a significant mean difference exists on ACT scores by participation in a co-curricular activity $F\ (1,\ 347) = 4.80$, $p < 0.05$, Partial $n = 0.01$, Power = 0.59" (p. 56).

Kilrea (2014) correlation study that examined the relationship between extracurricular activity participation and the academic achievement of higher secondary students was conducted by Academic achievement as measured by the ACT was the dependent variable in this study, while the independent variables were gender, number of activities, and total number of seasons in participation. Academic achievement was measured by composite ACT scores and was compared to two types of extracurricular activities: academic activities and non-academic activities. The research was limited to schools in one district and those who were willing to participate.

Miranda (2013) the final study on this topic was conducted. The purpose of this research study was to determine if a cause-effect relationship existed among the dependent variables of cumulative GPA, SAT score, and ACT score and the independent variable: participation in extracurricular activities. The design of this study was descriptive, causal-comparative in nature and included a sample of three hundred sixty-one students at a private school in north central Texas. The most relevant research questions addressed the effects of participation or non-participation in extracurricular activities on HSGPA and ACT scores. Gender was also addressed but didn't carry any significance to my study.

Pettigrew (2012) considered the impact of socioeconomic status on student achievement in rural east Tennessee. Pettigrew declared that "The achievement gap in the educational setting of economically disadvantaged and non-economically disadvantaged students... is hefty and unrelenting" (p. 11). For this reason, the researcher studied 5 dependent variables (the number of items students answered correctly on the math, language arts, science, and social studies portions of the test and the holistic writing test scores) and the independent variables of school classification and socioeconomic status to try and fill a void in literature that exists concerning the issue (Pettigrew, 2009). The Tennessee Comprehensive Assessment Program (TCAP) measured academic achievement for the population of

271 eighth graders and this data used in a two-way analysis of variance. When socioeconomic levels were taken into consideration in the two-way ANOVAs, "There was a significant difference in the mean number of language arts items answered correctly between students who were economically disadvantaged and those who were not, $F(1,263) = 8.07$, $p = .01$".

Anderson (2011) study, a similar descriptive, correlation study was conducted by St. Rose with the goal of filling a void in literature that exists when examining interrelationships between SES, gender, race/ethnicity, and SAT performance (St. Rose). In this study, St. Rose used a multiple regression to examine differences. St. Rose proposed that, "Empirical evidence indicates that not only gender, but also race/ethnicity and socioeconomic status are related to academic performance" (St. Rose, 2008, p. 13). The researcher used the same age group of participants that comprise the current study: high school seniors. The research questions focus on moderator effects, whereas my research question does not. However, St. Rose's (2008) study was still beneficial because of the similarity in standardized test type.

While the effects of extracurricular involvement on academic achievement have been considered, this section will specifically address athletic participation by reviewing three studies. Extracurricular activities and more specifically participation in athletic activities have numerous effects on a student mentally, physically and emotionally

Stencel (2010) stated that "Leadership, citizenship, and personal development qualities...are among the implications associated with extracurricular activities" (p. 21). In his work, Stencil examined the correlation between athletic participation and academic achievement. The dependent variables observed in this study were GPA, NCAA core GPA, composite ACT score, and attendance rates. The researcher's sample consisted of 507 students from 13 different high schools in west Tennessee. The following are two research questions posed by Stencel that were most relevant to my study: First, "Is there a correlation between interscholastic athletic participation and cumulative GPA?" (p. 44); Second, "Is there a correlation between interscholastic athletic participation and composite ACT scores?" (Stencel). To address the research questions, an ANOVA and MANOVA were conducted using SPSS with the significance level set as $p = .05$. In regards to the first research question posed, reports concluded that "at the multivariate level, significant difference existed for the status main effect [$F(2,502) = 4.922$, $p = .008$]"

Montgomery (2009) investigated the connection between high school athletics and academic performance. The researcher chose to compare a sample of African American males who participated in athletics to a sample of those who did not. This study was conducted with data gathered from the 2008-2009 academic year. One topic of debate that the researcher pointed out was the notion that athletic participation may detract too much from academic activities, resulting in lower academic performance.

Kaufmann (2007) also executed a study regarding athletic participation and academic achievement. As suggested in the previous study, Kaufmann also discussed the possibility that athletic activities detract from academic focus. This debate served as one motive for the research study which examined the dependent variable of academic performance in relation to the independent variables of HSGPA, ACT composite score, highest level of mathematics achieved, and attendance rate. The researcher suggested that the variable of highest level of math achieved helped to determine which students might be college bound as opposed to those who may not be college bound.

(Kaufmann, 2006). The conclusion of the study suggested that, "The data analysis yielded a positive and significant relationship between athletic participation and academic success, especially grade point average" (Kaufmann, p. 7). More specifically, Kaufmann reported that "The greatest single effect [in this study] was participation, F (1,357) = 149.204, p < .01" (p. 63).

Eccles (2003), children and adolescents in the United States spend more than half of their waking hours in leisure activities. Along with interest in how leisure time is being spent, researchers are wondering why there are high levels of disinterest, underachievement, disengagement, and increased amount of time teens spend unsupervised by adults. Participation in activities has been linked to social and academic success, yet over-participation may be too stressful for young adults as it may consume too much of their free time. There are pros and cons to both sides of the activity participation discussion.

There are different opinions of what is considered an extra-curricular activity. A few examples of activities outside the school day may include pro-social activities such as dances, team sports, and performing arts, while in-school involvement activities may include intramurals, and academic clubs. Different levels of activity involvement and participation may positively impact future success for those who participate. Research also indicated that both the type of extracurricular programs and level of participation may impact the individuals' development (Eccles, 2003).

Gardner et al. (2003), theory and research on positive youth development emphasizes the transition of human development, and suggest that cultivating positive, supportive relationships with people and social institutions encourages healthy development. Considering this perspective, organized activities, such as extra-curricular activities, can encourage healthy development because of the support and opportunities that are present compared to less positive after school options for teens. Students who participate in structured activities are more likely to respect diversity, play by the rules, and contribute as a member of a team whether it is sports, scouting or clubs.

Barber (2001) have noted possible negative consequences of some types of extracurricular activities. If a coach is degrading to the team, or if members of the club exclude others, or just over-involvement with every spare minute scheduled in multiple activities, students may find there are negative consequences for participation. Either way, it is important to why students should get involved in positive activities and how to avoid the negative impact of over-participation.

Morrissey (2000) stated that there is an established between adolescents extracurricular activities and educational attainment as adults in occupational choice and income. Morrissey also noted a reduction in delinquency and less engagement in risky behaviors. These factors explain why students should balance their lives with academics and activities as participating in these well-rounded activities may impact their success in the future. When stating some of the benefits of participating in extracurricular activities, some believe that this leads to positive youth development.

Morrissey (2000) describes positive youth development as encompassing five constructs: (1) competence in academic, social, and vocational areas; (2) confidence; (3) connection to family, community, and peers; (4) character; and (5) caring and compassion (cited in Roth, 2000). These are also known as the Five Cs of positive attributes for youth. This provides discussion and examples of some of the positive effects in development based on participating in extracurricular activities. In addition, this chapter will also highlight some of the negative effects that may also take place in adolescent development due to injury, limited opportunity or over-scheduled participation. Furthermore, this chapter will include what schools can do to encourage students to participate in extracurricular activities in hopes of reducing absenteeism, bullying, and high dropout rates. Lastly, this chapter will describe how extracurricular activities can effect personal, social and academic development in a positive manner. Benefits of Participation When looking at the variety of out-of-school options students may choose, it is important to consider how connecting with an activity might benefit them.

Eccles (2000), that participation in voluntary, school-based, extracurricular activities increase school participation and achievement (cited in Mahoney et al., in press). This happens because it facilitates:

a) The acquisition of interpersonal skills and positive social norms,

b) Membership in pro-social peer groups, and

c) Stronger emotional and social connections to one's school.

It then stands to reason that participation may contribute to an increase of wellness in mental health, improved students' engagement in school and achievement, strengthen their long-term educational outcomes and find that participation may decrease problem behaviors. One study in particular discussed how being involved in physical extracurricular activities that may actually improve self-perceptions. It is important to understand that participation in extracurricular physical activities may influence the mental well-being of young people by reducing stress, keeping fit and feeling overall better about their appearances.

Daley and Leahy (2000) did a study involving 126 randomly selected children who were 16 years old, who participated in physical extracurricular activities. All of these participants were involved in some form of physical extracurricular activity organized by the school at least once per week either during lunchtime or after school hours. The second group consisted of 63 additional children who did not participate in physical activities. Those who had regular physical activity perceived themselves in a positive manner. What the researchers found was a positive association between participation in various forms of physical activity and positive self-perception.

There has always been debate whether participation in extracurricular activities has a positive correlation with academic success. According to Reeves (2008), students who took part in three or four extracurricular activities during the academic year had dramatically better grades than those who participated in no extracurricular activities at all.

Darling, Caldwell, and Smith (2000) suggested that participation in athletics is related to the following positive academic related outcomes including higher grade point average, fewer disciplinary referrals, lower absentee rates, decrease in dropout rates, stronger commitment to the school, liking school better, being in the academic tract in coursework, taking more demanding coursework, more likely to attend college full time and graduate, holding higher aspirations for attending college, applying to more universities and colleges, and had better occupational status 1S-years after high school.

Olson (1999) found that students enrolled in fine arts activities had significantly lower absentee rates than those students who did not participate at all. Also, it was determined that dropouts were involved in fewer extracurricular activities than were those who stayed in school. Involvement in extracurricular activities is consistently and positively correlated with good school attendance, and good attendance is often correlated with a higher grade point average.

Gilman (1998) discussed the concept of structured extracurricular activities as a strategy for schools to build resiliency, support pro-social behavior, offer opportunities for engagement with school and related activities, and provide constructive academic performance and growth in subjective well-being. One of the methods discussed was trying to establish a school-identity for students. Students who identify with schools have an internalized sense of belonging, are discernibly part of the school environment, and the school constitutes an important part of their own experience. The structured extracurricular activities can help develop a sense of identification with the school and the community. Participation in activities can be important for students who are at-risk of dropping out of school, since these students are not likely to identify with their school or the values and norms that it fosters.

Eccles found that both the extracurricular programs and individual characteristics and leadership influenced the nature of the impact of participation on individuals' development. Knowing what activities adolescents are involved in may indicate who the adolescent is hanging out with, and who the adult coaches and mentors are that they can turn to when in need. Often when an adolescent is involved in an activity this may directly effects who is in their peer group because of the amounts of time spent with one another. It is likely that participation in these kinds of activities influences the kinds of relationships adolescents form with adults as well as improving the perspective and connection of the school. Overall, the development that occurs can contribute to an adolescents' identity and show the importance of contributing as a member of the school community.

CONCLUSION

A summary of the review of related literature is given this chapter. The outcome of the extracurricular activities in the researches has also discussed in this chapter Research methodology.

Chapter - III

Methodology

INTRODUCTION

Methodology "The analysis of the principles of methods, rules and postulates employed by a discipline"; "The systematic study of methods that are, can be, or have been applied within a discipline".

Research purifies human life. It improves its quality. It is search for knowledge. If shows how to Solve any problem scientifically. It is a careful enquiry through search for any kind of Knowledge. It is a journey from known to unknown. It is a systematic effort to gain new knowledge in any kind of discipline.

When it seeks a solution of any educational problem it leads to educational research. Curiosity, inquisitiveness is natural gifts secured by a man. They inspire him to quest, increase his thirst for knowledge / truth. After trial and error, he worked systematically in the direction of the desired goal. His adjustment and coping with situation makes him successful in his task. Thereby he learns something's, becomes wise and prepares his own scientific procedure while performing the same task for second time. So is there any relationship among science, education and educational Research.

Research is the voyage of discovery. It is the quest for answers to unsolved problems. Research is required in any field to come up with new theories or modify, accept, or nullify the existing theory. From time immemorial it has been seen so many discoveries and inventions took place through research and world has got so many new theories which help the human being to solve his problems.

EDUCATIONAL RESEARCH

Educational Research as nothing but cleansing of educational Research is nothing but cleansing of educational process. Many experts think Educational.

According to Mouly, Educational Research is the systematic application of scientific method for solving for solving educational problem.

According to Travers, Educational Research is the activity for developing science of behavior in educational situations. It allows the educator to achieve his goals effectively.

According to Whitney, Educational Research aims at finding out solution of educational problems by using scientific philosophical method.

Thus, Educational Research is to solve educational problem in systematic and scientific manner, it is to understand, explain, predict and control human behaviour.

Educational Research Characterizes as follows;

1. It is highly purposeful.
2. It deals with educational problems regarding students and teachers as well.
3. It is precise, objective, scientific and systematic process of investigation. It attempts to organize data quantitatively and qualitatively to arrive at statistical inferences. It discovers new facts in new perspective. i.e. It generates new knowledge. It needs interdisciplinary approach for solving educational problem. It demands subjective interpretation and deductive reasoning in some cases.
4. It uses classrooms, schools, colleges department of education as the laboratory for conducting researches.

RESEARCH DESIGN

Before starting a research, the investigator will look for problem; she will read books, journals, research reports and other related literature. Based on this, she will finalize the topic for research. During this process, she will be in close contact with his guide. As soon as the topic is decided, first task is to decide about design. Research design is a blue print or structure with in which research is conducted. It constitutes the blue print for the collection, measurement and analysis of data.

According to Gay and Airasian (2000), a design is general strategy for conducting a research study. The nature of the hypothesis, the variables involved, and the constraints of the real world all contribute to the selection of design.

Kothari (1988) says, Decisions regarding WHAT?, WHERE?, WHEN?, HOW MUCH?, by WHAT? means concerning an inquiry or a research study constitute research design.

Thus, it can be said that research design is an outline of what the researcher will do from writing of objectives, hypotheses and its operational implications to find analysis of data.

Thus, according to nature and type of study the components of design will be decided. In short, any efficient research design will help the researcher to carry out the study in a systematic way.

PURPOSE OF RESEARCH DESIGN

A research design helps the investigator to obtain answers to research problem and issues involved in the research, since it is the outline of entire research process.

Design also tells us about how to collect data, what observation are to be carry out, how to make them, how to analyze the data. Design also guides investigator about statistical techniques to be used for analysis. Thus, design guides the investigator to carry out research step by step in an efficient way. This chapter presents details regarding the following:

1. Selection of Dependent variables and Categorical variables.

Construction of tools to measure the*"A Study on Effect of Sound and Light Equipments in Eradicating Errors in Pronunciation among IXth Standard Students".*

2. Reliability, Validity of the tools Illustrated.
3. Explain the Sampling procedure adopted in this study.
4. Scheduling the survey and collecting the data for Interpretation.

STATEMENT OF THE PROBLEM

Over the years the costs and effect of extracurricular activities have generated many studies and numerous relations to academic performance. It is defined that traditional extracurricular activity in class instruction that impact academic achievement. Educationists are interested in the relationship between academic achievement and participation in extracurricular activities. Implying that these activities do have some sort of influence on how students perform academically. To find the involvement of the students the present study is entitled as *"A Study on Effect of Sound and Light Equipments in Eradicating Errors in Pronunciation Among IXth Standard Students".*

OBJECTIVES OF THE STUDY

The following are the objectives of the present study chosen;

1. To find out the significant difference between the mean scores on importance of Extra-Curricular Activities and Academic Achievement among Higher Secondary School Students in Tiruchirappalli District.
2. To find out the significant difference between the mean scores on importance of Extra-Curricular Activities and Academic Achievement among Male higher secondary school students.
3. To find out the significant difference between the mean scores on importance of Extra-Curricular Activities and Academic Achievement among Female higher secondary school students.
4. To find out the significant difference between the mean scores on importance of Extra-Curricular Activities and Academic Achievement among Rural Residential higher secondary school students.
5. To find out the significant difference between the mean scores on importance of Extra-Curricular Activities and Academic Achievement among Urban Residential higher secondary school students.
6. To find out the significant difference between the mean scores on importance of Extra-Curricular Activities and Academic Achievement among Government higher secondary school students.
7. To find out the significant difference between the mean scores on importance of Extra-Curricular Activities and Academic Achievement among Non-Government higher secondary school students.
8. To find out the significant difference between the mean scores on importance of Extra-Curricular Activities and Academic Achievement among Nuclear Family higher secondary school students.
9. To find out the significant difference between the mean scores on importance of Extra-Curricular Activities and Academic Achievement among Joint Family higher secondary school students.
10. To find out the significant difference between the mean scores on importance of Extra-Curricular Activities and Academic Achievement

among higher secondary school students with respect to their Literate Father.

11. To find out the significant difference between the mean scores on importance of Extra-Curricular Activities and Academic Achievement among higher secondary school students with respect to their Illiterate Father.
12. To find out the significant difference between the mean scores on importance of Extra-Curricular Activities and Academic Achievement among Average Economical Family higher secondary school students.
13. To find out the significant difference between the mean scores on importance of Extra-Curricular Activities and Academic Achievement among Good Economical Family higher secondary school students.

HYPOTHESES OF THE STUDY

Hypothesis is usually considered as the principal instrument in research. The derivation of a suitable hypothesis goes hand in hand with the selection of a research problem.

The following are the hypotheses of the present study chosen;

1. There is no significant difference between the mean scores on importance of Extra-Curricular Activities and Academic Achievement among Higher Secondary School Students in Tiruchirappalli District.
2. There is no significant difference between the mean scores on importance of Extra-Curricular Activities and Academic Achievement among Male higher secondary school students.
3. There is no significant difference between the mean scores on importance of Extra-Curricular Activities and Academic Achievement among Female higher secondary school students.
4. There is no significant difference between the mean scores on importance of Extra-Curricular Activities and Academic Achievement among Rural Residential higher secondary school students.
5. There is no significant difference between the mean scores on importance of Extra-Curricular Activities and Academic Achievement among Urban Residential higher secondary school students.
6. There is no significant difference between the mean scores on importance of Extra-Curricular Activities and Academic Achievement among Government higher secondary school students.

7. There is no significant difference between the mean scores on importance of Extra-Curricular Activities and Academic Achievement among Non-Government higher secondary school students.
8. There is no significant difference between the mean scores on importance of Extra-Curricular Activities and Academic Achievement among Nuclear Family higher secondary school students.
9. There is no significant difference between the mean scores on importance of Extra-Curricular Activities and Academic Achievement among Joint Family higher secondary school students.
10. There is no significant difference between the mean scores on importance of Extra-Curricular Activities and Academic Achievement among higher secondary school students with respect to their Literate Father.
11. There is no significant difference between the mean scores on importance of Extra-Curricular Activities and Academic Achievement among higher secondary school students with respect to their Illiterate Father.
12. There is no significant difference between the mean scores on importance of Extra-Curricular Activities and Academic Achievement among Average Economical Family higher secondary school students.
13. There is no significant difference between the mean scores on importance of Extra-Curricular Activities and Academic Achievement among Good Economical Family higher secondary school students.

DELIMITATIONS OF THE STUDY

Delimitations for this study include

1. The independent variables to be manipulated.
2. The time frame to complete this research study was limited.

Data was gathered solely from students of the 2014-2015 academic years since data was gathered from higher secondary students of Thiruchirappalli District.

RESEARCH METHOD

The investigator preferred Survey Method for the present study. In this study, the investigator used stratified Random sampling method to collect data on *"Importance of Extra-Curricular Activities and Academic Achievement among Higher Secondary School Students"*.

RESEARCH TOOLS

In the present study the investigation selected questionnaire as the most important tools for collecting data because it is used increasingly to enquire into the current conditions, opinions and attitude of a groups.

W. Best observes that the questionnaire is the most tools in collecting both quantitative and qualities information, for the present study questionnaire was prepared with view to gather information in details regarding on *Importance of Extra-Curricular Activities and Academic Achievement among Higher Secondary School Students.* The selection of suitable tool for the investigation is very important for successful Research. Questionnaire is a tool used to collect data from the selected sample.

A research tool plays a major role in any worthwhile research is the sole factor in determining the sound data and in arriving at perfect conclusion about the problem or study on hand, which ultimately, helps in providing suitable remedial measures to the problem concerned.

CONSTRUCTION OF RESEARCH TOOLS

The research tool on *"Importance of Extra-Curricular Activities and Academic Achievement among Higher Secondary School Students"* was constructed by the investigator. All the question items are open type. The responded, which respondent the correct answers were given scores and these score were considered for data analysis.

The investigator used the following tools in this study.

1. Personal Data Sheet developed by the Investigator herself for suitability.

2. "Importance of Extra-Curricular Activities and Academic Achievement among Higher Secondary School Students" related enquiry as questioner was taken for survey.

It has Total 25 numbers of questions respectively to seek information needed from the students. Here the Extra-Curricular Activities scores was distributed as per the students response obtained using the Likert type 4 point scale. And the Academic Achievement scores of the students selected as their previous annual achievement marks obtained in the examination. The marks out of 500 are converted into 100% then the scores were manipulated.

SAMPLES OF THE STUDY

Sampling is the process of selecting a sample from the population. For this population 200 samples were observed form Tiruchirappalli District. and it was divided into a number of parts called Sampling Units.

DESCRIPTION OF RESEARCH TOOL AND SCORING PROCEDURE

Scoring of the response sheets were done as per the scoring scheme. The scores obtained in all questionnaires along with the personal data are consolidated and tabulated on consolidation sheet for the purpose of analysis. Scoring pattern strongly Agree, Agree, Disagree & Strongly Disagree has scores as 4, 3, 2 & 1 correspondingly.

PILOT STUDY

The pilot study is an initial study to test 50 peoples from Tiruchirappalli District Higher Secondary School Students which is conducted by the investigator to know more about the research problem in various aspects. Based on the pilot study, the main study was conducted by the investigator while administering the research in the pilot study, some relationship between test anxiety and mental health, and the investigator clarified all of their doubts and difficulties. Based on that, the investigator modified the items.

The pilot stage is concerned with refining the items collected. The collected items were presented before the expert with a request to offer their considered opinion regarding the suitability objectivity clarity and relevancy of the statement collected from different sources. The opinion of the experts was taken into consideration to refine the items.

The pilot study, the main study was conducted by the investigator while administering the research in the pilot study, some doubts were raised by the school students, and the investigator clarified all of their doubts and difficulties.

After getting response from the respondents, the investigator gave frequencies for the correct response and these frequencies were converted into scores and those scores.

VALIDITY OF THE TOOL

In preparing a research tool is to develop a pool of item. This is followed by item analysis which involves computing difficulty index and discrimination index of each item. This is followed by ascertaining the validity of the tool. Validity is the most important consideration in the selection and use of any testing procedures. The validity of a test, or of any measuring instrument, depends upon the degree of exactness with which something is reproduced/copied or with which it measures what it purports to measure.

The validity of a test may be defined as "the accuracy with which a test measures what it attempts to measure." It is also defined as "The efficiency with which a test measures what it attempts to measure".

Lindquist has defined validity – "As the accuracy with which it measures that which is intended to as the degree to which it approaches infallibility in measuring what it purports to measure". On the basis of the preceding definitions, it is seen that Validity is a matter of degree. It may be high, moderate or low. Validity is specific rather than general. A test may be valid for one specific purpose but not for another Valid for one specific group of students but not for another.

RELIABILITY OF THE TOOL

Garett (1979) Reliability is the consistency with which a tool measures what it measure. In the present study, the typical Split-Half was employed to evaluate the stability of the measurement the tools were administered to a group of Higher Secondary School Student and the score were computed.

The co-efficient of correlation between the odd and even numbers scores is found to be 0.89 by using the Spareman-Brown prophecy formula. The Reliability value has been calculated using the below formula;

$$r_{11} = 2r^{oe}$$
$$1 + r^{oe}$$
$$2x0.89$$
$$=$$
$$1 + 0.89$$
$$= 0.94$$

Hence the reliability value is 0.94.

The reliability of the tool refers to the internal consistency observed in measurement of reliability.

SAMPLING TECHNIQUE USED

After finalizing the variables of present study, consideration was given to whether the entire population is to be made the subject for data collection or a particular group is to be selected as representative of the whole population. The population of 200 data here refers to check the "Importance of Extra-Curricular Activities and Academic Achievement among Higher Secondary School Students". The above techniques, the selection of a group as a representative of the whole population was found to be more convenient and suitable.

This technique leads to a considerable save of time, effort and finance. The number of students selected will be small, and so it is possible to make a detailed and intensive study. This generally leads to more accurate and reliable results. As this sampling technique has many advantages, it was selected for the collection of data. In any behavioral research, various methods are utilized for selection and drawing of samples. After a detailed study of all these methods and considering the variables selected for the research work, the stratified Random sampling method was found to be most suitable.

COLLECTION OF DATA

Questionnaire

A questionnaire is a form prepared and distributed to secure responses to certain questions. It is a device for securing answers to questions by using a form which the respondent fills by himself. It is a systematic compilation of questions that are submitted to a sampling of population from which information is desired. Questionnaires rely on written information supplied directly by students in response to questions. The information from questionnaires tends to fall into two broad categories facts and opinions. It is worth stressing that, in practice, questionnaires are very likely to include questions about both facts and opinions.

Purpose

The purpose of the questionnaire is to gather information from widely scattered sources. It is mostly used in uses in cases where one can not readily see personally all of the people from whom he desires responses. It is also used where there is no particular reason to see them personality.

The investigator herself met each and every student. Before going to administer the research tool, the investigator revealed the purpose of the present study to the Higher Secondary Students and then asked them to give their responses for each and every item that are given in the questionnaire. The responses of the students were collected and recorded.

ANALISIS OF DATA

Descriptive Data Analysis

Descriptive statistics are used to present quantitative descriptions in a manageable form. In a research study, we may have lots of measures. Or we may measure a large number of people on one measure. Descriptive statistics help us to simply large amounts of data in a sensible way.

Measures of Central Tendency

These include Mean, Median and Mode which indicate the average value of the variable being studied (Mean), the value above and below which lie 50% of the sample values (Median) and the value which occurs the maximum number of times in the sample (Mode). These help in determining the extent of normality of the distribution of scores on the variable being studied.

Measures of Variability

These include the standard deviation, skewness and kurtosis. The standard deviation indicates the deviation of each score from the Mean. Skewness indicates whether majority of the scores lie to the left of the Mean (positively skewed), to the right of the Mean (negatively skewed) or bell-shaped (normally distributed). Kurtosis indicates whether the distribution of the scores is flat (platykurtic), peaked (leptokurtic) or bell-shaped (mesokurtic).

STATISTICAL TECHNIQUES USED

In the present study the investigator followed the statistical procedure mentioned earlier to analyze the data and to arrive the meaningful conclusions.

The 't' value has been to find out the Importance of Extra-Curricular Activities and Academic Achievement among Higher Secondary School Students in terms of their Gender, Residential Place, Type of School, Family Nature, Father's Educational Qualification, Family Economical Status and Achievement Score.

Statistical Techniques serves the fundamental purpose of the description and inferential analysis. It is concerned with numerical description of a particular group observed. Any similarity to those outside the group cannot be taken for granted.

The data describe one group only. Simple educational research involves descriptive statistics and provides valuable information about the nature of a particular group or class.

Data collected from tests have little meaning or significance until they have been classified or rearranged in a systematic way.

The following Statistical Techniques were used in this study.

1. Mean (M)
2. Standard Deviation (S.D.)
3. 't' – test for determine the significance of difference between means of two sub-groups.

ARITHMETIC MEAN

The mean of a distribution is commonly understood as the arithmetic average. It is computed by dividing the sum of all scores by the number of scores.

STANDARD DEVIATION (S.D)

Standard Deviation is the square-root of the mean of the squares of the deviations of all the items from the arithmetic mean. It is represented by the letter 'ó'.

't'- TEST

The test of significance of the difference between two mean is known as 't'- test. It involves the computation of the ratio between experimental variance (observed difference between two sample means) and error variance (the sampling error factor).

When small samples are involved the t-table is used to determine statistical significance, rather that the normality, probability table.

This concept of small sample size was developed around 1915 by William, carefully calculated for small samples area reproduced in the t-distribution table.

The t- critical values necessary for rejection of a null hypothesis are higher for the samples of a given level of significances. Each t – critical value for rejection is based upon the appropriate number of degrees of freedom.

The **t – test** would be used upon this formula.

M1= Mean of First Group

M2 = Mean of Second Group

S1 = SD of the first

S2 = SD of the second group

N1 = No. of students in first Group

N2 = No. of Students in Second Group

THE LEVEL OF SIGNIFICANCE

The rejection or acceptance of a null hypothesis is based upon some level of significance as a criterion.

TWO – TAILED TEST

If a null hypothesis is established that there is no significant difference between the mean I.Q. scores one would be concerned only with a difference.

CONCLUSION

In this chapter the methodology of the study was explained clearly. Each and every step was carefully planned and executed. The research strategies and the collection procedures have been explained. To find out the Higher Secondary School students Importance of Extra-Curricular Activities and Academic Achievement the above said scale was administrated to collect 200 samples from Higher Secondary School Students and all the 200 students' observations were computed. The scores were subjected to statistical treatment that is described in the upcoming chapter.

Chapter - IV

Analysis and Interpretation of Data

INTRODUCTION

"Research data becomes meaningful in the process of being analyzed and interpreted" key phases of every thesis is the proper analysis and interpretation of the data.

Barr and Scates, suggest four helpful models to get started in analyzing the gathered data.

1. To think in terms of significant tables that data permits.
2. To examine carefully the statement of the problem and the earlier analysis and to study the originality of the data.
3. To get away from the data and to think about the problem or to discuss the problem with others.
4. To attack the data by making various simple statistical calculations.

This chapter highlights the analysis of the data obtained regarding the variable of the present study using appropriate techniques verifying hypothesis framed for the present study.

The finding were interpreted and discussed in the light of finding of other research studies.

The data of the present study were collected from 200 students studying in the Higher Secondary School level. Standards have been analyzed by using the statistical techniques.

ANALYSIS OF DATA

According to Kaplan, "Analysis attempts to characterize the meaning in a given body to discourse in a systematic and quantitative fashion.

According Barr and Others "Analysis is an important phase of the classification and summation of data into a summary".

After, collecting the data from the respondents, the investigator gave frequencies for the correct responses and these frequencies were converted into scores.

The scores were used to identify the present topic "A study on importance of extra-curricular activities and academic achievement among higher secondary school students in Tiruchirappalli district".

TESTING OF HYPOTHESES

The hypotheses formulated for the present study taken as "A study on importance of extra-curricular activities and academic achievement among higher secondary school students in Tiruchirappalli district" were tested using statistical techniques. Descriptive and inferential analyses were used.

HYPOTHESIS : 1

There is no significant difference between the mean scores on importance of Extra-Curricular Activities and Academic Achievement among Higher Secondary School Students in Tiruchirappalli District.

TABLE : 1

The following table shows the 'r' value of Extra-Curricular Activities and Academic Achievement among Higher Secondary School Students in Tiruchirappalli District.

Findings of Higher Secondary School Students In Tiruchirappalli District					xy	N	'r' value
Extra-Curricular Activities	x	250	x2	17820	4519	200	0.19
Academic Achievement	y	1616	y2	46428			

INTERPRETATION

Since the calculated 'r' value **0.019** is smaller than the table value 0.113 at 0.05 level of significance. It is inferred that, there is no significant difference between the mean scores of Extra-Curricular Activities and Academic Achievement among Higher Secondary School Students in Tiruchirappalli District.

RESULT

Hence the null hypothesis is accepted.

HYPOTHESIS: 2

There is no significant difference between the mean scores on importance of Extra-Curricular Activities and Academic Achievement among Male higher secondary school students.

TABLE: 2

The following table shows the mean scores, standard deviation and 't' value of Extra-Curricular Activities and Academic Achievement among Male higher secondary school students.

Male	N	M	SD	df	't' value	Level of Significance at 0.05
Extra-Curricular Activities	45	78.29	12.04	43	1.21	Not Significant
Academic Achievement	45	75.24	11.03			

INTERPRETATION:

Since the calculated 't' value **1.21** is smaller than the table value 1.96 at 0.05 level of significance. It is inferred that, there is no significant difference between the mean scores of Extra-Curricular Activities and Academic Achievement among Male higher secondary school students.

RESULT:

Hence the null hypothesis is accepted.

HYPOTHESIS: 3

There is no significant difference between the mean scores on importance of Extra-Curricular Activities and Academic Achievement among Female higher secondary school students.

TABLE : 3

The following table shows the mean scores, standard deviation and 't' value of Extra-Curricular Activities and Academic Achievement among Female higher secondary school students.

Female	N	M	SD	df	't' value	Level of Significance at 0.05
Extra-Curricular Activities	155	78.89	8.49	153	1.79	Not Significant
Academic Achievement	155	76.80	11.71			

INTERPRETATION:

Since the calculated 't' value **1.79** is smaller than the table value 1.96 at 0.05 level of significance. It is inferred that, there is no significant difference between the mean scores of Extra-Curricular Activities and Academic Achievement among Female higher secondary school students.

RESULT:

Hence the null hypothesis is accepted.

HYPOTHESIS: 4

There is no significant difference between the mean scores on importance of Extra-Curricular Activities and Academic Achievement among Rural Residential higher secondary school students.

TABLE : 4

The following table shows the mean scores, standard deviation and 't' value of Extra-Curricular Activities and Academic Achievement among Rural Residential higher secondary school students.

Rular Residential	N	M	SD	df	't' value	Level of Significance at 0.05
Extra-Curricular Activities	142	78.55	9.19	140	2.53	Significant
Academic Achievement	142	75.39	11.66			

INTERPRETATION:

Since the calculated 't' value **2.53** is higher than the table value 1.96 at 0.05 level of significance. It is inferred that, there is significant difference between the mean scores of Extra-Curricular Activities and Academic Achievement among Rural Residential higher secondary school students.

RESULT:

Hence the null hypothesis is rejected.

HYPOTHESIS: 5

There is no significant difference between the mean scores on importance of Extra-Curricular Activities and Academic Achievement among Urban Residential higher secondary school students.

TABLE : 5

The following table shows the mean scores, standard deviation and 't' value of Extra-Curricular Activities and Academic Achievement among Urban Residential higher secondary school students.

Urban Residential	N	M	SD	df	't' value	Level of Significance at 0.05
Extra-Curricular Activities	58	79.24	9.89	56	0.18	Not Significant
Academic Achievement	58	79.06	10.95			

INTERPRETATION:

Since the calculated 't' value **0.18** is smaller than the table value 1.96 at 0.05 level of significance. It is inferred that, there is no significant difference between the mean scores of Extra-Curricular Activities and Academic Achievement among Urban Residential higher secondary school students.

RESULT:

Hence the null hypothesis is accepted.

HYPOTHESIS: 6

There is no significant difference between the mean scores on importance of Extra-Curricular Activities and Academic Achievement among Government higher secondary school students.

TABLE : 6

The following table shows the mean scores, standard deviation and 't' value of Extra-Curricular Activities and Academic Achievement among Government higher secondary school students.

Government School	N	M	SD	df	't' value	Level of Significance at 0.05
Extra-Curricular Activities	55	79.27	10.12	53	3.25	Significant
Academic Achievement	55	73.43	8.64			

INTERPRETATION:

Since the calculated 't' value **3.25** is higher than the table value 1.96 at 0.05 level of significance. It is inferred that, there is significant difference between the mean scores of Extra-Curricular Activities and Academic Achievement among Government higher secondary school students.

RESULT:

Hence the null hypothesis is rejected.

HYPOTHESIS: 7

There is no significant difference between the mean scores on importance of Extra-Curricular Activities and Academic Achievement among Non-Government higher secondary school students.

TABLE : 7

The following table shows the mean scores, standard deviation and 't' value of Extra-Curricular Activities and Academic Achievement among Non-Government higher secondary school students.

Non-Government School	N	M	SD	df	't' value	Level of Significance at 0.05
Extra-Curricular Activities	145	78.55	9.11			
Academic Achievement	145	77.59	12.31	143	0.75	Not Significant

INTERPRETATION:

Since the calculated 't' value **0.75** is smaller than the table value 1.96 at 0.05 level of significance. It is inferred that, there is no significant difference between the mean scores of Extra-Curricular Activities and Academic Achievement among Non-Government higher secondary school students.

RESULT:

Hence the null hypothesis is accepted.

HYPOTHESIS: 8

There is no significant difference between the mean scores on importance of Extra-Curricular Activities and Academic Achievement among Nuclear Family higher secondary school students.

TABLE : 8

The following table shows the mean scores, standard deviation and 't' value of Extra-Curricular Activities and Academic Achievement among Nuclear Family higher secondary school students.

Nuclear family School	N	M	SD	df	't' value	Level of Significance at 0.05
Extra-Curricular Activities	121	78.94	8.94			
Academic Achievement	121	76.37	12.13	119	1.87	Not Significant

INTERPRETATION:

Since the calculated 't' value **1.87** is higher than the table value 1.96 at 0.05 level of significance. It is inferred that, there is no significant difference between the mean scores of Extra-Curricular Activities and Academic Achievement among Nuclear Family higher secondary school students.

RESULT:

Hence the null hypothesis is accepted.

HYPOTHESIS: 9

There is no significant difference between the mean scores on importance of Extra-Curricular Activities and Academic Achievement among Joint Family higher secondary school students.

TABLE :9

The following table shows the mean scores, standard deviation and 't' value of Extra-Curricular Activities and Academic Achievement among Joint Family higher secondary school students.

Joint Family	N	M	SD	df	't' value	Level of Significance at 0.05
Extra-Curricular Activities	79	78.46	10.06			
Academic Achievement	79	76.58	10.68	77	1.11	Not Significant

INTERPRETATION:

Since the calculated 't' value **1.11** is smaller than the table value 1.96 at 0.05 level of significance. It is inferred that, there is no significant difference between the mean scores of Extra-Curricular Activities and Academic Achievement among Joint Family higher secondary school students.

RESULT

Hence the null hypothesis is accepted.

HYPOTHESIS: 10

There is no significant difference between the mean scores on importance of Extra-Curricular Activities and Academic Achievement among higher secondary school students with respect to their Literate Father.

TABLE : 10

The following table shows the mean scores, standard deviation and 't' value of Extra-Curricular Activities and Academic Achievement among Male higher secondary school students.

Literate Father	N	M	SD	df	't' value	Level of Significance at 0.05
Extra-Curricular Activities	110	78.15	9.46	108	2.77	Significant
Academic Achievement	110	74.36	10.75			

INTERPRETATION

Since the calculated 't' value **2.77** is higher than the table value 1.96 at 0.05 level of significance. It is inferred that, there is significant difference between the mean scores of importance of Extra-Curricular Activities and Academic Achievement among higher secondary school students with respect to their Literate Father.

RESULT

Hence the null hypothesis is rejected.

HYPOTHESIS: 11

There is no significant difference between the mean scores on importance of Extra-Curricular Activities and Academic Achievement among higher secondary school students with respect to their Illiterate Father.

TABLE : 11

The following table shows the mean scores, standard deviation and 't' value of Extra-Curricular Activities and Academic Achievement among Male higher secondary school students.

Illiterate Father	N	M	SD	df	't' value	Level of Significance at 0.05
Extra-Curricular Activities	90	79.48	9.28			
Academic Achievement	90	79.00	12.04	88	0.29	Not Significant

INTERPRETATION

Since the calculated 't' value **0.29** is smaller than the table value 1.96 at 0.05 level of significance. It is inferred that, there is no significant difference between the mean scores of importance of Extra-Curricular Activities and Academic Achievement among higher secondary school students with respect to their Illiterate Father.

RESULT:

Hence the null hypothesis is accepted.

HYPOTHESIS: 12

There is no significant difference between the mean scores on importance of Extra-Curricular Activities and Academic Achievement among Average Economical Family higher secondary school students.

TABLE : 12

The following table shows the mean scores, standard deviation and 't' value of importance of Extra-Curricular Activities and Academic Achievement among Average Economical Family higher secondary school students.

Average Economical Family	N	M	SD	df	't' value	Level of Significance at 0.05
Extra-Curricular Activities	123	77.54	10.14			
Academic Achievement	123	75.47	11.24	121	1.51	Not Significant

INTERPRETATION

Since the calculated 't' value **1.51** is smaller than the table value 1.96 at 0.05 level of significance. It is inferred that, there is no significant difference between the mean scores of importance of Extra-Curricular Activities and Academic Achievement among Average Economical Family higher secondary school students.

RESULT:

Hence the null hypothesis is accepted.

HYPOTHESIS: 13

There is no significant difference between the mean scores on importance of Extra-Curricular Activities and Academic Achievement among Good Economical Family higher secondary school students.

TABLE :13

The following table shows the mean scores, standard deviation and 't' value of importance of Extra-Curricular Activities and Academic Achievement among Good Economical Family higher secondary school students.

Good Economical Family	N	M	SD	df	't' value	Level of Significance at 0.05
Extra-Curricular Activities	77	80.68	7.70	75	1.63	Not Significant
Academic Achievement	77	78.03	11.94			

INTERPRETATION

Since the calculated 't' value **1.63** is smaller than the table value 1.96 at 0.05 level of significance. It is inferred that, there is no significant difference between the mean scores of importance of Extra-Curricular Activities and Academic Achievement among Good Economical Family higher secondary school students.

RESULT

Hence the null hypothesis is accepted.

CONCLUSION

In this chapter the collections of data were tabulated, analyzed and interpreted. The next chapter deals with the summary findings and conclusion of the investigation.

Chapter - V

Summary of Findings and Conclusion

INTRODUCTION

After finalizing the calculation the investigator now moves on to the summarization of the research work undertaken. Summary is the most used part of research report because it guides not only research scholars but also educationists and people who are interested in that particular problem. The important findings of the present study are summarized below.

The most important of any research is its findings. The findings lead the investigator in drawing conclusion and in offering appropriate suggestions and recommendation. This chapter is a summary of the research work including the statement of the problem, objectives of the study, findings and conclusion of the study. In this chapter the results are discussed in accordance with the hypothesis formulated.

NEED AND SINGNIFICANCE OF THE STUDY

"Participation in extracurricular activities in higher secondary school appears to be one of the few interventions that benefit low-status, disadvantaged students those less well served by traditional educational programs as much as or more than their more advantaged peers" - **Everson and Millsap (2012)**

Student's classroom engagement is related to student participation in activities, especially among students from poor families. Activities help students to build supportive relationships on academic achievement. This component in classroom engagement and aspire students. This activity programs create higher secondary school students with higher aspirations and more commitment to academic success. This programs help promote healthy physical, psychological, emotional and social health. For the above reason the present study is taken to find *"A Study on Effect of Sound and Light Equipments in Eradicating Errors in Pronunciation Among IXth Standard Students."*

STATEMENT OF THE PROBLEM

Over the years the costs and effect of extracurricular activities have generated many studies and numerous relations to academic performance. It is defined that traditional extracurricular activity in class instruction that impact academic achievement. Educationists are interested in the relationship between academic achievement and participation in extracurricular activities.

Implying that these activities do have some sort of influence on how students perform academically. To find the involvement of the students the present study is entitled as "A Study on Importance of Extra-Curricular Activities and Academic Achievement among Higher Secondary School Students in Tiruchirappalli District".

OBJECTIVES OF THE STUDY

The following are the objectives of the present study chosen

1. To find out the significant difference between the mean scores on importance of Extra-Curricular Activities and Academic Achievement among Higher Secondary School Students in Tiruchirappalli District.
2. To find out the significant difference between the mean scores on importance of Extra-Curricular Activities and Academic Achievement among Male higher secondary school students.
3. To find out the significant difference between the mean scores on importance of Extra-Curricular Activities and Academic Achievement among Female higher secondary school students.
4. To find out the significant difference between the mean scores on importance of Extra-Curricular Activities and Academic Achievement among Rural Residential higher secondary school students.
5. To find out the significant difference between the mean scores on importance of Extra-Curricular Activities and Academic Achievement among Urban Residential higher secondary school students.

6. To find out the significant difference between the mean scores on importance of Extra-Curricular Activities and Academic Achievement among Government higher secondary school students.
7. To find out the significant difference between the mean scores on importance of Extra-Curricular Activities and Academic Achievement among Non-Government higher secondary school students.
8. To find out the significant difference between the mean scores on importance of Extra-Curricular Activities and Academic Achievement among Nuclear Family higher secondary school students.
9. To find out the significant difference between the mean scores on importance of Extra-Curricular Activities and Academic Achievement among Joint Family higher secondary school students.
10. To find out the significant difference between the mean scores on importance of Extra-Curricular Activities and Academic Achievement among higher secondary school students with respect to their Literate Father.
11. To find out the significant difference between the mean scores on importance of Extra-Curricular Activities and Academic Achievement among higher secondary school students with respect to their Illiterate Father.
12. To find out the significant difference between the mean scores on importance of Extra-Curricular Activities and Academic Achievement among Average Economical Family higher secondary school students.
13. To find out the significant difference between the mean scores on importance of Extra-Curricular Activities and Academic Achievement among Good Economical Family higher secondary school students.

HYPOTHESES OF THE STUDY

1. There is no significant difference between the mean scores on importance of Extra-Curricular Activities and Academic Achievement among Higher Secondary School Students in Tiruchirappalli District.
2. There is no significant difference between the mean scores on importance of Extra-Curricular Activities and Academic Achievement among Male higher secondary school students.
3. There is no significant difference between the mean scores on importance of Extra-Curricular Activities and Academic Achievement among Female higher secondary school students.

4. There is no significant difference between the mean scores on importance of Extra-Curricular Activities and Academic Achievement among Rural Residential higher secondary school students.
5. There is no significant difference between the mean scores on importance of Extra-Curricular Activities and Academic Achievement among Urban Residential higher secondary school students.
6. There is no significant difference between the mean scores on importance of Extra-Curricular Activities and Academic Achievement among Government higher secondary school students.
7. There is no significant difference between the mean scores on importance of Extra-Curricular Activities and Academic Achievement among Non-Government higher secondary school students.
8. There is no significant difference between the mean scores on importance of Extra-Curricular Activities and Academic Achievement among Nuclear Family higher secondary school students.
9. There is no significant difference between the mean scores on importance of Extra-Curricular Activities and Academic Achievement among Joint Family higher secondary school students.
10. There is no significant difference between the mean scores on importance of Extra-Curricular Activities and Academic Achievement among higher secondary school students with respect to their Literate Father.
11. There is no significant difference between the mean scores on importance of Extra-Curricular Activities and Academic Achievement among higher secondary school students with respect to their Illiterate Father.
12. There is no significant difference between the mean scores on importance of Extra-Curricular Activities and Academic Achievement among Average Economical Family higher secondary school students.
13. There is no significant difference between the mean scores on importance of Extra-Curricular Activities and Academic Achievement among Good Economical Family higher secondary school students.

MAJOR FINDINGS OF THE RESEARCH

1. There is no significant difference between the mean scores of Extra-Curricular Activities and Academic Achievement among Higher Secondary School Students in Tiruchirappalli District.

2. There is no significant difference between the mean scores of Extra-Curricular Activities and Academic Achievement among Male higher secondary school students.
3. There is no significant difference between the mean scores of Extra-Curricular Activities and Academic Achievement among Female higher secondary school students.
4. There is significant difference between the mean scores of Extra-Curricular Activities and Academic Achievement among Rural Residential higher secondary school students.
5. There is no significant difference between the mean scores of Extra-Curricular Activities and Academic Achievement among Urban Residential higher secondary school students.
6. There is significant difference between the mean scores of Extra-Curricular Activities and Academic Achievement among Government higher secondary school students.
7. There is no significant difference between the mean scores of Extra-Curricular Activities and Academic Achievement among Non-Government higher secondary school students.
8. There is no significant difference between the mean scores of Extra-Curricular Activities and Academic Achievement among Nuclear Family higher secondary school students.
9. There is no significant difference between the mean scores of Extra-Curricular Activities and Academic Achievement among Joint Family higher secondary school students.
10. There is significant difference between the mean scores of importance of Extra-Curricular Activities and Academic Achievement among higher secondary school students with respect to their Literate Father.
11. There is no significant difference between the mean scores of importance of Extra-Curricular Activities and Academic Achievement among higher secondary school students with respect to their Illiterate Father.
12. There is no significant difference between the mean scores of importance of Extra-Curricular Activities and Academic Achievement among Average Economical Family higher secondary school students.
13. There is no significant difference between the mean scores of importance of Extra-Curricular Activities and Academic Achievement among Good Economical Family higher secondary school students.

RECOMMENDATIONS

The following recommendations were made:

1. It was recommended that Teacher's need to be aware of the importance of their role of their Student's academic performance, extra-curricular activities participation. So that they can provide the necessary facilities at class room and school environment will promote the students aesthetic talents.
2. Many parents may not be aware of the influence of various home environmental factors on the performance and extra-curricular activities of their students especially in cultural and in sports activities.
3. It is recommended that teachers, educationists and leaders should try to create awareness in parents on the importance of the home environment on encourage using motivation factors which can improve the students performance.
4. Parents need to be informed that they can contribute to the education of their students through encouragement, provision of extra-curricular activity participating facilities and active assistance among other strategies.
5. Parents need to know their role in the education of their students also give importance to their interest so that they do not put the blame entirely on teachers when their students do not perform well in school extra-curricular activities.

SUGGESTION FOR FURTHER RESEARCH:

1. A study may be taken up to assess the motivational and extra-curricular activity participation interest to students various schooling level.
2. Similar studies may be taken up at state and national levels.
3. Comparative studies may be taken up between Secondary school and Higher secondary school students.
4. Comparative studies may be taken up between two or more districts particularly to the rural area students.
5. Comparative studies may be taken up between UG and PG Students also.

CONCLUSION

Definitely those activities in schools by encouraging the students to participate in cultural and sports activities will develop the student's progressiveness in their life. Hence this study useful to check the Extra-curricular interest that will be stimulated by the Motivation hence the academic achievement improved among them.

The present research study reveals that there is no significant difference founded between the mean scores of Extra-Curricular Activities and Academic Achievement among Higher Secondary School Students in Tiruchirappalli District in terms of Male higher secondary school students, Female higher secondary school students, Urban Residential higher secondary school students, Non-Government higher secondary school students, Nuclear Family higher secondary school students, Joint Family higher secondary school students, with respect to their Illiterate Father, Average Economical Family higher secondary school students, Good Economical Family higher secondary school students. But there is significant difference founded between the mean scores of Extra-Curricular Activities and Academic Achievement among Rural Residential higher secondary school students because of their living environment. There is significant difference between the mean scores of Extra-Curricular Activities and Academic Achievement among Government higher secondary school students is because of their school environment. There is significant difference between the mean scores of importance of Extra-Curricular Activities and Academic Achievement among higher secondary school students with respect to their Literate Father is founded because of their parental care.

BIBLIOGRAPHY

1. Ames, C. (1992). Journal of Educational Psychology. Classrooms: Goals, structures and student Achievement.
2. Ames, Carol. "The Enhancement of Student Achievement." In *Advances in Achievement and Cultural proof: Enhancing Achievement*, edited by Martin L. Maher and Douglas A. Kleberg. 123-48. Greenwich, Connecticut: Academic Press, 1987.
3. Atkinson JW, Feather NT (Eds) (1966). The Theory of Achievement. New York: John Wiley and sons.
4. Atkinson, John W., and Norman T. Feather (eds.). *A Theory of Achievement and Extra Curricular Activity.* Huntington, New York: R. E. Kiger,
5. Broh, B. (2002). *Sociology of Education.* Linking extracurricular activity programming to academic achievement: Who benefits and why?
6. Crow, L. & A., How to Study, Collier Books, New York, New York (1971). Kornhauser, A.W., How to Study, University of Chicago Pres, Chicago, Illinois (1957).

7. Condry, John. "Enhancing Achievement: A Social Developmental Perspective." In *Advances in Achievement and Achievement, Vl 5: Enhancing Achievement*, edited by Martin L. Maehr and Douglas A. Kleiber.. Greenwich, Connecticut: Academic Press.

8. Chiu, L.H. (1997). *Educational & Psychological Measurement.* Development and validation of the School Achievement Rating Scale.

9. Dowson, M., & McInerney, D. M. (2001). *Journal of Educational Psychology.* Psychological parameters of students' social and work avoidance goals: A qualitative investigation.

10. Entwistle, N. J. (1968). *British Journal of Educational Psychology.* Academic Achievement and extracurricular activity school attainment.

11. Fulk, B. M. (2003). *American Secondary Education.* Concerns about ninth grade students' poor academic performance: One school's action plan.

12. Heckhausen H (1967). The Anatomy of Achievement. New York: Academic Press.

13. Kaplan, A. and Maehr, M. (2002). *Academic Achievement of Adolescents.* Greenwich, Adolescents' achievement goals: Situating Achievement in socio cultural contexts. In F. Pajares & T. Urdan (Eds.), CT: Information Age Publishing.

14. Holloway, H. John (1999) "Understanding Youth Culture: Extra-Curricular Activities the Path to Academic Success?" 57 (4): 87-88.

15. Holloway, H. John (2002) "Extra-Curricular Activities and Student Motivation" 60 (1): 698-713.

16. Jenkins, J.E. (1996) "The Influence of Peer Affiliation and Student Activities on Adolescent Involvement." 31(122):197–306. Kaufman, Phillip (2000). Washington, DC: U.S. Department of Education and Justice.

17. Khan, I. and Khan, M. J. (2011) "ECA of Students and achievement used in Examinations in Urban Areas of District Peshawar." 49 (4): 601-609.

18. Kombo, D. Kisilu and Tromp, L. A. Delno (2006) Nairobi: Pauline's Publications Africa. Lockwood, Daniel (1997) .

19. Washington, DC: U.S Department of Justice, National Institute of Justice. Manning, Anita.

20. McNeal, R. "Extra-Curricular Activities and High School Dropouts" 68: 62-81.

21. Merton, K and Nisbert R. 3rd ed. New York: Harcourt Brace. Ministry of Education (1996) Zambia Education Publishing House.

22. Moriana, J. A., Alós, F., Alcalá, R., Pino, M. J., Herruza, J. and Ruiz, R. (2006) "Extra- Curricular Activities and Academic Performance in Secondary Students.

23. Maehr, Martin L., and Larry A. Braskamp. *The Achievement Factor: A Theory of* extracurricular activity *participation.* Lexington, Massachusetts: Lexington Books.

24. Morgan, C.T., 1956. An introduction to Psychology. McGraw-Hill Book Co., Inc. N.Y., USA.

25. Patel., B.V., 1976, Study habits inventory. In: *Second Handbook of Psychology and Social Instruments,* Ed. Pestonjee, D.M., Concept Publishing Company, New Delhi

26. Ryan, A. M. (2001). The peer group as a context for the development of young adolescent Achievement and achievement. *Child Development.*

27. Roeser, R. and Galloway, M. (2002). Studying Achievement to learn during early adolescence: A holistic perspective. In F. Pajares & T. Urdan (Eds.), *Academic Achievement of Adolescents.* Greenwich, CT: Information Age Publishing.

28. Urdan, T. C., & Maehr, M. L. (1995). A case for social goals. *Review of educational research,* Beyond a two-goal theory of Achievement and achievement:

29. Wigfield, A. and Tonks, S. (2002). *Academic Achievement of Adolescents* expectancies for success and extracurricular activity during the middle and high school years.

30. Weiner, Bluma. "A Theory of Achievement for Some Classroom Experiences." *Journal of Educational Psychology.*

4. Relationship Between The Reading and achievement

Chapter - I

Elementary Education in India

The universalization of elementary education in India has been a long - cherished but unrealized goal which India has been striving towards ever since her independence in 1947. As the British government expanded its rule in India, education for Indians gradually became their concern. However, their main purposes were, as stated in Macaulay's infamous Minute on Education in 1835, creating a class of people who would be interpreters between the British rulers and the Indian masses, and preparing government employees to bolster and further the imperialist aims of the raj. Sir Charles Wood's Education Dispatch of 1854 suggested that the government should abandon the strategy of providing only higher education and promote mass education. However, teacher training for elementary education progressed at a very slow pace.

Indigenous Indian elementary education, whose features were popularity in the community and flexibility in its setup, was on the decline under the sluggish expansion of modern elementary school system. Although many reports under the British rule stressed the importance of elementary teacher training and recommended establishing more normal schools, elementary schools were woefully insufficient.

In the final analysis, the British Government never accepted responsibility for educating the masses in India, and the problem of wastage and stagnation in school education remained unsolved. Further examination on the educational policy after independence for universalization of elementary education requires careful consideration regarding the historical background of school education in India.

RECENT TRENDS IN ELEMENTARY EDUCATION

1. Elementary Education is recognized as a fundamental right of all citizens in India. The Supreme Court of India in its judgment in Unnikrishnan's case has held that all citizens have a fundamental right to education up to the age of 14 years. The Government of India has introduced 83^{rd}constitutional Amendment Bill in Parliament in 1997 to make education a fundamental right of all children up to the age of 6-14 years.

2. Greater emphasis on Decentralization of Educational planning and administration. The 73rd and 74th constitutional amendments have provided a statutory base for decentralized educational planning.

3. Multi – sector holistic approach to Unviersalisation of Elementary Education (UEE).

4. Greatest stress on creation of conditions that would encourage increased community participation in effective school management and supervision.

5. Re-examination of relationship among the government, NGOs and private institutions to harness potential of non – governmental institutions in pursuit of UEE.

6. Recognition of limitations of market forces is ensuring equity and equality in elementary education. The Government is committed to enhance financial allocation for education to 6% of GDP.

7. Greater thrust on community – based support structures, educational planning and monitoring & evaluation to improve delivery of elementary education.

There is a strong consensus today about the importance of elementary education in Indian public policy. It is hard to imagine how productive and income growth can come about for the 45 per cent of India which is illiterate. Going beyond economies, there are significant returns to education as far as social development and politics are concerned. It is hard to imagine how social progress can be obtained with 45 per cent illiteracy.

From this perspective, one common theme that has emerged is that while the liberalization of the 1990 has involved taking the state out of myriad aspects of the Indian economy, there remains a major role for the state in elementary education. Indeed, the withdrawal of the state from other areas should help free up resources for education and health.

Why is elementary education special? Why should the State spend on elementary education? A common reason that is supplied is the poor people are too backward to invest in education by themselves; hence the only way to ensure that their children grow up educated is through large government interventions. This argument is highly suspect. The second and more defensible rationale for public expenditures for elementary education is based upon the "externalities" of education. Each educated person generates myriad benefits for all those around him, and he, individually, cannot capture the full benefits of his education that accrue to society. Hence, individuals have an incentive to under invest in education, generate these positive benefits, and take away part (but not all) of these benefits are taxes.

NEWSPAPERS

The daily newspapers can also be taken as an effective teaching aid if it is used in right and conscientious perspective. They are full of information about the general economic and social life of the people. They are, in fact, the minimum text book for the study of current affairs. In spite of all the difficulties which they present for the immature reader, still they remain the all indispensable source.

Modern teaching aims at correcting different subjects among themselves and also the daily life. Very often he has to relate certain topics in history, geography, arithmetic, science, economics, commerce, agriculture etc. with the daily life through the medium of the newspaper. It is a common experience that pupils find it difficult to understand such topics as discount, stock and shares, Government budget etc. They newspaper furnishes many examples which can be used to introduce lessons of these types. Newspaper can motivate the children for knowing the past events. There is no doubt that the pupil is interested in what is now happening. Since he is already interested in his own preferences it becomes easy to lead him to those very things and correlating them with his education. That means newspaper serve as a wonderful motivational aid, it is the process of going from know to the unknown, from the familiar to the unfamiliar which are the most important maxims of teaching.

Newspapers contain a reservoir of resources and illustrations. Contemporary occurrences help to clarify and exemplify the realities described in the text books Newspapers may be – used to augment other instructional resources and as a means of sensitizing the class to the need for up – to – date information.

Newspapers can provide a point of contact and as a means of approach. Since much of history, civics, geography and other contents are remote in time and place and also in the experience of pupils, current news happenings can serve as a starting point to stimulate interest in these fields. On social studies newspapers are particularly significant. Many newspapers items can vitalize a unit and connect the past with the present, they can express the extension and exemplification of the major topics in the curriculum. A study of newspapers not only integrates the past with the present but reveals the relationship of specific events to the larger current scene.

Occurrences in the teaching of various languages mathematics or even in science are reported in the newspapers which can vitalize instruction. The teachers may reflect upon the maximum and minimum temperatures, the rainfall of various places, the weather forecast as well as the time of sunrise and sunset of a particular place. News regarding earth quakes, cyclones, tidal waves, new planets etc., may be made known to the pupils. The special issues of the newspapers – republic day issues, industrial supplements, etc, are full of information. The life sketches of great personalities and the description of historical buildings and places can enrich the curriculum. Important articles appearing on Sundays have been found very useful for educational purposes. The special features, the editorials, the cartoons, the advertisements all can enlighten the students.

Newspapers help in fulfilling the gap between information contained in books and changing developments of the world. With changes occurring as rapidly as they do in the dynamic world of today to text books are likely to become obsolete in terms of changing conditions. They only way of the learner of today can keep himself up – to – date in knowledge is to develop and maintain a continuing interest in current affairs as reported through the various news mediums.

Newspapers are filled with affairs, ephemeral and permanent, trivial and important. There are incidents and scandals merely sensational of passing interest. That means the teacher has to be careful in selecting suitable material to be used by the pupils. Movements, trends, ideas and changes in politics, international relations, labour the important. The sputnik age, with inventions, discoveries, research and news development in industries and significant scientific progress is always of interest to the students. Sports have become so much a part of modern life that the phase of our society is important in the life of a youth. The material selected should be readable and should be related to the objectives of the different grade levels.

ROLE OF A TEACHER

How the teacher should deal with the news items is summarized briefly here;

1. Daily discussion of news topics.
2. Use of news bulletin board
3. News map
4. Use of a variety of activities like panel discussion, round table discussions, debates, preparing charts, maps, graphics, building, scrap books of news, stories, pictures puzzles, drawing cartoon to illustrate news, dramatizing news events.

DAILY DISCUSSION OF NEWS TOPICS

It is advisable if the news items can be discussed in the morning assembly. At the beginning of each social day, children reports news items. Happenings close to the children, however, trivial they seem, have value for discussion. They usually are details of living and working together. As children advances in age and ability the collection of news may become of general interest.

It is the duties of the teacher of help the child develop his power of critical thinking and his ability to discriminate between significant news and the sensational. Without guidance of the teacher, children are likely to report the sensational news like murders, rapes, robberies etc. it is the teacher to help children evaluate news stories in terms of the social significance affecting people by the event and the reasons why it received in the attention it did.

It is necessary to build the child's interest in news to the extent that the child voluntarily brings news clippings whenever he finds – one – which he feels is worthwhile to bring to schools. The teachers' role in this respect is one of the leadership and encouragement.

Dealing with controversial issues, every effort should be made to develop the scientific approach to problem solving in the handling of various issues. Teachers have to use objective approach to such problems in a spirit of reasonableness. An objective point of view, sound, judgment and proper guidance are most essential in any discussion. In teaching controversial issues, the teacher has a special responsibility to help children develop habits of critical judgment and open mindedness, to evaluate sources of information and to judge the soundness of facts presented.

USE OF NEWS BULLETIN BOARD

News Bulletin Board may be used for displaying interesting news pictures and news stories. The display may contain news of local interest, news of national and international problems, even jokes for bringing variety.

NEWS MAP

A large world map is placed on the bulletin board with sufficient space around it to post clippings, pictures, charts etc. Coloured string or narrow, strips of paper may then be used to connect the news story with the location of spot where the event occurred.

THE PANEL DISCUSSION

A selected group of students are four to eight and a chairman may present a previously prepared subject before an audience. After the presentation, the other students of the class could ask questions, clarify points or add to what the panel his said. Members of the group may raise questions, or express their opinions. At the close of the discussion, the chairman summarizes what has been discussed, and summing up all into an integrated whole.

DEBATE

Two group - of students are present argument for and against, for a given proposition. The opposing sides must possess equivalent intellectual capacity. The proposition is usually the solution to a problem rather than the problems itself. After both sides have determined the issue, they select and present the evidence that will prove the issues true a false.

MAKING CHARTS, MAPS AND GRAPHS

Charts, maps, graphs can also help to show components of an event that had best to the climax.

BUILDING SCRAP BOOKS OF NEWS STORIES OR PICTURES

Collections of news clippings are also a useful activity careful selection of articles in the scrap book will allow the pupils to follow the development of the news story on a continuing basis.

DRAWING CARTOONS TO ILLUSTRATE NEWS

Cartoons dealing with some catastrophe, safety or health habits, good citizenship, ill effects of war etc, can provide a good deal of interest. The procedure can be used with older children. The teacher should avoid having children draw cartoons which might be offensive to individuals or groups

DRAMATIZING NEWS EVENTS

The items like festivals, meetings, conferences. Negotiations, if dramatized, can create a good deal of interest among students.

READING SKILLS

Bacon said, "Reading make a full man, writing an exact man". Reading skill is, undoubtedly of unique importance in the learning of a language. A W Frisby says. "Reading for those who have been guided to a appreciate it, is one of the most important activities of life to bring to us not only a pleasant way of spending the time, but a way of entering into the life of the world and helping us to contemplates spiritual matters. Many of those who do not approach reading in this life have probably not received in their youth the right encouragement. "Thus we find that the ability to read well is very much expected from every person. R.S. Trivedi and D.A. Ghanchi write in their books 'Teaching English'... "In fact, the education of a child is imperfect, unless he is equipped with ability to read, to decipher, to interpret and to understand properly the contents of a reading material. The intellectual advancement of a child is strictly limited if he is unable to read".

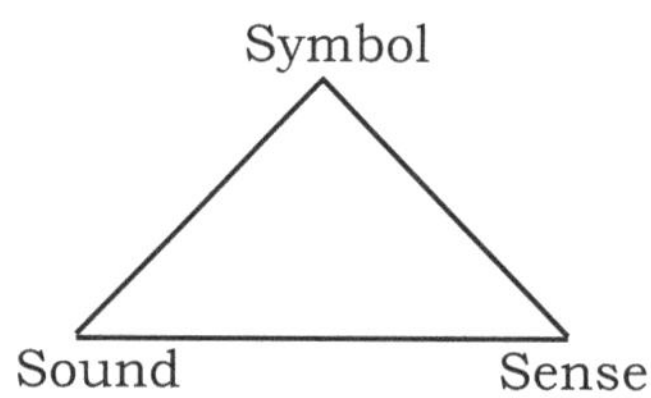

Reading involves recognition of sound and written symbols. Recognition of sounds is needed for listening or speaking of the language. Recognition of written symbols is important for reading purposes. Let us first of all, study what is meant by reading.

READING: DEFINITION

Reading is process of looking at a written or printed symbol and translating it into an appropriate sound. This spoken symbol is further associated with an object for which it stands. Thus reading consists of three elements... the symbol (written or printed), the sound and the sense. For example, the child reads the word 'dog' in his reader. First of all, he looks at the symbol, translates it into a specific sound which stands for some animal called 'dog' and at the same time he visualizes the concrete object or idea for which they said symbol stands.

Reading in fact is the ability which enables the pupils sooner or later, to read with the purpose of extracting from the printed page, the thoughts, facts and information that it has to give him. We are enlightened by reading. By reading our written message is interpreted by the other person.

READING MECHANICS

When a person reads anything his eyes go on moving along with the printed or written symbols. If we are watch carefully, the eyes do not move smoothly in one even movement. They move by jumps separated by short stops. He reads when the eyes are having a pause and not when the eyes are in movement. The number of words read in one complete movement of the eyes is called the Eye – Span.

While reading, we do not look at the various letters of a word. We rather look at the words as a whole e.g. (Chair not c-h-a-i-r). The span can help develop the art of reading. There are fact readers and slow readers. The reason behind it is that a fast reader has wider eye- span, whereas a poor reader has short eye-span.

While reading, some students put their four fingers under every world. It is a bad habit because it has adverse effect on the speed of reading. So the teacher should check this bad habit at the initial stages.

TEACHING OF READING

People generally feet that the ability to read fluently is the primary aim of learning English. Before 1900, the major aim in teaching reading was just word recognition. But in due course of time, the concept underwent a change. In the modern times, there have been many social changes and so the purposes of teaching reading have increased. So much so is the change that even the methods of teaching reading have been modified accordingly. At present reading is taught so that a person is able.

1. To recognize words.
2. To understand the meanings of words.
3. To react to what has been read. In other words, the child laughs, feels sad, waits for the ending etc. as the case may be. And he will disagree on false statement.
4. To change ideas and behaviour of the students.

Reading of mother tongue and reading of a foreign language are fundamentally the same processes. The learners face problems in both the cases. However in case of mother tongue, the problems are few because he has already learnt listening and speaking at home. In case of a foreign language, practice in listening or speaking is given in the school. Comparatively, the learners have less practice in aural – oral aspect of the language. Besides, English is not a phonetic language. It spelling system create problems in reading. So it is very essential that reading should be started after giving sufficient practice in listening and speaking.

READING IN PREPARATION

Preparatory reading means preparing the students for reading from the books. When the students come to the school, they should not be taught reading on the first or the second day. Rather they should be given language training in listening, and speaking for some days. Thus oral work and its practice of one type or the other should continue for a number of days.

In preparatory stage, the teacher should teach the students how to produce certain sounds. They should be taught how to speak the words. Those words should be taken up in oral work which the students will conic across in their books at the later stage. This stage when the students are prepared for the stage of reading is also called pre-reading stage.

Thus we notice that preparatory reading is of utmost importance in the teaching of a language. The following steps are suggested for conducting it:

1. By showing actual objects, the teacher tells the names of the things. In case of verbs, actions are performed and the teacher speaks the words. The students simply watch and listen carefully.

2. The teacher makes use of charts or pictures for those items which cannot be actually shown by their sketches or diagrams can be drawn easily.

3. Flash cards can also be used for this purpose. On one flash card the name of the object is written and on the other, sketch is drawn. The teacher shows the flash cards and makes the students speak the words. By and by, he makes the picture disappear. It helps the students to have some recognition of the words or letters as the case may be.

4. In case the flash cards are not available, the black – board can be used for the same purpose. Some of the pictures may be drawn and words or sentences describing them are written. Then the pupils are asked to read them, Later, only words or sentences may be written and pupils are helped to read them.

5. Some drills of words o sentences may be given in chorus, in groups and then to individuals.

6. By using black – boards or flash cards, simple comprehension drills may be conducted as mentioned below;

7. The learners may be asked to pick up one of the objects provided.

8. Some pictures may be provided, and the learner is asked to find one mentioned by the teacher.

9. First halves of a few sentences may be written on the black board. The second halves may be written on the flash cards. The students

may be asked to pick – it the corresponding halves on the flash cards.

10. Some of the reading games by are introduced. These games are of two types (i) Recognition games. (ii) Comprehension games

READING AS A SKILL

When reading starts in the child's mother tongue, he or she does not face any trouble. Because the child already knows the sounds, words, phrases and structure in their spoken form. The only effort that the child has to make is to associate those sound with their written symbols. The child has to learn to identify the 'language signals' or 'visual images'.

But the reading a second language poses a different set of difficulties to the learner. The child does not know the sounds, vocabulary or structure of the new language. So, he has to learn all these things first and then only he can start reading.

Reading in English should be started only after the child has been given a thorough practice in listening and speaking. The child should have had enough 'oral practice' of the text that he is going to read. His speech should be free from errors. The vocabulary should also be fixed for various stages and classes. The scripts in English also present some problems in reading. The child should be taught two types of scripts – the lower case and the upper case used in printing of books, newspapers, magazines etc., the child also finds it difficult to read certain worlds that are similar in spelling but different in pronunciation. The sounds in words like cut, but hut etc., are similar. But the word, 'put' has a different sound though it is similar to 'but'. Further, the words with the same spelling are sometimes read differently when used as a noun, a verb, an adjective or an adverb. For example, the word, 'conduct' should be spoken or read as 'conduct in its noun form and conduct in its verb form. The children also face some difficulty to read words where there are silent letters. In words like knife, 'k' is silent. Similarly, children find it difficult to read words like island, calm etc.

In order to overcome the above difficulties, the children should be given a thorough training in the development of 'listening' and 'speaking' skills before we help them read.

AIMS OF TEACHING READING

The teacher of English should bear in mind the following aims while teaching reading to their pupils in the classroom.

1. To enable the pupils to recognize words.

2. To get them to comprehend the meaning of words, phrases and sentences.
3. To help them to guess the meanings of unfamiliar words from the context in which they are used.
4. To enable them to react to what has been read.
5. To enable them to infer the mood of the author / writer.
6. To get them read at a normal speed.
7. To enable them to use proper stress, intonation and pauses suitable to the context.

PROCESS INVOLVED IN TEACHING READING ALOUD

Reading aloud is a process of identifying the written or printed symbols and translating them into appropriate sound components. These symbols are associated with the objects which they stand for. Thus, 'reading' consists of three important elements, namely, the symbols, the sound and the sense. These three elements of reading can be represented by the three vertices or a triangle as shown hereunder.

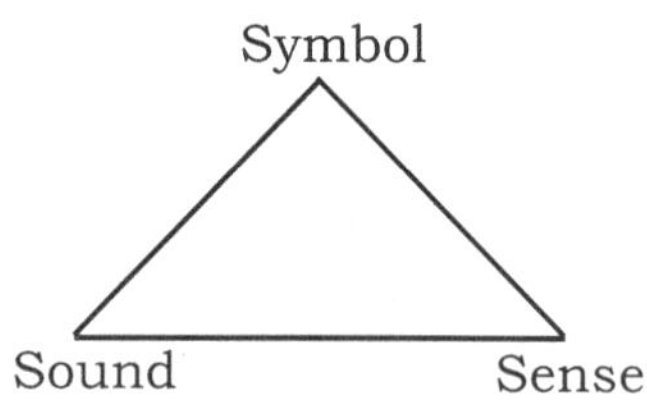

For example, when the child wants to read a word like 'building', he follows all the three stages in reading. First, the child looks at the symbol (the object), translates it into a specific sound pattern that stands for the object and then tries to understand the meaning of the word, 'building'. This is how the child completes the process of 'reading' aloud.

TYPES OF READING

Depending on the nature and purpose, reading may be classified into various categories;

READING ALOUD

Much of the early reading should be reading aloud. It is necessary to ensure that the child associates the spoken word with the printed symbols correctly.

Reading aloud provides practice in good speech habits among the children and gives the teacher an opportunity to find out whether the children can read with correct stress, intonation and pronunciation or not. This kind of reading also help in including among the children the right habits of reading words are group.

SILENT READING

Along with the ability to read aloud, the children may be encouraged to read silently. Most of the reading done at the higher stage of learning should be of this kind only.

The purpose of silent reading is to encourage the students to read with comprehension. The speed when one reads silently is more than that when one reads aloud. This enables the students to read more materials in less time when they read silently.

The following are the advantages of silent reading

1. Silent reading keeps the whole class busy.
2. It helps the students read at their own pace.
3. It prepares the students for independent reading.

INTENSIVE READING OR CRITICAL READING

Intensive reading or critical reading is done while the students try to gather facts or arrive at some conclusions on the basis of the facts. This is done mostly when the students prepare for the examinations. This kind of reading is done with thinking and comprehensions. Hence, it is also known as 'Critical Reading' or 'Reading for comprehension'.

EXTENSIVE READING

Extensive reading is a kind of wide reading based on the large field from where we gather the desired information of the purpose of our survey or report. This is an advanced stage in reading, which emphasizes the expansion of vocabulary and the advanced skills of comprehension. Most of the time, it would be silent reading and it is at this level that the speed of reading beings to increases. The students start reading independently at this stage. The reading at this stage is need – based and hence the reading becomes multi – dimensional in nature. This kind of reading is also known as 'Reading for information'. The students may be encouraged to read a good number of journals, magazines, newspapers etc. besides the prescribed textbooks.

READING FOR COMPREHENSION

The students should be encouraged to read with comprehension. Reading with comprehension involves a number of activities like recognizing words, understanding the meanings of words, associating the meaning of different words, understanding the meaning of the whole passage and finally forming ideas on what has been read.

There are three important aspects involved in reading for comprehension.

When the students read, they should understand

1. The purpose of their reading (why they read)
2. The method or procedure followed by them in reading (how they read)
3. The content or the material they read (what they read)

Reading for comprehension also involves certain sub - skills like skimming, scanning and in-depth reading.

Skimming is related to the speed of the reading. One should read the material at a reasonable speed. When you read the passage fast to get the gist, you try to skim through the passage. Scanning involves findings out the required information from the text or other reading material you go through. Looking at the page of a dictionary to arrive at the required entry is scanning. In – depth reading involves reading of extra material like reading magazines, journals, newspapers etc., for pleasure or information.

READING SKILLS

Reading is a major objective of the English course in schools. Reading aloud helps pronunciation. Reading is source of pleasure and profit. The abilities involved in reading are

1. Comprehension
2. Recognition of the syllabus.

Intensive and Extensive Reading

A detailed story of the prescribed reader or text book is intensive reading. The deals are with the study of new structures and new vocabulary items. This is in fact a study where a student is attempting to master language skills even if it is to a limited extent. But after the school or college course nobody makes an intensive study of anything unless it specifically demands such a study. Otherwise all reading that takes place in life like study of newspapers, novels etc are all by extensive study only.

All that a person attempts to know in the extensive study is to know the main points. Its main aim is to get information's. Intensive reading prepares the student for extensive reading. Extensive reading, if properly guided will:

1. Reinforce what was already learnt as structure or vocabulary.
2. Increase the speed in silent reading
3. Create love for extra – reading
4. Help to read for pleasure and get information.

GENERAL PRINCIPLES OF TEACHING READING

1. Time of staring
2. Choice of primer
3. Speech before reading
4. Training, in both oral and silent reading
5. Using a psychological method
6. Play – way
7. Teacher as model reader
8. Procedural variety
9. Insisting on correct reading habits from the beginning
10. Reading with comprehension.

TEACHING TAMIL PROSE

According to Coleridge, "Prose is best words in their best order". The aims, methods and nature of teaching prose lesson are different from those of poetry. Prose is for knowledge, information and language. Poetry is for enjoyment, aesthetic, sensuousness and imagery. Appreciation of prose involves comprehending the central experience beauty, and property of phraseology, the allusions and the images in the presentation of the experience.

CHARACTERISTIC OF PROSE

1. Prose consists of philosophical ideas, social problems, historical description of events, geographical, concepts etc.
2. Prose is the most important aspect of literature. Thoughts on a

topic, story, drama, novels, auto biography and biography, narration and explanation of concepts, theories and principles are major aspects of prose.

3. Prose develops listening, reading, speaking and writing skills.
4. The purpose of literature is best served by prose.
5. Prose develops the expressional and interpretative ability of students.
6. Prose develops cognitive and affective aspects of students.
7. Prose is the best way of preserving human knowledge experiences, imagination and ideas and transmits to new generations.

GENERAL OBJECTIVES OF TEACHING PROSE

1. To enable students understand the passage or lesson.
2. To develop their imaginative powers.
3. To enable students enjoy reading English literature.
4. To enrich students active and passive vocabulary.
5. To enable pupils read the passage with correct pronunciation, intonation, pause and articulation of voice.
6. To develop students imaginative power and prepare them for world citizenship.

VARIOUS FORMS OF PROSE

1. Essay: Essay may be personal, philosophical, historical or critical. They may be lengthy or short in size. Samuel Johnson defined it as a "loose sally of the mind, an irregular, undigested piece, not a regular and an order composition.

2. Novel: The term originally meant a 'Fresh story' but gradually come to signify a story in prose as distinguished from a story in verse which continued to be called a romance. W.E.William defines it as "a long narrative in prose details the actions of fictitious people.

3. Short story: It is a recent development in Tamil literature. It shares the usual constituents of all fiction – plot, character and setting – but they cannot be treated with the same detail as in a novel.

4. Play or Drama: Drama presents fiction of fact in a form that could be acted before the audience. A play has a plot, characters, dialogue, an atmosphere and an outlook on life much as a novel has, but it is as a rule intended to performed in public, not to be read in private. There are some other kinds of prose such as biography, paragraph writing, composition, etc.

PROCEDURE OF TEACHING PROSE LESSON

There is every need for pre-planned lesson plan for teaching prose. Different scholars have suggested different types of lessons. Generally, Herbart ion steps are followed in teaching and planning a prose lesson. These steps are strictly on "Apperceptionistic view, according to which "Learning to link an old idea with a new idea". These steps should be followed after insisting the marginal entries in the lesson plan as – data, school, class period, subject, topic etc.

A. PREPARATION

1. Teaching Aids
2. Previous knowledge
3. Introduction

B. PRESENTATION

1. Model Reading
2. Loud reading or Imitation Reading by Teacher (Single)
3. Loud reading or Imitation reading by students
4. Exposition and explanation
5. Silent Reading

MODEL READING

The teacher gives a model reading to enables students to know the exact way of reading. So the teacher should try to read with correct pronunciation, intonation and stress. He should be particular about pause, articulation and expression. While reading the teacher should not almost absorbs him completely in the books but gives some attention to students.

LOUD READING OR IMITATION READING BY THE TEACHER

For this the selection of words must be on the basis of the general pronunciation of students. Those words which can be pronounced wrongly by students should be selected and written on the black board one by one and get drilled.

SECOND MODEL OF TEACHING PROSE

The class text book or reader in English is meant to be taught intensively. In the intensive teaching under structural approach which is followed in schools a teacher has to adopt a particular procedure or pattern. The steps a teacher has to follow in teaching pros are:

1. Motivation or Introduction (Previous knowledge)
2. Introduction of New Grammatical structure.
3. Introduction of New vocabulary.
4. Model reading or pattern reading by the teacher.
5. World study or explanation of different worlds.
6. Silent reading by the pupils
7. Testing comprehension or comprehension questions
8. Reading aloud by the pupils.
9. Assignment oral or written

   The detailed procedure adopted under each step is discussed hereunder.

READING INVOLVES THE FOLLOWING PROCESSES

1. Recognizing the printed Symbols
2. Uttering their correct Sounds and
3. Understanding their sense

Thus when a pupil being to read, he has to see they symbols, say their sounds and understand the sense. The first two items of this process are mechanical (physical) and the third viz. comprehensions or understanding is an act of mind (mental). By drill and practice the mechanical process may be speeded up. Thus the first relates to the mechanics of reading.

A few sentence forms and patterns have been taught in standard three which were solely devoted to the listening and peaking practice. Regular reading is begun after getting proficiency in listening and speaking skills. Reading in the early stages is a means of fixing more family what the pupils when already learnt. The act of reading has been defined as sight – sound – sense co-ordination.

Reading is a tool – an important tool – in everyday life in the world. It is the first item in the scheme of the 3 R's (viz. reading, arithmetic and writing). When the pupil goes out of school to enter life or to join a college, he is going to use this tool for life's purpose. The more than sharp the tool is, the more efficient will be its use. Reading ability serves life's purpose in many ways. Reading is useful

1. gathering knowledge from the books
2. getting pleasure
3. Producing effect upon the hearers. Reading without getting at the meaning is useless. Reading in important in life. The faster one reads with comprehension the quicker will be one's success in life.

ORAL READING

Reading aloud: Oral reading is that in which, there is vocalization of every world that we read. In order words, it is reading aloud. The early reading is necessarily oral. Oral reading has to be taught for a time so that the pupils may get mastery of the English language forms. Oral reading gives quick command over a large number of words.

Pupils learn the meaning of what they read fully and correctly. Apart from these advantages, pupils learn pronunciation, articulation, intonation, stress, etc. only through oral reading. It is the basis for reading meaningfully, correctly and fluently. But one cannot be reading aloud all through life, pronouncing every word. Such a course is unnecessary, wasteful and tiresome. So after some practice in oral reading, we have to train children in silent reading.

TECHNIQUES TO TEACHING SILENT READING

Most of the reading in the class should be silent. The lesson in the course book, the prescribed supplementary readers and other non – textural passages can be used for the purpose. When the pupils read silently, the teacher must ask them

1. Not to move their lips
2. Not to whisper out the words and
3. Not to pass their fingers under each world. He must ask them to read fast and give them just enough time only.

SPEED IN SILENT READING

This is reckoned as so many words per minute. So far the minimum speed has not been fixed.

Tentative speed is given below

1. Std, 4.75 wpm (Words per minute)
2. Higher Std, 150 wpm (Words per minute)

Speed in reading is gaining greater emphasis, and as it has to be tested objectively, norms have to be built up.

1. Speed must be reckoned accurately for each pupil and efforts taken to improve his speed.
2. Understanding is also important. It should not be scarified to improper speed in reading.

Silent reading is for comprehension and speed. So after silent reading, the teacher must set some comprehensions questions. These questions are simply to find out how much the pupils have understood. Yes or No, True or False. It's difficult; question may be put in Tamil occasionally. The pupils should be encouraged to find out the answer to questions set by the teacher even before the pupils starting silent reading. This will help read with a purpose.

STAGES OF DEVELOPING READING SKILLS

From what we have studies so far, it is possible to summaries the stages in the development or reading skill. They are;

1. Saying the sounds represented by letters and letter combinations.
2. Recognizing and saying sentences and words presented with illustrative pictures and drawings.
3. Recognizing and saying sentences and words without visual associations or pictures.
4. Silent reading of words and sentences from the reader and the supplementary reader with understanding.
5. Occasional reading aloud of words and sentences from the course book.
6. Answering questions based on what is read.
7. Reading silently on own speed.
8. Guessing the meaning of unfamiliar words from the context in which they are used.
9. Finding information from a given passage in response to questions set before reading.

AIMS OF SILENT READING

1. The chief aims of silent reading are comprehension and speed. Pupils should get at the information quickly through silent reading.
2. To pave the way for the adult way of reading.
3. To get the essentials and leave off the non – essentials.
4. To develop a taste for reading.

THE DEVELOPMENT OF LANGUAGE THROUGH READING

Language is a phenomenon that is unique to human species. Ideas and language are inseparable. Communication of ideas and the subsequent embellishment and improvement of ideas demand the medium of language. Without effective language and languages skills, learning is retarded. The acquisitions of effective language skills are essential if the learner is to move successfully through one's school experiences. The science that investigates the content and the process of language learning is related to linguistics and psychology. Linguistics is an ancient preoccupation of scholar and a relative science as is psychology. They relate the influence of the 'switches and changes' in theoretical orientations in linguistics and psychology on the teaching of second language.

Today's professional teacher and tomorrow's practitioner of that art need the skills, the controls, the understandings and the knowledge of teaching to enable the student's language grow and his/ her ability to learn. The language skills namely – Listening, Speaking, Reading and Writing have been called as skilled process. This infers that these are similar to any other skill that is learnt. However, the teacher would discover that the third factor of language learning, i.e. reading is perhaps the most complex and discrete of all instructional attempts. First of all, the teacher as well as the student needs to understand the concept that reading is another form of communication. The words which are spoken can be recorded (encoded) in written form; and that what has been written can read (decoded); and further what the students says, writes and reads can be read by others. Hence the process of reading can be seen as a developmental process, a leaned process and as a responding process.

A Developmental Process the term as it refers to reading instruction deals with the order in which certain tasks and learning activities are presented in order to lead the student from the simplest skills to the increasingly more difficult ones required for independence and fluency. The length of words, the length of sentences and paragraphs as well as the story being read, the introduction of a new words, the acquisition of decoding skills and such other instructional considerations are necessarily and basically matters of progressing nature. Hence, the idea of reading being a development process is a valid one.

A Learned Process This process simply indicates that the ability to read is an acquired one. It must be taught or learned. It is not something inherent; it is the result of conditioning. Literacy, the ability to read and write comes as a result of learning. The very word 'learn' connotes that which is acquired by study, experience or instruction. Certainly in learning to read, the student receives from all three types of input – the actual study; experience be it firsthand or explicit; and instruction be it individual or group – oriented; the student moves naturally into the potential of this learned ability.

As soon as the student learns the mechanics and responses of reading, she proceeds to find new information, further knowledge, and expanded learning. Along with these developing powers, the other tasks such as reference skill or the use of more sophisticated tools – the dictionary, the encyclopedia, the card catalogue, the index, the glossary, and the subject matter of the text are unconsciously learnt. Certainly one would not minimize the effectiveness and value of the other media – the illustration, the animation of the film, and the availability of listening and recording devices. Even these tools require a level of learned 'reading' to be effective in the classroom. The student uses reading as a means of expanding one's store of knowledge as well as strengthening one's skills power. Since reading is basically communication, all the intellectual skills that are used in receiving and reacting to message are necessary in the total process of understanding and assessing the written materials.

A Responding Process Since communicating is not a unilateral process one could readily say that reading is a responding process. Not only does the writer have something to say, to tell or to share, the reader must respond by being interested, by feeling the message being given; and by receiving and becoming involved with that which is being offered by the writer. It is this affective responding that makes reading such an important tool for communication. Further, the reading process must being about the response, an arousal, a resultant action, in which the reader feels the emotive quality of the materials, so that the student smells, tastes, and touches the description related to these responses. The student must experience the pathos, the hilarity, or the danger of the narrative by the appropriate reactions. The interest and reading taste must be so catered to and so captivated that the student is carried along from page to page, topic to topic, or selection to selection without boredom or frustration. A vital facet of reading is interest.

READING

Reading is an interpretation of graphic symbols as it involves an interaction between the writer and reader. One has to decode the sign system and extract the meaning from the graphic symbols. Decoding occurs only when the meaning that the writer wanted to share with the reader has been received by the reader. During the decoding the reader transforms the visual representation of language into meaning. Decoding is affected through syntax; syntax mediates between the visual surface structure and meaning. (Smith, 1971: 222) Further, meaning is supplied by the reader as he processes the symbols by relating them to experiences. Meaning is both output (what the reader brings by way of past experience of the printed page) and also input (the new meaning that the reader gets from the printed page). Words get meaning as a consequence of occurring in sentences.

A team of experts, under the sponsorship of the United States Office of Education defined reading as 'a term used to refer to an interaction by which meaning encoded in visual stimuli by an author becomes meaning in the mind of the reader'. Reading is the recognition and perception of language structures as wholes in order to comprehend both the surface and deep meaning which these structures communicate.

Reading is a unidirectional process from letters to sounds to meaning. **Gough** (1972)

Reading is involving flexible processing and multiple information sources, depending upon contextual circumstances. **-Rumelhart** (1977)

Reading is a selective process, involving partial use of available minimal language clues (graphic, semantic and syntactic) selected from perceptual input on the basis of the readers' expectation.**-Goodman** (1967)

Kamala Nanda (1989) in her book 'Developing English Comprehension' highlights the definition of reading by Spache and Spache (1973) and Stauffer (1967)

Reading in obviously a multifaceted process that like at chameleon changes its nature from one development stage to another. **-Spache and Spache**(1973).

His definition emphasizes two important points about reading. Primarily it is a process and then it is a changing development phenomenon.

Reading is a mental process requiring accurate word recognition, ability to recall to mind particular meaning, and ability to shift or reassociate meaning until the constructs and concepts present dare clearly grasped, critically evaluated, accepted and applied or rejected. **- Stauffer** (1967)

Ahuja and PramilaAhuja (1987) in their book 'How to Increase Reading Speed' highlight the following definitions of Reading.

Reading is an art and what is read is a form of art... The sentence is the heartbeat of the mind. **-Mark Van Doren** (1962)

Reading means plucking out all the subtle threads of meaning from sentence, paragraphs and pages and weaving them into one's own personality. - **Artley** (1953)

Reading is a very complex process in which the recognition and comprehension of written symbols are influenced by the perceptual skills, the word analysis skills, the experience, the language background, the mindset and the reading ability of the reader. - **Harris** (1970)

Reading clarifies, formulates, and hence helps to express ideas born of the reader's common experience. In short, reading is a social process. - **Processor Douglas Waples** (1940)

Reading is a subtle and complex act which involves more or less simultaneously, the following: sensation of light rays on the retina of the eye reaching the brain, perception of separate words and phrases, functioning of the eye muscles with the exact controls, immediate memory for what has been read, remote memories based on the reader's experience, interest in the context read, and organization of the material so that it can be used in some way. These various features operate more or less concurrently. **-Russell** (1949)

1. Reading is the ability of the vocal cords to pronounce correctly the written materials.
2. Reading is n expression of sentences in correct forms.
3. Reading is the media of expressing words and sentences in correct intonation.
4. Reading means silent and loud reading.
5. Reading is a fine art of speech**- Abuja and Pramila Abuja** (1987 : 5)

   A complex system of deriving meaning from print that requires all of the following

i) The skills and knowledge to understand how phonemes or speech sounds are connected to print.

ii) The ability to decode unfamiliar words.

iii) The ability to read fluently.

iv) Sufficient background information and vocabulary to foster reading comprehension.

v) The development of appropriate active strategies to construct meaning from print.

vi) The development and maintenance of a motivation to read.

GOAL OF READING INSTRUCTION

The goal of reading instruction should be to develop the reading skills among the learners. Some of the basic component skills in reading are:

1. Skill in using the language read
2. Skill in getting at the sound structure of words
3. Skill in deciphering the letters of the alphabet in its various forms of printing and handwriting.
4. Skill in the physical act of visual coordination between the two eyes.
5. Skill in recognizing the patterns of correspondence between letters and sounds.
6. Skill in comprehending the whole meaning.
7. Skill in the correlation of the visual act of reading with reasoning and thinking, evaluating, and reacting.
8. Skill in regulating the speed of reading to the level of difficulty of the reading material.
9. Skill in regulating the speed of read, and establishing its relevance to the underlying purpose.
10. Skill in utilizing one's individual resources for effective reading. **(Kamala Nanda**1989 : 29)

All these components conjure up a mental picture. The sharper the outline, the better is the level of understanding either immediately or at later points enabling the learners to arrive at the meaning. The skill in comprehending the whole meaning s seen as a tool to help learners to think inwardly and to reflect, thereby leading to enhancement in reading comprehension.

Enforcing to these ideas Ahuja and ParmilaAhuja (1987:3) highlight the views of LwarenceHafner (1967) who stated reading has the following values;

1. Reading material is readily accessible
2. Reader can react as an individual.
3. Reading allows time for reflection
4. Information is easily checked.
5. Memories can be renewed

6. One can select segments of materials he wants.
7. Sources can be compared readily.
8. One can readily skin a wide range of materials.
9. One can check on the credentials of the author.
10. Reading provides excellent contexts for concept development and vocabulary study Hence, reading is a tool and serves as a means to an end.

THE NATURE OF THE READING PROCESS

Reading is a process by which a person reconstructs a message encoded graphically by a writer. The reader goes from the written language, visually perceived, to a reconstruction of the message encoded in the written language by the writer. When the reconstruction agrees with the writer's intended message, comprehension of the passage occurs. Further, reading requires that the reader makes visual contact with the stimulus or graphic cues and that he forms a perceptual image of the graphic stimulus. Reading thus is a sensory process and a word identification process, as the reader picks up the graphic cues (stimulus input). This is the signal in reading, and reading requires as sign system in which messages are formulated (the graphic system). Without graphic input there would be no reading. Reading thus is a sensory process, requiring discriminative visual responses to graphic symbols. Further, each language has a surface structure (the sound and written representation of language) and a deep structure which gives meaning. The basic requirement for reading is for the reader to be able to deal efficiently with both the surface and the deep structure, so that the reader can concentrate on the auditory – vocal language which is the communicative vehicle for meaning.

Reading researchers have tended to define reading as an interaction between the text and the reader. The text has been defined by Wallace (1992: 8) as "any chunk of written language which carries a whole meaning". The text is usually considered to be a meaningful potential language stimulus, whose meaning is influenced by two major textual factors: language and content and reader factors. The content – textual factors which affect the reading include genre, cultural familiarity, and coherence of the text while the reader – factors comprise background knowledge and the reading purpose. The unfamiliarity in any one of these areas will make reading comprehension difficult. Hence reading comprehension can be viewed as is interaction between the resources of the reader and the characteristics of the text.

When a learner reads a text, the reader's intent has significant role in understanding the message. The level of the reader, and the nature of information learned from the text will vary with the reader's intent. For example, when one reads a novel or short story for pleasure, the reader will report the general details such as the plot and gist with ease, whereas, while reading a professional article, one would report in great detail he logic, citation, specific procedural outcomes, and conclusions of the article they have read. These two examples reveal that the level of detail in a text depends on what the reader wants to comprehend from the text. Further, reading intent can also affect the nature of information that is acquired from the text.

As reading is act of communication in which information is transferred from a transmitter to a receiver, it is an active process. The reader must make an active contribution, so as to acquire the available information. One has to look at the text, and assign meaning to the text, as well as, to the written symbols in that text. From the above situation, it is clear that reading includes visual and non - visual information. To gather visual information from the printed page, the reader relies on the eyes, and background knowledge to make concrete the abstract information n the printed page.

ACHIEVEMENT

St.W.Jones

The art of achievement the art of arriving at or reading hence, the art of obtaining by efforts, the achievement of every desired object.

WEBSTER'S UNABRIDGED DICTIONARY (1913)

That which is attained to, or obtained by exertion, acquirements, knowledge as literary and scientific attitudes.

Tamil is a part of prose lesson that based on experimentation. Reading is one of the most important branches of Tamil.

All parts definition of Tamil, namely a mental and natural. State of readiness, organized through experience, exerting a directive and dynamic influence upon the individuals, response to all objects and situations with which it is related.

Tamil has been identified as a very important school subject and its important in scientific and technological development.

Tamil is defined as the learned patterns for thinking, feeling and acting that are transmitted via the acquisition of chemistry theory, skills and values.

Students, those who are entering the curriculum activities to learn education are called students. Students a person studying under relatively close supervision and tutelage of a teacher.

Studies refer to the activities carried out be learners during the learning process of improving learning. Study habits in Tamil are intended to elicit and guide one's cognitive processes during learning.

Higher secondary school, pupils enter higher school education when they are about sixteen years old. Higher school education is provided by specialist teacher for each subject. The curriculum construction help students develop a sense of competence, responsibility and purpose to foster and understanding of ethical principles, and to build a sense of social responsibility in school. The purpose of secondary education can be to give common knowledge, to prepare for higher education or to train directly in a profession.

PUDUKKOTTAI EDUCATIONAL DISTRICT

Pudukkottai Educational district is a one of the Educational district in Pudukkottai, Tamilnadu in India.

SCOPE OF THE STUDY

Values are actually a very special power in the universe. It is one our mind can grasp for the purpose of uplifting life values are actually spiritual skill a divine gift that comes to use from the infinite source of things. The highest of principles such as oneness, love, beauty and others descend from the heavens and are reinterpreted values by our mind.

STATEMENT OF THE PROBLEM

The problem of the statement as follows *"A Study On Relationship Between The Habit Of Reading News Papers And Achievement In Prose – Lessons among IXth Standard Students In Pudukkottai District."*

OBJECTIVES OF THE STUDY

The following are the objectives of the present Study

1. To Find out significant difference between the Habit of Reading Newspapers Mean Scores of IXthStandard Students on the Basis their **Boys and Girls**

2. To Find out significant difference between the Habit of Reading Newspapers Mean Scores of IXth Standard Students on the Basis their **Rural and Urban**

3. To Find out significant difference between the Habit of Reading Newspapers Mean Scores of IXthStandard Students on the Basis their **Government School and Private School.**

4. To Find out significant difference between the Habit of Reading Newspapers Mean Scores of IXth Standard Students on the Basis their **Parents Educated and Un Educated**

5. To Find out significant difference between the Habit of Reading Newspapers Mean Scores of IXth Standard Students on the Basis their **Parents Government Employee and Private Employee**

6. To Find out significant difference between the Achievement in Prose - Lessons Mean Scores of IXth Standard Students on the Basis their **Boy and Girls**

7. To Find out significant difference between the Achievement in Prose - Lessons Mean Scores of IXth Standard Students on the Basis their **Rural and Urban**

8. To Find out significant difference between the Achievement in Prose - Lessons Mean Scores of IXth Standard Students on the Basis their **Government School and Private School.**

9. To Find out significant difference between the Achievement in Prose - Lessons Mean Scores of IXth Standard Students on the Basis their **Parents Educated and Un Educated.**

10. To find out significant difference between the Achievement in Prose - Lessons Mean Scores of IXth Standard Students on the Basis their **Parents Government Employee and Private Employee.**

11. To find out Significant Relationship in the Habit of Reading News Papers and Achievement in Prose Lessons in respect to Gender (Boys and Girls) of Mean Scores between IXth Standard Students

12. To find out Significant Relationship in the Habit of Reading News Papers and Achievement in Prose Lessons in respect to Boys Mean Scores between IXth Standard Students

13. To find out Significant Relationship in the Habit of Reading News Papers and Achievement in Prose Lessons in respect to Girls Mean Scores between IXth Standard Students

HYPOTHESIS OF THE STUDY

1. There is no significant difference between the Habit of Reading Newspapers Mean Scores of IXth Standard Students on the Basis their **Boys and Girls**

2. There is no significant difference between the Habit of Reading Newspapers Mean Scores of IXth Standard Students on the Basis their **Rural and Urban**
3. There is no significant difference between the Habit of Reading Newspapers Mean Scores of IXth Standard Students on the Basis their **Government School and Private School.**
4. There is no significant difference between the Habit of Reading Newspapers Mean Scores of IXth Standard Students on the Basis their **Parents Educated and Un Educated**
5. There is no significant difference between the Habit of Reading Newspaper Mean Scores of IXth Standard Students on the Basis their **Parents Government Employee and Private Employee**
6. There is no significant difference between the Achievement in Prose - Lessons Mean Scores of IXth Standard Students on the Basis their **Boys and Girls**
7. There is no significant difference between the Achievement in Prose - Lessons Mean Scores of IXth Standard Students on the Basis their **Rural and Urban**
8. There is no significant difference between the Achievement in Prose - Lessons Mean Scores of IXth Standard Students on the Basis their **Government School and Private School.**
9. There is no significant difference between the Achievement in Prose - Lessons Mean Scores of IXth Standard Students on the Basis their **Parents Educated and UN Educated.**
10. There is no significant difference between the Achievement in Prose - Lessons Mean Scores of IXth Standard Students on the Basis their **Parents Government Employee and Private Employee.**
11. There is no Significant Relationship in the Habit of Reading News Papers and Achievement in Prose Lessons in respect to Gender (Boys and Girls) of Mean Scores between IXth Standard Students
12. There is no Significant Relationship in the Habit of Reading News Papers and Achievement in Prose Lessons in respect to Boys Mean Scores between IXth Standard Students
13. There is no Significant Relationship in the Habit of Reading News Papers and Achievement in Prose Lessons in respect to Girls Mean Scores between IXth Standard Students

LIMITATIONS OF THE STUDY

This study has identified the important Newspapers in Relationship to Achievement in Prose – Lessons. The investigation of Newspapers in relationship to achievement in prose lesson, at Pudukkottai District is restricted to 300 Sample of Higher Secondary students Pudukkottai district. The present educational study survey was conducted in the duration of 2014-2015.

CONCLUSION

The first chapter deals, with the significance of the problems, title of the study, operation definition of the key terms, objectives of the study, Major hypotheses, limitation of the study, plan and procedure of the study organization of the study. The review of related literature and research studies related with the present investigation are included in the next chapter.

Chapter - II

Review of Related Literature

INTRODUCTION

The present chapter summarizes the research studies related to the problem under investigation. Review of research studies is of fundamental importance to prove insight into the problem, to familiarize the researcher with the studies previously done, to make the researcher adopt suitable design and to ensure perfection in the study to be made. With this view, the researcher has attempted to review numerous relevant and pertinent studies that have been undertaken by the educational researchers.

IMPORTANCE OF REVIEW OF RELATED LITERATURE

In the words of Good, "The key to the vast store house of published literature may open doors to sources of significant problems and explanatory hypothesis and provide helpful orientation for definition of the problem, background for selection of procedure, and comparative data for interpretation of results". (John. V.Best, James, V.Khan, 1993, P-155) in order to be truly creative and original, one must read extensively and critically, one must read extensively and critically as a stimulus to think. "Besides enlarging the knowledge about the topic, writing a literature review will give the investigator to gain and demonstrate skills in two areas.

INFORMATION SEEKING

The ability to scan the literature efficiently using manual or computerized methods, to identity a set of useful articles and books.

CRITICAL APPRAISAL

The ability to apply principles of analysis to identify unbiased and valid studies.

1. It enables the researcher to define his problem. The knowledge of related literature brings the researcher up – to – date on the work which others have done and thus to state the objective clearly used concisely.
2. It helps the researcher to avoid unfruitful and useless problem area.
3. It helps the researcher to avoid duplications of well established facts.
4. It helps the researcher to understand the research methodology which refers to the way; the study is to be conducted.
5. It helps the researcher to known about tool and instruments which proved to be useful in the previous studies.
6. The final and important specific reason for reviewing the related literature is to known about the recommendations of previous researchers listed in their studies for further research.

One of the essential aspects of research process is the review of related literature. It plays a crucial role in planning of the study.

Review of the related literature, besides, allowing the researcher to acquaint himself with current knowledge in the field or area in which he is going to conduct his research, serves the following specific purpose.

1. By reviewing the related literature the researcher can avoid unfruitful and useless problem areas. He can select those areas in which positive findings are very, likely to result and his endeavors would be likely to add to the knowledge in a meaningful way.
2. Through the review of related literature the researcher can avoid unintentional duplication of well established findings. It is no use to replicate a study when the stability and validity of its results have been clearly established.
3. The review of related literature gives the researcher an understanding of the research methodology which refers to the way the study is to be conducted. It helps the researcher to know about the tools and instruments which proved to be useful and promising the previous studies. The advantages of the related literature are also to provide insight into the statistical methods through which validity of results is to be established.

4. The final and important specific reason for reviewing the related literature is to know about the recommendations of previous researcher listed in their studies for further research.

NEED OF REVIEW IN RELATED LITERATURE

The review of literature is essential due to the following reasons

1. One of the early steps in planning a research work is to review research done previously in the particular area of interest and relevant area quantitative and qualitative analysis of this research usually gives the worker an indication of the direction.
2. It is very essential for every investigator to be up – to – date in his information about the literature, related to his own problem already done by others. It is considered too most important pre-requisite to actual planning and conducting the study.
3. It avoids the replication of the study of findings to take an advantage from similar of related literature and regards to methodology, techniques of data collection, procedure adopted and conclusions drawn. He can justify his own endeavor in the field.
4. It provides as source of problem of study, an analogy may be drawn for identifying and selecting the problem of research. The researcher formulates his hypotheses on the basis of review of literature. It also provides the rationale for the study. The result and findings of the study can also be discussed at length.

The review of literature indicates the clear picture of the problem to be solved. The scholarship in the field can be developed by reviewing the literature of the field.

OBJECTIVES OF REVIEW OFRELATED LITERATURE

The review of literature serves the following purposes in conducting research work.

1. It provides theories, ideas, explanations or hypothesis which may prove useful in the formulating of a new problem.
2. It indicated whether the evidence already available solves the problem adequately without requiring further investigation. It avoids the replication.
3. It provides the sources for hypotheses. The researcher can formulate research hypotheses on the basis of available studies.
4. It suggests method, procedure, source of data and statistical techniques appropriate to the solution of the problem.

5. It locates comparative data and findings useful in the interpretation and discussion of results. The conclusions drawn in the related studies may be significantly compared and may be used as the subject for the findings of the study.
6. It helps in developing experts and general scholarship of the investigator in the area investigated.
7. It contributes towards the accurate knowledge of the evidence or the literature in one's area of activity of Good Avenue towards marking oneself. This knowledge is an institution of higher learning or a research organization.

SOURCES OF REVIEW OF RELATED LITERATURE

There are several of literatures which may be used for this purpose. These sources can be broadly classified into these heads.

(i) Books and Text – Books materials.

(ii) The Periodical literature and

(iii) General References.

BOOKS AND TEXT - BOOKS MATERIALS

The most useful lift of books published in the English language is the cumulative book index and book review index, books review digest, subject guide to books indicated that books are in print or press or forthcoming books. National union catalogue is also useful for this purpose. There are a number of publications that locate specific reference that cover particular area of knowledge. The cumulative book index is published in the English language.

Sources of information in the social sciences 'organized' by subject area and indexed by author and title, this work contains comprehensive list of reference books and monographs.

PERIODICALS

A periodical is defined as a publication issued in successive parts, usually at regular intervals, and as a rule, intended to be continued indefinitely. These include Yearbook, Documents, Almanacs, and the cumulative book index, international Abstracts, Journals, Newspapers, Magazines and International Index to periodicals.

Periodicals are generally placed in open shelves in the Periodical room. Their effective use is predicted on the use of an index to identity the articles on subjects matter under the study.

ABSTRACTS

Another type of reference guide is the abstracts, reviews, or digest. In addition to provide a systematized list of reference sources, it includes a summary of the contents. Usually the brief summaries of research studies are given from the abstract – Educational abstracts in humanities.

PURPOSES OR REVIEW OF LITERATURE

The purpose of review of literature are given below

1. Discovering important variable.
2. Distinguishing what has been done from what needs to be done.
3. Synthesizing the available studies to have perspective.
4. Determining meanings, relevance of the study and relationship with the study and its deviation from the available studies.
5. The main purpose of this review is to put the hypothesis to be examined in the research report into its proper context.
6. Secondary purpose of this part of the report are to provide readers with guidelines regarding where they can look to find more information and to establish the author's credential by letting readers know that the researcher is aware of what has been going on with regard to the current and related topics.

PRINCIPLES AND PROCEDURES FOR THE REVIEW OFRELATED LITERATURE

The principles and procedures for the review of literature are given below :

1. It is generally advisable to get first and over all view by consulting a general source, such as a text – book which is more likely to provide the meaning and nature of the concepts and variables or theoretical framework of the field. The logical starting point is to get a clear picture of the problem to be solved. A text – book usually provides the theoretical aspects of the problem. It is very essential to develop deep understanding about the variables and the field.
2. After developing the insight about the general nature of his problem. The investigator should review the empirical researches of the area. The best reference for this phase is the handbook of research. Encyclopedia of Educational research, the review of educational research and international abstracts for more up to – date findings.

3. The research for library material must be systematic and thorough. The investigator generally should start by collecting his references from the educational index. When a large number of references are to be copied, they should be types because precision is required here.

4. The researcher should take not systematically in the light of such criteria as uniformity, accuracy and ease of assembly. The notes should be taken on the card.

- Each entry should be made separately; references should be recorded with complete bibliographic data.
- It should be recorded on front side of the card and content should be taken below and reverse side of it. Each note should be recorded carefully and accurately.

5. The investigator should take as complete notes as he might need. On the other hand, taking unnecessary notes is wasteful. The useful and necessary material should be recorded precisely. It would be better that similar sources are gathered. It is necessary that a general education of each sources, rather than simply a summary of its content be made. Such evaluation is necessary both in presenting the study in the review of literature, and in using the study as background for the interpretation of the findings of the study.

6. The actual note – taking process is always a difficult task for the researcher. He has to spend long hours in the library taking notes by hand. It is very tedious job and leads to importance to carelessness and illegibility. He should make use of the facilities available in the library for this purpose.

Studies conducted in India and aboard

Pillay, G.S. and Anandan, K. (2008) made an analysis of the educational Newspaper programmers produced in India at the higher educational level. The survey revealed that very few Newspaper programmers were produced in subjects like law, anthropology and veterinary sciences. In general, educational subjects like economics, sociology, and management, educational received greater attention but not geography or political science. The researchers felt that there was no coordination between various production agencies.

Idayavani,S. (2008) developed two video programmers, one on weathering and another on rivers, and made a study to see how viewing of the Newspaper affects their achievements. It was found that students who were exposed to the video method performed better than students taught by the traditional lecture method.

Anuradha, K.(2008) observed that student's television viewing behaviour and its impact on personal and educational development. The study also showed that students like watching advertisement and programmers on sport.

Narayanasamy, M. (2008) prepared a video programmed for sixth grade students to teach Tamil vocabulary. He found that the experimental group learnt more Tamil words using the programmed than the control group.

Ghose,S. (2007) looked into, the reporting in Tamil Nadu. The survey goes – beyond education and covers programmers on health agriculture and adult, education. It was found that although time – duration of the programmers was generous; the telecast did not come at a convenient hour with the result that the targeted audience had to miss the programmers. A conspicuous neglect was pointed out in the training of teachers, both in Reading in utilizing school broadcasts. All teachers agreed that school broadcasts were useful and helpful to students.

Dharunkar, V.L (2007) looked into the research potentials and priorities the educational broadcasts. He suggests that comparative studied be taken up to assess the effectiveness of educational broadcasts in South Asian countries another point that needs attention is the need to fuse together folk and electronic media.

Lal, H (2006) conducted a study on quality educational television programs for students and found out that use of news papers purposes enriches learning experiences. They also suggested that production on quality educational media programmes relevant to the subject and to different stages of education would facilitate enriched learning experiences.

Ponnusamy, P. and Natesan, M. (2006) attempted to study instructional media and their effect on class room learning and concluded that use of instructional media on high schools and enrich classroom learning experiences of high school students. They also attempted to measure the frequency of use of different media by teachers of primary and upper high schools and concluded that most of the primary teachers were utilizing only models and newspaper in their classroom activities and needed a proper training.

Golani, T.P. (2000) attempted to study the awareness and to present the other measures in the form of concrete proposals and their implications for secondary schools as well as for the professional courses in training teachers. The findings of the study indicated that according to opinions of the secondary schools under survey, the teaching aids were essential and useful in developing clear concepts and in stimulating learning and use of aids are useful in teaching subjects like Tamil language.

Biswal, B. (1998) studied the reaction of students and teachers towards effective utilization of school broadcast programmers. The study revealed that the strategies developed for effective utilization of school Broadcast Programmes were significantly effective when compared to the radio broadcast alone. Students and teachers favored the strategies and the strategies were feasible in terms of time, schedule and cost involved.

Passi, B. K. et al. (1980) studied the facilities available, reasons and opinions for broadcasting educational programmes for teachers. The main findings was that a majority of the teachers (95%) had facilities for listening to radio broadcasts and they liked to listen to broadcasts related to the ways of motivation and creating interest among students for teaching language and science, maintaining discipline in classrooms as well as in school.

Phutela, R.L (1980) attempted to investigate the utilization and comprehensibility of school Television Programmers in Reading skills the part of the students of different classes. The result of four out of five comprehension tests regarding utilization programmers showed real difference in the learning of the subject matter, indicating that these lessons were well understood.

Goel (1980) studied the school broadcast in the country covering all the 35 AIR stations engaged in producing school broadcast programmers and it was revealed that there was no coordination between the broadcast divisions and state departments of educations. But the study concluded that indeed there is a positive effect of new paper and prose lesson.

Rao, R.R. and Subrahmanyam, S. (1980) estimated the relative influence of certain factors on reading attainment of students and suggested remedial measures to improve the reading skills. The study found out that among the personal attributes, general mental ability, visual discrimination of words, auditory discrimination of sounds, clarity of speech, reading habits and interest in reading influenced their reading attainment positively.

Apel, K. and Apel, L. (2011) conducted a study, "Identifying Intra individual differences in students' Reading Language Abilities" Topics in language Disorders. Students must be able to consciously use their knowledge of phonology, orthography, morphology, semantics, syntax and pragmatics to successfully read and write. Difficulties in the conscious awareness of I or more of these 6 linguistic knowledge components may lead to reading and Reading deficits. In this article, we present a componential model of spoken and Reading language that can guide literacy educators in their assessment of students Reading language skills. We then provide some general assessment strategies that measures students' conscious awareness of these different linguistic components to read and write. To demonstrate the use of this model and the assessment strategies, we present 3 student profiles that illustrate how difficulties with Reading language ability can be the result of different underlying linguistic awareness deficits. On the basis of these individual deficits, we also provide initial suggestions for prescriptive professionals from varying backgrounds share a common knowledge base and vocabulary so that meaningful clinical and educational services are provided to students who struggle in the area of Reading language.

Celina, P. (2010) conducted a study on stimulating linguistic, aesthetic and objectified pre – reading skills of pre –scholars and found out that a child has to acquire a lot of skills at the physical, intellectual and emotional levels and these skills can be developed through playful activities. The skills develop not in isolation but as an integral part of the total development of an individual. A multimode programmer both in school and non – school environment was implemented for developing basic skills among the pre – scholars. It was found that the programmed was very effective in enhancing majority of the pre- reading skills among the pre – scholars.

Arndt, E.J. and Foorman, B.R. (2010) conducted a study, "Second Graders as Spellers: What Types of Errors Are They Making?" In their study beginning second – grade students (N = 60) were administered a researcher – developed, dictated spelling test. Spelling errors of students were analyzed by grade – level spelling patterns and linguistic characteristics: phonological, orthographic, orthographic image, transposition, and morphological. Results revealed that morphological spelling pattern errors occurred most frequently. The frequency of linguistic category errors for this sample, ranging from least to most, was transposition, phonological, orthographic image, orthographic, and morphological.

De, S. and Roger, J. (2009) in perspective on the Research and purpose of Reading Comprehension Study Skills and Techniques stated that the primary purpose of reading is to drive the meaning of an author's which has been transmitted through print, as it relates to the readers personal need to go from a point of lesser to greater information. The four perspectives cross both basic and applied research needs in comprehension assessment technique, methods and materials.

Mayer and Gallini (2007) found that coordinating text with pictures improved learning. They found that students who were present text with a narration by the teacher scored significantly higher on retention, matching and transfer texts.

Koppar, B. (2006) investigated the factors affecting reading comprehensive and found out the relationship of reading comprehension with attitude towards academic motivation. The study found out that the reading comprehension was related positively to the reading attitude and academic achievement.

George, E. I., Mathew, V.G and Nair, K. S (2005) conducted a pilot study to develop suitable instruments and techniques and determined the relationship of language and play development and academic achievement. The communicative language and play patterns of the three groups were arrived at and compared to obtain the developmental norms.

Michael, P. (2000) in an article "Comprehension Instruction: What works" opines that without a strong background in basic skills like decoding and vocabulary – building, comprehension is impossible. This article offers research based strategies for building on these and other skills to increase student understanding of what is rad.

Attewell (2000) found out that through the use of text, graphics, audio, video and animation, edutainment steers away from the traditional teaching method. These multimedia appliances help to reinforce learning, and make learning more fun rather than a hassle. Another advantage of edutainment is that it allows the students to control their own learning pace. When students have the ability to control the speed at which they learn the material, it usually requires less time to learn it.

CONCLUSION

The review reveals that, so far none of research has been conducted to find out Reading News Paper in Understanding Prose lesson in Tamil Language for Ninth Standard Students. The review of related literature has helped the investigator to formulate the relevant hypotheses and suitable methodology, which are discussed in the next chapters to follow.

Chapter - III

Methodology

INTRODUCTION

This chapter deals with the description of research design and procedure. The research design is the plan, structure and strategy of answer of research question and to control the variance. It is at this stage that circuital decisions are made for how the objective is to be achieved and how the work to be executed. So, in this context this chapter explains design of the study. Population, size of the sample and how they are subjected as variables.The source and techniques of gathering data as soon.

RESEARCH DESIGN

This chapter presents details regarding the following

1. Selection of Dependent variables and categorical variables.
2. Construction of tools to measure the IXth standard students relationship between the habit of reading newspapers and achievement in prose lessons
3. Methods of establishing the reliability and validity of the tools constructed.
4. Sampling procedure adopted in this study.
5. Scheduling the survey and collecting the data.

The world survey indicated the gathering of data regarding current condition. Survey is an important type of study. It involves a clearly defined problem and defined objectives of the research. Strategy employed, tool used, sample technique employed and data collection produces followed are outlined.

RESEARCH PROCEDURE

1. Choosing a problem
2. Identification of the variables
3. The learning outcome
4. Selection and development of the tools
5. Selection of sample of high school IXth standard students.
6. Administration of the tools
7. Collection of data
8. Data analysis
9. Test of the Hypothesis
10. Findings and Evaluation
11. Implications

STATEMENT OF THE PROBLEMS

The title of the present investigations precisely stated thus relationship between the Habit of Reading newspapers and achievement in prose lessons among IXth standard students.

TOOLS OF SURVEY RESEARCH METHOD AND ITS PROBLEMS

To carry out any type of educational research, data are required because answers to the research problem are sought on the basis of empirical data. Data are gathered using readily available tools or those which are modified or developed by the research. The investigator must take important decisions concerning the selection of appropriate data collecting tools. There are many types of tools and each type has it's unique characteristics and each should be considered for the appropriateness of collecting certain kind of data on a selected research problem. It is necessary for the researcher to become familiar with the different types of research tools so that he could select his tool wisely form the available one or modify one of these or construct one for him/her.

The suitable tool for the data collection depends upon the type of surveys the time and resources available. Usually in survey research interview schedule questionnaire in survey method and yes or no type questions test inventory and observation schedule are used. As the questionnaire can be easily administered and also they consume less time and effort than the interviews they are widely used.

OBJECTIVES OF THE STUDY

The following are the objectives of the present Study

1. To Find out significant difference between the Habit of Reading Newspapers Mean Scores of IXthStandard Students on the Basis their **Boys and Girls**
2. To Find out significant difference between the Habit of Reading Newspapers Mean Scores of IXth Standard Students on the Basis their **Rural and Urban**
3. To Find out significant difference between the Habit of Reading Newspapers Mean Scores of IXthStandard Students on the Basis their **Government School and Private School.**
4. To Find out significant difference between the Habit of Reading Newspapers Mean Scores of IXth Standard Students on the Basis their **Parents Educated and Un Educated**
5. To Find out significant difference between the Habit of Reading Newspapers Mean Scores of IXth Standard Students on the Basis their **Parents Government Employee and Private Employee**
6. To Find out significant difference between the Achievement in Prose - Lessons Mean Scores of IXth Standard Students on the Basis their **Boy and Girls**
7. To Find out significant difference between the Achievement in Prose - Lessons Mean Scores of IXth Standard Students on the Basis their **Rural and Urban**
8. To Find out significant difference between the Achievement in Prose - Lessons Mean Scores of IXth Standard Students on the Basis their **Government School and Private School.**
9. To Find out significant difference between the Achievement in Prose - Lessons Mean Scores of IXth Standard Students on the Basis their **Parents Educated and Un Educated.**
10. To find out significant difference between the Achievement in Prose - Lessons Mean Scores of IXth Standard Students on the Basis their **Parents Government Employee and Private Employee.**

11. To find out Significant Relationship in the Habit of Reading News Papers and Achievement in Prose Lessons in respect to Gender (Boys and Girls) of Mean Scores between IXth Standard Students
12. To find out Significant Relationship in the Habit of Reading News Papers and Achievement in Prose Lessons in respect to Boys Mean Scores between IXth Standard Students
13. To find out Significant Relationship in the Habit of Reading News Papers and Achievement in Prose Lessons in respect to Girls Mean Scores between IXth Standard Students

HYPOTHESIS OF THE STUDY

1. There is no significant difference between the Habit of Reading Newspapers Mean Scores of IXth Standard Students on the Basis their **Boys and Girls**
2. There is no significant difference between the Habit of Reading Newspapers Mean Scores of IXth Standard Students on the Basis their **Rural and Urban**
3. There is no significant difference between the Habit of Reading Newspapers Mean Scores of IXth Standard Students on the Basis their **Government School and Private School.**
4. There is no significant difference between the Habit of Reading Newspapers Mean Scores of IXth Standard Students on the Basis their **Parents Educated and Un Educated**
5. There is no significant difference between the Habit of Reading Newspaper Mean Scores of IXth Standard Students on the Basis their **Parents Government Employee and Private Employee**
6. There is no significant difference between the Achievement in Prose - Lessons Mean Scores of IXth Standard Students on the Basis their **Boys and Girls**
7. There is no significant difference between the Achievement in Prose - Lessons Mean Scores of IXth Standard Students on the Basis their **Rural and Urban**
8. There is no significant difference between the Achievement in Prose - Lessons Mean Scores of IXth Standard Students on the Basis their **Government School and Private School.**
9. There is no significant difference between the Achievement in Prose - Lessons Mean Scores of IXth Standard Students on the Basis their **Parents Educated and Un Educated.**

10. There is no significant difference between the Achievement in Prose - Lessons Mean Scores of IXth Standard Students on the Basis their **Parents Government Employee and Private Employee.**
11. There is no Significant Relationship in the Habit of Reading News Papers and Achievement in Prose Lessons in respect to Gender (Boys and Girls) of Mean Scores between IXth Standard Students
12. There is no Significant Relationship in the Habit of Reading News Papers and Achievement in Prose Lessons in respect to Boys Mean Scores between IXth Standard Students
13. There is no Significant Relationship in the Habit of Reading News Papers and Achievement in Prose Lessons in respect to Girls Mean Scores between IXth Standard Students

LIMITATIONS OF THE STUDY

This study has identified the important Newspapers in Relationship to Achievement in Prose – Lessons. The investigation of Newspapers in relationship to achievement in prose lessons, at Pudukkottai District is restricted to 300 sample of IXth Standard students Pudukkottaieducational district. The present educational study survey was conducted in the duration of 2014-2015.

RESEARCH METHOD

The investigator preferred stratified sampling method for the present study. In this study, the investigator used cross sectional survey method to collect data and to identify the intensity of the study has identified the important Newspaper in Relationship to Achievement in prose – lessons.

RESEARCH TOOLS

In the present study the investigation selected questionnaire as the most important tools for collecting data because it is used increasingly to enquire into the current conditions, opinions and attitude of a students at Ninth standard level.

For the present study questionnaire was prepared with view to gather information in details regarding on "Newspapers in Relationship to achievement in Prose – lessons at Pudukkottai District". The selection of suitable tool for the investigation is very important for successful. Research, questionnaire is a tool used collects data from the selected sample.

CONSTRUCTION OF RESEARCH TOOLS

The research tool on "Newspapers in Relationship to Achievement in Prose – Lessons at Pudukkottai District" was constructed by the investigator in the present study. All the question items are closed type. The responded that respondents the correct answers were given scores and these score were considered for data analysis.

SAMPLES OF THE STUDY

A sample is a small proportion of a population selected for observation and analysis a sample is a smaller representation of the higher secondary school at Pudukkottai educational District. The investigator selected 300 samples from the study by using stratified sampling techniques. The sample should be selected at random from the Population. The stratified sampling is purely based on defined principles and is a scientific technique. In this, every individual unit in the population gets a chance to be selected.

Sample distribution

S. No	Category	Groups	No. of Samples Total	No. of Samples
1.	Gender	Male	147	300
		Female	153	
2	Locality	Rural	149	300
		Urban	151	
3	School	Government	151	300
		Private	149	
4	Parents educational qualification	Educated	125	300
		Uneducated	175	
5	Parents Employments	Government Job	114	300
		Private Job	186	

DESCRIPTION OF RESEARCH TOOL AND SCORING PROCEDURE

The response sheets of the subjects were scored according to the guidelines given by the constructors of the tool. Scoring of the response sheets were done a per the scoring scheme. The scores obtained in all questionnaires along with the personal data are consolidated and tabulated on consolidation sheet for the purpose of analysis. It is a two point (Yes or No) scales and one wait question types of tool.

PILOT STUDY

The pilot stage is concerned with refining the items collected. The collected items were presented before the expert with a request to offer their considered opinion regarding the suitability objectivity clarity and relevancy of the statement collected from different sources. The opinion of the experts was taken into consideration to refine the items.

The pilot study is an initial study which is conducted by the investigator to know more about the research problem in various aspects. Based on the pilot study, the main study was conducted by the investigator while administering the research in the pilot study, some doubts were raised by the higher secondary school students, and the investigator clarified all of their doubts and difficulties. Based on that, the investigator modified the items.

Further, the investigator obtained some ideas from the experts and modified the irrelevant item that is coming in the present study. After getting response from the respondents, the investigator gave frequencies for the correct response and these frequencies were converted into scores and those scores were used to establish reliability.

VALIDITY OF THE TOOL

The validity of tool depends upon the fidelity with which it measures what is purports to measure Nunnaly (1978) Maintains that rather than established the validity of the measures after they are constructed, it is highly meaningful that one should ensure the validity of the tool by the plan and producer of test construction. This can be done through a representative collection of items and a sensible method of test construction. The different procedures followed in developing the tools are outline in this chapter.

RELIABILITY OF THE TOOL

The reliability of questionnaire on indentifying the problems encountered by Higher secondary school students in News papers in Relationship to Achievement in Prose – Lessons at Pudukkottai District was established by making a rational equivalence method. In this method, the investigative used KuderRicherdson formula. The reliability of the tool refers to the internal consistency observed in measurement of reliability.

SAMPLING TECHNIQUE USED

After finalizing the variables of present study, the stratified sampling method is used consideration was given to whether the entire population is to be made the subject for data collection or a particular group is to be selected as representative of the whole population. The entire population here refers to all the higher secondary school students studying in Pudukkottai District.

Of the above techniques, the selection of a group as a representative of the whole population was found to be more convenient and suitable. This technique led to a considerable save of time, effort and finance. The number of students selected will be small, and so it is possible to make a detailed and intensive study. This generally leads to more accurate and reliable results. As this sampling technique has may advantages, it was selected for the collection of data.

In any behavioural research, various methods are utilized for selection and drawing of samples. After a detailed study of all these methods and considering the variables selected for the research work, the stratified sampling method was found to be most suitable.

In the stratified sampling method, the entire population will be divided into smaller homogenous groups or strata, and then a sample is selected within each group. Every sampling unit in the population is placed in one of the strata prior to the selection of the sample so that the sum of the strata is identical with the population.

Stratified sampling method has certain merits as a technique of sampling. Auckoff has rightly said that 'stratified sampling enables the researcher to make a composition of properties of the strata as well as to estimate population characteristics'.

In this stratified sampling method, the investigator has greater control over the selection of the sample when compared with simple random sampling. In simple random sampling, although every group has a chance of being selected and included in the sample, there is every possibility, and sometimes it does not happen, that certain important groups are left unrepresentative. But in stratified sampling methods no important group is likely to be left out.

Stratified sampling method is the ideal one when comparsion between different variable has to be made. For example, if comparison has to be made between arts and science students or rural and urban students, it would be very difficult to select the required number of units through any other method of sampling. If any other is used, the problem of bias and prejudice creeps in.

Replacement of units is also possible in the stratified sampling method. Normally, if a particular unit is not accessible for a study, it is difficult to replace it by another, but in this method it is possible. Stephen states that stratification automatically brings about a replacement of persons lost in the sample, by persons of the same stratum, thus partly correcting the bias that would result if there were no replacement of losses.

As the entire population is divided into particular strata it is easy and convenient to replace an in accessible case by an accessible one. In stratified sampling method, much depends on stratification process.

The following precaution were taken while stratifying the population: the variables involved in the study were taken note of; care was taken to see that each stratum in the universe was large enough in size so that selection of items could be done on random basis; the strata formed were definite and clear cut; each stratum was free from influence of the other; and there was no overlapping.

COLLECTION OF DATA

The investigator himself met each and every school students who are studying in various higher secondary schools (IXth Standard Students) located at Pudukkottai District. The investigator met the Headmaster of various schools and got permission from them to administer the research tool. Before going to administer the research tool, the investigator revealed the purpose of the present study to the school students and then asked them to given their responses for each and every item that are given in the questionnaire. The responses of the school students were recorded.

ANALYSIS OF DATA

The term analysis refers to the compilation of certain measures along with searching for pattern and relationship that among groups. For the present study the investigator collected the data from higher secondary students using the tool developed to find out questioner of sample to identify the "Newspaper in Relationship to Achievement in Prose – Lesson at Pudukkottai District". This involves computing measures of central tendency like Mean and the measures of variability like standard deviation and t – test.

STATISTICAL TECHNIQUES USED

The following statistical techniques have been proposed for the present study.

THE ARITHMETIC MEAN (M)

The mean of the distribution is commonly understood as the arithmetic average. The term guide – point averages familiar to student is a Mena value.

It is computed by dividing the sum of all the scores by the number of scores. It is probably most useful of all statistical measures for in addition to the information that it provides. It is the base from which many others in important measures are computed.

$$M = \frac{\Sigma \bar{x}}{N}$$

Where,

M = Mean

Ex = The sum of the scores of the distribution

N = Number of Scores

ARITHMETIC MEAN FROM A FREQUENCY DISTRIBUTION

Sometimes it is more convenient to desire mean from a frequency distribution. An additional column may be opened to record the products of frequency distribution. The total of this frequency distribution will be divided by the total of 'F' (i.e.) N to get Mean.

Formula

$$M = A + \frac{\Sigma fd}{N} X\, CI$$

Where,

A - Assumed mean value

CI - Class Interval

N - Total Number of scores

THE STANDARD DEVIATION

Standard deviation most widely used measure of dispersion of a series and is commonly denoted by the symbol 123 (sigma) standard deviation is defined as the square root of the average of squares of deviations when such deviations for the values of individuals items in a series are obtained from the arithmetic average.

Standard deviation Formula

$$\sigma = ci\ X \sqrt{\left(\frac{\Sigma fd^2}{N}\right) - \left(\frac{\Sigma fd}{N}\right)}$$

Standard deviation

fd^2-The squared Sum of the scores

fd - The sum of the score of the distribution

N - Number of scores

'T' - TEST

The test of significant of the difference between two mean is known as't' – test. It involves the computation of the ratio between experimental variance (observed difference between two sample means) and error variance (the sampling error factors).

When small samples are involved the t-tables is used to determine statistical significance, rather that the normality, probability table. This concept of small sample size was developed around 1915 by William SealyGossest, consulting acticians for Guinness Breweries of bubluin, Ireland, Gusset critical values, carefully calculated for small samples area reproduced in the t- distribution table. The t- critical values necessary for rejection of a null hypothesis are higher for the samples of given level of significance. Each t- critical value for rejection is based upon the appropriate number of degrees of freedom.

The t- test would be used upon this formula $t = \frac{M1 \sim M2}{SEd}$

$$SEd = \sqrt{\frac{SD1^2}{N1} + \frac{SD2^2}{N2}}$$

M1 = Mean of First Group

M2 = Mean of Second Group

S1 = SD of the first group

S2 = SD of the second group

N1 = No. of students in first Group

N2 = No. of students in second group.

CORRELATION CO - EFFICIENT

Correlation Co – Efficient

$$r = \frac{N\sum xy - \sum x \sum y}{\sqrt{[N\sum x^2 - (\sum x)^2][N\sum y^2 - (\sum y)^2]}}$$

CONCLUSION

The III chapter gives the details research mythology and the procedure of varies aspects of data collection. The chapter also explains techniques used for the study. It has also been clearly mentioned about tools of the study. Statistical inferences will be given in the next chapter.

Chapter IV

Analysis and Interpretation of Data

INTRODUCTION

The next steps in the process of research after collection of data are the organization and interpretation of data formulation of conclusions and generalizations to meaningful picture the raw information collected. The analysis and interpretation are subjective reaction and desires to derive from the inherent meanings in their relationship to the problem.

Gay (1976) states the analysis of the data is as important as any other component of the research process. According to Mouly (1964) "Research data becomes meaningful in the process of being analyzed and interpreted". Regardless of how well the study in conducted an inappropriate analysis can lead to inappropriate conclusions. The data collected was subjected to statistical calculation and the hypotheses formulated for the study have been verified.

ANALYSIS OF DATA DEFINITION

Analysis of data usually studying the material in order to determine inherent facts or meanings it involves, breaking down the excision complex factors into simple parts and putting these parts together in new arrangements for the purpose of interpretation.

The present chapter includes the analysis and interpretation of data and the results that emerge out the analysis of data.

NALYSIS OF DATA

Analysis of data means studying the tabulated materials in orders to determine inherent facts of meanings. It involves the breaking down of the existing complex faders into simple parts and putting them together in a now arrangement for the purpose of interpretation.

According toBerelson "Analysis is a research technique for objective, systematic and quantitative description of the manifest content of communication."

Analysis is a technique of social research which presents qualitative data in an objective, systematic and quantitative form.

According to Kaplan, "Analysis attempts to characterize the meaning in a given body to discourse in a systematic and quantitative fashion. **According Barr and Others** "Analysis is an important phase of the classification and summation of data into a summary".

According to Wolfe, "The discovery of order in the phenomena of nature, not withstanding their complexity and apparent confusion is rendered possible by the process of analysis and synthesis which are foundation stone of all scientific methods"

After, collecting the data from the respondents, the investigator gave frequencies for the correct responses and these frequencies were converted into scores and then the investigator calculated the percentage scores. The percentage scores were used to identify the level of Problems encountered by higher secondary students in achieving certain competencies in chemistry. The investigator also used test of significance to find out the significant difference between the various groups of demographic variables in Problems encountered by higher secondary students in achieving certain competencies in chemistry.

HYPOTHESIS: 1

There is no significant difference between the Habit of Reading News papers Mean Scores of IXth Standard Students on the Basis their **Boys and Girls**

TABLE: 1

The Table shows Mean, Standard Deviation and 't' value Habit of Reading News papers Mean Scores of Ninth Standard Students on the Basis their **Boys and Girls**

Gender	N	M	S.D	't' Value	Significance at 0.05 Level
Boys	147	82.63	5.78		
Girls	153	78.50	4.07	7.12	Significant
df = 298				Critical Value for 0.05 for level : 1.96	

INTERPRETATION

Since the calculated 't'Value **(7.12)** is larger than the **Table Value (1.96)** it is inferred that there is significant difference between the Habit of Reading News papers Mean Scores of IXth Standard Students on the Basis their **Boys and Girls**

RESULT

Hence the null hypothesis is **rejected.**

HYPOTHESIS: 2

There is no significant difference between the Habit of Reading News papers Mean Scores of IXth Standard Students on the Basis their **Rural and Urban**

TABLE: 2

The Table shows Mean, Standard Deviation and 't' value Habit of Reading News papers Mean Scores of IXth Standard Students on the Basis their **Rural and Urban**

Locality	N	M	S.D	't' Value	Significance at 0.05 Level
Rural	149	79.09	4.47		
Urban	151	81.93	5.84	4.73	Significant
df = 298			Critical Value for 0.05 for level : 1.96		

INTERPRETATION

Since the calculated 't'Value **(4.73)** is larger than the **Table Value (1.96)** it is inferred that there is significant difference between the Habit of Reading News papers Mean Scores of IXth Standard Students on the Basis their **Rural and Urban**

RESULT

Hence the null hypothesis is **rejected.**

HYPOTHESIS: 3

There is no significant difference between the Habit of Reading News papers Mean Scores of Ninth Standard Students on the Basis their **Government School and Private School**

TABLE: 3

The Table shows Mean, Standard Deviation and 't' value Habit of Reading News papers Mean Scores of IXth Standard Students on the Basis their **Government School and Private School**

School	N	M	S.D	't' Value	Significance at 0.05 Level
Government	151	80.35	8.43	2.26	Significant
Private	149	78.56	4.68		

df = 298 Critical Value for 0.05 for level : 1.96

INTERPRETATION

Since the calculated 't'Value **(2.26)** is larger than the **Table Value (1.96)** it is inferred that there is significant difference between the Habit of Reading News papers Mean Scores of Ninth Standard Students on the Basis their **Government School and Private School**

RESULT

Hence the null hypothesis is **rejected.**

HYPOTHESIS: 4

There is no significant difference between the Habit of Reading News papers Mean Scores of IXth Standard Students on the Basis their **Parents Educated and Un Educated**

TABLE: 4

The Table shows Mean, Standard Deviation and 't' value Habit of Reading Newspapers Mean Scores of IXth Standard Students on the Basis their **Parents Educated and Un Educated**

Parents Education	N	M	S.D	't' Value	Significance at 0.05 Level
Educated	125	79.72	5.42		Significant
Un Educated	175	81.10	5.31	2.22	

df = 298 Critical Value for 0.05 for level : 1.96

INTERPRETATION

Since the calculated 't'Value **(2.22)** is larger than the **Table Value (1.96)** it is inferred that there is significant difference between the Habit of Reading News papers Mean Scores of IXth Standard Students on the Basis their **Parents Educated and Un Educated**

RESULT

Hence the null hypothesis is **rejected.**

HYPOTHESIS: 5

There is no significant difference between the Habit of Reading News papers Mean Scores of IXth Standard Students on the Basis their **Parents Government Employee and Private Employee**

TABLE: 5

The Table shows Mean, Standard Deviation and 't' value Habit of Reading News papers Mean Scores of IXth Standard Students on the Basis their **Rural and Urban**

Parents Education	N	M	S.D	't' Value	Significance at 0.05 Level
Government	114	80.44	5.82		
Private	186	80.58	5.12	0.22	Not Significant
df = 298			Critical Value for 0.05 for level : 1.96		

INTERPRETATION

Since the calculated 't'Value **(0.22)** is smaller than the **Table Value (1.96)** it is inferred that there is no significant difference between the Habit of Reading News papers Mean Scores of IXth Standard Students on the Basis their **Parents Government Employee and Private Employee**

RESULT

Hence the null hypothesis is **accepted.**

HYPOTHESIS: 6

There is no significant difference between the Achievements in Prose - Lessons Mean Scores of IXth Standard Students on the Basis their **Boys and Girls**

TABLE: 6

The Table shows Mean, Standard Deviation and 't' value Achievement in Prose - Lessons Mean Scores of IXth Standard Students on the Basis their **Boys and Girls**

Gender	N	M	S.D	't' Value	Significance at 0.05 Level
Boys	147	54.22	9.90		
Girls	153	50.55	11.40	3.39	Significant
df = 298			Critical Value for 0.05 for level : 1.96		

INTERPRETATION

Since the calculated 't'Value **(3.39)** is larger than the **Table Value (1.96)** it is inferred that there is significant difference between the Achievement in Prose - Lessons Mean Scores of IXth Standard Students on the Basis their **Boys and Girls**

RESULT

Hence the null hypothesis is **rejected.**

HYPOTHESIS: 7

There is no significant difference between the Achievements in Prose - Lessons Mean Scores of IXth Standard Students on the Basis their **Rural and Urban**

TABLE: 7

The Table shows Mean, Standard Deviation and 't' value Achievement in Prose - Lessons Mean Scores of IXth Standard Students on the Basis their **Rural and Urban**

Locality	N	M	S.D	't' Value	Significance at 0.05 Level
Rural	149	55.68	11.85		
Urban	151	48.54	8.49	6.00	Significant

df = 298 Critical Value for 0.05 for level : 1.96

INTERPRETATION

Since the calculated 't'Value **(6.00)** is larger than the **Table Value (1.96)** it is inferred that there is significant difference between the Achievement in Prose - Lessons Mean Scores of IXth Standard Students on the Basis their **Rural and Urban**

RESULT

Hence the null hypothesis is **rejected.**

HYPOTHESIS: 8

There is no significant difference between the Achievement in Prose - Lessons Mean Scores of IXth Standard Students on the Basis their **Government School and Private School.**

TABLE: 8

The Table shows Mean, Standard Deviation and 't' value Achievement in Prose - Lessons Mean Scores of IXth Standard Students on the Basis their **Government School and Private School**

School	N	M	S.D	't' Value	Significance at 0.05 Level
Government	151	51.39	10.59		
Private	149	55.89	12.08	3.43	Significant
df = 298			Critical Value for 0.05 for level : 1.96		

INTERPRETATION

Since the calculated 't'Value **(3.43)** is larger than the **Table Value (1.96**) it is inferred that there is significant difference between the Achievement in Prose - Lessons Mean Scores of IXth Standard Students on the Basis their **Government School and Private School**

RESULT

Hence the null hypothesis is **rejected.**

HYPOTHESIS: 9

There is no significant difference between the Achievement in Prose - Lessons Mean Scores of IXth Standard Students on the Basis their **Parents Educated and Un Educated**

TABLE: 9

The Table shows Mean, Standard Deviation and 't' value Achievement in Prose - Lessons Mean Scores of IXth Standard Students on the Basis their **Parents Educated and Un Educated**

Parents Education	N	M	S.D	't' Value	Significance at 0.05 Level
Educated	123	53.96	9.49		
Un Educated	177	53.73	13.30	0.17	Not Significant
df = 298		Critical Value for 0.05 for level : 1.96			

INTERPRETATION

Since the calculated 't'Value **(0.17)** is smaller than the **Table Value (1.96**) it is inferred that there is no significant difference between the Achievement in Prose - Lessons Mean Scores of Ninth Standard Students on the Basis their **Parents Educated and Un Educated**

RESULT

Hence the null hypothesis is **accepted.**

HYPOTHESIS: 10

There is no significant difference between the Achievements in Prose - Lesson Mean Scores of IXth Standard Students on the Basis their **Parents Government Employee and Private Employee**

TABLE: 10

The Table shows Mean, Standard Deviation and 't' value Achievement in Prose - Lessons Mean Scores of IXth Standard Students on the Basis their **Parents Government Employee and Private Employee**

Parents Education	N	M	S.D	't' Value	Significance at 0.05 Level
Government	112	57.93	14.02		
Private	188	51.93	13.67	0.91	Not Significant
df = 298			Critical Value for 0.05 for level : 1.96		

INTERPRETATION

Since the calculated 'tValue (0.91) is smaller than the Table Value (1.96) it is inferred that there is no significant difference between the Achievement in Prose - Lessons Mean Scores of IXth Standard Students on the Basis their Parents Government Employee and Private Employee

RESULT

Hence the null hypothesis is **accepted.**

HYPOTHESIS: 11

There is no Significant Relationship in the Habit of Reading News Paper and Achievement in Prose Lessons in respect to Gender (Boys and Girls) of Mean Scores between IXth Standard Students.

TABLE: 11

The Table Shows the Relationship in the Habit of Reading News Paper and Achievement in Prose Lessons in respect to Gender (Boys and Girls) of Mean Scores between IXth Standard Students

Group	N	$\sum xy$	$\sqrt{\sum x^2y^2}$	'r' Value	Significance at 0.05 Level

Habit of Reading News Papers Student (Boys and Girls) Achievement in Prose – Lessons Students (Boys and Girls)	300	-3456.59	17953.26	-0.19	Not Significant

df = 298 Critical Value for 0.05 for level : 0.113

INTERPRETATION

Since the calculated 'r' Value (-0.19) is smaller than the Table Value (0.113) it is inferred that there is no significant Relationship in the Habit of Reading News Paper and Achievement in Prose Lessons in respect to Gender (Boys and Girls) of Mean Scores between IXth Students. Hence the r value is Very Low Negative Correlation.

RESULT

Hence the Null Hypothesis is **accepted.**

HYPOTHESIS: 12

There is no Significant Relationship in the Habit of Reading News Papers and Achievement in Prose Lessons in respect to Boys Mean Scores between IXth Standard Students.

TABLE: 12

The Table Shows the Relationship in the Habit of Reading News Papers and Achievement in Prose Lessons in respect to Boys Mean Scores between IXthStandard Students

Group	N	$\sum xy$	$\sqrt{\sum x^2 y^2}$	'r' Value	Significance at 0.05 Level
Habit of Reading News Paper Student of Boys Achievement in Prose – Lesson Students of Boys	147	7907.18	8420.04	0.94	Significant

df = 145 Critical Value for 0.05 for level : 0.159

INTERPRETATION

Since the calculated 'r' Value (0.94) is larger than the Table Value (0.16) it is inferred that there is significant Relationship in the Habit of Reading News Papers and Achievement in Prose Lessons in respect to Gender Boys Mean Scores between IXthstandard students. Hence the r value is Very High Positive Correlation.

RESULT

Hence the Null Hypothesis is **rejected.**

HYPOTHESIS: 13

There is no Significant Relationship in the Habit of Reading News Papers and Achievement in Prose Lessons in respect to Girls Mean Scores between IXth Standard Students.

TABLE: 13

The Table Shows the Relationship in the Habit of Reading News Papers and Achievement in Prose Lessons in respect to Girls Mean Scores between IXth Standard Students

Group	N	$\sum xy$	$\sqrt{\sum x^2 y^2}$	'r' Value	Significance at 0.05 Level
Habit of Reading News Paper Student of Girls Achievement in Prose – Lesson Students of Girls	153	6446.48	7115.99	0.91	Significant
df = 151	Critical Value for 0.05 for level : 0.138				

INTERPRETATION

Since the calculated 'r' Value (0.91) is larger than the Table Value (0.138) it is inferred that there is significant Relationship in the Habit of Reading News Paper and Achievement in Prose Lessons in respect to Gender Girls Mean Scores between IXthstandard students. Hence the r value is Very High Positive Correlation.

RESULT

Hence the Null Hypothesis is **rejected.**

CONCLUSION

Findings of the present of the study has been consolidated and given in this chapter. Suggestions to come over the Relationship between the Habit of Reading Newspapers and Achievement in Prose Lessons among IXth Standard Students have also been given in this chapter. Therefore, this study will certainly enhance the competence of the students as well teachers

Chapter - V

Summary of Findings and Conclusion

INTRODUCTION

To attainment of the students vary based on the individual difference. The difference of individual exists in the process of achievement in Prose Lessons also. The Academic Achievement in Prose Lessons many influence the achievement of students. The present study attempt to find out relationship in the reading newspapers and achievement in prose – lessons mean score between parent's qualification and parents type of work in IXth the Standard.

STATEMENT OF THE PROBLEMS

The present study is states as *"A Study On Relationship Between The Habit Of Reading News Papers And Achievement In Prose – Lessons among IXth Standard Students In Pudukkottai District."*

ASSUMPTION

The individual difference is a key concern towards the locality of mankind. The individual difference only influence in the classroom and total education system through there are practices to the teachers to handle the students carefully in learning situation. The behavior of the students may have same impact. The reading newspaper and achievement in prose – lessons of the student may have a close relationship. Hereby it is assumed that the achieving in prose – lessons may be equally propionate to the reading newspaper. It is also assumed that the achieving in Prose lesson may vary in accordance with different reading newspapers.

OBJECTIVES OF THE STUDY

The following are the objectives of the present Study

1. To Find out significant difference between the Habit of Reading Newspapers Mean Scores of IXthStandard Students on the Basis their **Boys and Girls**
2. To Find out significant difference between the Habit of Reading Newspapers Mean Scores of IXth Standard Students on the Basis their **Rural and Urban**
3. To Find out significant difference between the Habit of Reading Newspapers Mean Scores of IXth Standard Students on the Basis their **Government School and Private School.**
4. To Find out significant difference between the Habit of Reading Newspapers Mean Scores of IXth Standard Students on the Basis their **Parents Educated and Un Educated**
5. To Find out significant difference between the Habit of Reading Newspapers Mean Scores of IXth Standard Students on the Basis their **Parents Government Employee and Private Employee**
6. To Find out significant difference between the Achievement in Prose - Lessons Mean Scores of IXth Standard Students on the Basis their **Boy and Girls**
7. To Find out significant difference between the Achievement in Prose - Lessons Mean Scores of IXth Standard Students on the Basis their **Rural and Urban**
8. To find out significant difference between the Achievement in Prose - Lessons Mean Scores of IXth Standard Students on the Basis their **Government School and Private School.**
9. To Find out significant difference between the Achievement in Prose - Lessons Mean Scores of IXth Standard Students on the Basis their **Parents Educated and Un Educated.**
10. To find out significant difference between the Achievement in Prose - Lessons Mean Scores of IXth Standard Students on the Basis their **Parents Government Employee and Private Employee.**
11. To find out Significant Relationship in the Habit of Reading News Papers and Achievement in Prose Lessons in respect to Gender (Boys and Girls) of Mean Scores between IXth Standard Students.

12. To find out Significant Relationship in the Habit of Reading News Papers and Achievement in Prose Lessons in respect to Boys Mean Scores between IXth Standard Students

13. To find out Significant Relationship in the Habit of Reading News Papers and Achievement in Prose Lessons in respect to Girls Mean Scores between IXth Standard Students

HYPOTHESIS OF THE STUDY

1. There is no significant difference between the Habit of Reading Newspapers Mean Scores of IXth Standard Students on the Basis their **Boys and Girls**

2. There is no significant difference between the Habit of Reading Newspapers Mean Scores of IXth Standard Students on the Basis their **Rural and Urban**

3. There is no significant difference between the Habit of Reading Newspapers Mean Scores of IXth Standard Students on the Basis their **Government School and Private School.**

4. There is no significant difference between the Habit of Reading Newspapers Mean Scores of IXth Standard Students on the Basis their **Parents Educated and Un Educated**

5. There is no significant difference between the Habit of Reading Newspaper Mean Scores of IXth Standard Students on the Basis their **Parents Government Employee and Private Employee**

6. There is no significant difference between the Achievement in Prose - Lessons Mean Scores of IXth Standard Students on the Basis their **Boys and Girls**

7. There is no significant difference between the Achievement in Prose - Lessons Mean Scores of IXth Standard Students on the Basis their **Rural and Urban**

8. There is no significant difference between the Achievement in Prose - Lessons Mean Scores of IXth Standard Students on the Basis their **Government School and Private School.**

9. There is no significant difference between the Achievement in Prose - Lessons Mean Scores of IXth Standard Students on the Basis their **Parents Educated and Un Educated.**

10. There is no significant difference between the Achievement in Prose - Lessons Mean Scores of IXth Standard Students on the Basis their **Parents Government Employee and Private Employee.**

11. There is no Significant Relationship in the Habit of Reading News Papers and Achievement in Prose Lessons in respect to Gender (Boys and Girls) of Mean Scores between IXth Standard Students
12. There is no Significant Relationship in the Habit of Reading News Papers and Achievement in Prose Lessons in respect to Boys Mean Scores between IXth Standard Students
13. There is no Significant Relationship in the Habit of Reading News Papers and Achievement in Prose Lessons in respect to Girls Mean Scores between IXth Standard Students

MAJOR FINDINGS

1. There is significant difference between the Habit of Reading Newspapers Mean Scores of IXth Standard Students on the Basis their **Boys and Girls**
2. There is significant difference between the Habit of Reading Newspapers Mean Scores of IXth Standard Students on the Basis their **Rural and Urban**
3. There is significant difference between the Habit of Reading Newspapers Mean Scores of IXthStandard Students on the Basis their **Government School and Private School.**
4. There is significant difference between the Habit of Reading Newspapers Mean Scores of IXth Standard Students on the Basis their **Parents Educated and Un Educated**
5. There is no significant difference between the Habit of Reading Newspapers Mean Scores of IXth Standard Students on the Basis their **Parents Government Employee and Private Employee**
6. There is significant difference between the Achievement in Prose - Lessons Mean Scores of IXth Standard Students on the Basis their **Boy and Girls**
7. There is significant difference between the Achievement in Prose - Lessons Mean Scores of IXth Standard Students on the Basis their **Rural and Urban**
8. There is significant difference between the Achievement in Prose - Lessons Mean Scores of IXth Standard Students on the Basis their **Government School and Private School.**
9. There is no significant difference between the Achievement in Prose - Lessons Mean Scores of IXth Standard Students on the Basis their **Parents Educated and Un Educated.**

10. There is no significant difference between the Achievement in Prose - Lessons Mean Scores of IXth Standard Students on the Basis their **Parents Government Employee and Private Employee.**

11. There is Significant Relationship in the Habit of Reading News Papers and Achievement in Prose Lessons in respect to **Gender** (Boys and Girls) of Mean Scores between IXth Standard Students

12. There is Significant Relationship in the Habit of Reading News Papers and Achievement in Prose Lessons in respect to **Boys** Mean Scores between IXth Standard Students

13. There is Significant Relationship in the Habit of Reading News Papers and Achievement in Prose Lessons in respect to Girls Mean Scores between IXth Standard Students

EDUCATIONAL IMPLICATION

From the findings of the study, it is evident that there is significant difference in the Reading News Paper and Achievement in Prose Lesson mean scores between high school students compared have developed.

The teachers can play various subjects in developing scientific achievement among their students the major role. This can be done providing various situations according to the subjects than infuse certain characteristics of scientific achievement among their students. Usually students get may opportunities during reading periods.

Students have to utilize reading periods fully develop scientific achievement students have to give freedom to plan and implement their co-curricular activities both in the classes and outside the classroom. Teacher should be interested in contributing the development of proper classroom atmosphere so that the increase in the consistency of the environment can be developed in the schools to inculcate scientific achievement.

SUGGESTIONS FOR FURTHER RESEARCH

The following students may be under taken for further research into his area.

1. Comparative study of Reading News Papers and achievement in prose lesson in different professional arts college.

2. Find out the reading News Papers and achievement in prose lessons Neural, prose, poem, composition subject like.

3. The effect of various activities related to reading News Papers and achievement in prose lesson in the examination.

4. Reading News Papers and achievement in prose lessons and creativity of different level of students.
5. The effect of preparation of teaching aids developing reading News Papers and achievement in prose lessons.

CONCLUSION

The present study focus open the achieving in prose lesson and reading News Paper of the Ninth standard students, hence it will be helpful to the science teacher to enhance the proper achieving in Prose lesson among Ninth standard students.

As the present study analysis, the reading news paper in Relations to achievement in prose lesson the result of the study will guide the teacher also as to enrich the quality of the classroom teaching.

Achieving prose lesson is the social goal for education. Hence, the study wills he helpful for the social uplift for the society. As the study confirms the relationship between reading news paper and achievement in prose lesson among boys and girls, students it will be helpful for guidance and counseling among poor students. According to the present study achievement, prose lesson ill improve the students.

BIBLIOGRAPHY

1. Adamu, H. (1998). Examination malpractices in Nigeria tertiary institutions; types, causes, effects and solution, ethnology, effect and control of malignancies in Nigeria education. Zaria: S. Asekome.
2. Agbezree, L.(2001) Library Facilities and their use in Ghanaian Secondary School. Case study of St. Peters. Unpublished MA dissertation, University of Ghana: Legon. pp 70
3. Akinboye, J.O. 1980. A study of self-concept study behaviour and health attributes of male and female Nigerian adolescents. Journal of African Child Studies, 1 (2), 21-27
4. Babbie, E. (2005) The Basics of Social Research. 3rd ed, Belmont: Thomson Wadswort pp 265, 274.
5. Bakare, C.G.M. (1977). Study habits inventory. Ibadan: Psycho.
6. Bakare, C.G.M. 1975. Some psychological correlates of academic success and failure. African Journal of Educational Research, 2 (20), 11-22.
7. Bakare, C.G.M.(ed) 1970. Study habit inventory. Department of Guidance and Counselling, University of Ibadan, Ibadan, Nigeria.

8. Bashir , I.& Mattoo, N. H.(2012) A Study on Study Habits and Academic Performance Among Adolescents (14-19) years. International Journal of Social Science Tomorrow. Vol.1, No. 5, pp. 1-5.

9. Bhan, K. S., & Gupta, R. (2010) Study Habits and Academic Achievement among the students belonging to scheduled caste and non scheduled caste group. Journal of Applied Research in Education 15(1) pp. 1-9

10. Dadzie, P. S. (2008) Reading for Education: The roles of Libraries. Ghana Library Journal Vol. 20. No. 1. pp. 1-14

11. Deavers, R. (2000) The Effect of Instruction on Early Non-Word Reading Strategies. Journal of Research in Reading. No.23, pp 267-286.

12. Ekwe, E.U. 2005. Empowering Nigerian Learning Through Counselling for Stress Management. Conference Proceeding of the 29th Annual Conference of the Counselling Association of Nigeria (CASSON), 1-8.

13. Ezekie, A.I.A. (1977). Teacher and student factors encouraging examination malpractice in the Nigerian educational system: a case study of six southern states in Nigeria. J. Professional Studies in Education, 5, 43- 48.

14. Fagbemi J.O. (2001). Assessment and examination malpractice (pp. 231-245). In: Aghenta, J.A. & Lassa, P.N (Eds). Proceeding of the 16th annual congress of the Nigerian Academy of Education. Jos: University of Jos.

15. Gallo, D. (2007) Reading Interests and Habits of Connecticut Students in Grades Four through Twelve. The Reading Matrix. Vol. 2, No.3 pp 1-20.

16. Greene, B. (2001) "Testing Reading Comprehension of Theoretical Discourse with Close" Journal of Research in Reading. 24 (1) pp. 32-98

17. Guthrie J.T. Benneth, L & McGough, K (2007), Concept-oriented Reading Instruction: An Integrated Curriculum to Develop Motivations and Strategies for Reading http://curry.virginia.edu/go/clic/nrrc/corri_rlo.html Retrieved on November, 28 2013.

18. Higginbothan, S. (1999). Reading Interest of middle school students and preferences by gender of middle school students in a South Eastern State Atlanta Georgia, Master's Dissertation. Mercer University. pp. 140

19. Isangedighi, A.J. (1997). A comparison of study habits among the underachieving, the achieving and over-achieving junior secondary one students. West African J. Educ. Res., 1, 114-119.

20. Issa, A. O., Aliyu, M. B., Akangbe, R. B. & Adedeji, A. F.(2012) Reading Interest and Habits of the Federal Polytechnic Students. International Journal of Learning & Development.Vol.2, No.1, pp 470-486.

21. Kagu, B. 2000. The effect of group counseling on study habit patterns of adult learners. The Counsellor, 18 (10), 148-155.

22. Nwobi, P.C. 1997. Study Habit Skills as predictors of Academic performance among students of Anambra State College of Education, Nsugbe. Journal of Educational Studies and Research, 1 (1) 167-177.

23. Ogbodo, R.O. (2010) Effective Study Habits in Educational Sector: Counseling Implications. Edo Journal of Counseling, Vol. 3, No.2. pp. 1-11

24. Okafor, F.C.(ed.) 1981. Philosophy of Education and Third World Perspective Law. Rencesville Virginia; Brunsivide Publishing Company

25. Omoegun, O.M. 2000. Effects of remedial guidance on the academic achievement of Lagos state adolescents in English comprehension. Ilorin Journal of Education, 20,87-93.

26. Palani, K. K. (2012) Promising Reading Habits and Creating Literate Social. International Reference Research Journal Vol. III Issue 2(1) pp 91.

27. Salami, S.O. 2002. Effects of age, gender, and ecological background on the study behaviour patter of adolescents in Nigeria schools. African Journal of Educational Planning and Policy Studies, 3 (1) 83-94.

28. Salami, S.O. and S. Aremu, 2006. Relationship between problem-solving ability and study behaviour among school-going adolescents in southwestern Nigeria. Electronic Journal of Research in Educational Psychology 4 (1) 139-154

29. Singh, Y. G. (2011) Academic Achievement and Study Habits of Higher Secondary Students. International Referred Research Journal 3 (27) pp. 2

30. Tukur, A.H. & Musa, A.K.J. (2001). Examination malpractices among undergraduate students of University of Maiduguri: conditions and

forms (pp.349-363). In: Aghenta, J.A. & Lassa, P.N. (Eds). Proceeding of the 16th annual congress of the Nigerian Academy of Education. Jos: University of Jos.

31. Ugodulunwa, C.A. (2001). The attitude of students to cheating in examination. In: Aghenta, J.A. & Lassa, P.N. (Eds). Proceeding of the 16th annual congress of the Nigerian Academy of Education. Jos: University of Jos.
32. Ukwueze, A.C. 2009. The effect of Cognitive Restructuring on Study Habits among Secondary School Students. Journal of Education and Applied Psychology 2 (1) 183-189
33. Ward, M. L. (1997) Reader and Library Users: A Study of reading habits and public library use. Unpublished MA dissertation, University of Ghana: Legon. pp 70
34. West African Examination Council, (2008) Chief Examiners Report Ghana. pp. 3
35. Wilhite, S.C. 1990. Self-efficacy, locus of control, self-assessment of memory ability and study activities as predictors of college course achievement. Journal of Educational Psychology 82 (4), 696-700.

5. Awarness of Leadership Qualities District

Chapter-I

Introduction

"The purpose of education is not to produce people who loiter for jobs, but to produce responsible citizens" - **Sardarvallabaipatel**

Education is the learning process by which values, awareness, information and skills are acquired and integrated. Education is bound up with human race. Its boundaries are as wide as those of life. Its implications are rich and varied. It is a continuous process that occurs from birth to death. It is imparted in oral and written form. The UNESCO (United Nations Educational, Scientific and Cultural Organization) has defined "literacy in very clear terms that literate is an individual who is able to read development of students. It should impart knowledge and information and also develop character and personality. It should broaden the outlook, develop skill and abilities and prepare the students for life and world.

Education is the cornerstone of Economic, social and cultural development of a country. An appropriate education system cultivates knowledge, better Qualities, positive values and awareness among the people, especially those who acquire it. Education is the main force which influences the quality of life. It has assumed more importance today than even before because in its present role, it is adding new dimensions to our present and future scenario.

Education is a unique feature that plays the most dominant role is the life of the areal human source and is considered as an important, valuable and tangible asset to the country. The economic development of the country depends fully upon such real assets. For the reconstruction of the society, education can be modified and made realistic. The aim of the education is not only the acquisition of information but also the development of that best of mind and awareness, which will make us responsible citizens. Education itself is the basic human right and used as a tool to make sensitive about issues and problems. It uses culturalization, conditioning, re-conditioning, learning or re-learning techniques to bring people within the redline zone to change behavior.

The Latin word "education" means "bringing out the potentialities of the individual or self development". It has a very wide connotation. In its fundamental sense it is life itself.

Need and significance of the study

1. Awareness have a subject – object relationship i.e. they always involve the relationship between the individual and specific objects, persons, groups institutions, values or norms related to the environment.
2. Awareness is learned and acquired by experience and not inborn and inherent.
3. Awareness are relatively, enduring state of readiness. For example once they are gratified. But awareness on the other hand is relatively stable of readiness.
4. Awareness has motivational affective characteristics.
5. Awareness are numerous and varied as the stimuli to which they refer.
6. Awareness range from strongly positive to strongly negative. When a person shows some tendency to approach an object, he is said to have positive awareness. When he shows a tendency to avoid the object, his awareness is negative.
7. Awareness usually is considered as consisting three basic components thinking, feeling and reacting. The first aspect pertains to belief. It involves the thought of a person has about to a value here we are talking about whether the person feels attracted, repelled or is natural regarding the topic in question. The third element is a predisposition to behavior.

8. Awareness is developed right from childhood through the process of conditioning, imitation and instruction.
9. Awareness formed earlier could undergo changes in the light of new experiences, but this process is very slow and that is why we say awareness is more or less stable.
10. We view the different components of our environment only through the lens of our present awareness leadership them. We refuse to look at the food features present in objects leadership which we have negative awareness.

Scope of the study

The concept of serving is fundamental to the leadership role. Good leadership involves serving the organization or group and the people within it. Ineffective leaders tend to invert these principles and consider merely that the leader must be served by the people. Good leadership in the modern age more importantly requires awareness and behaviors which characterize and relate to humanity.

Statement of the problem

The present investigation entitled "*Awareness of leadership qualities among B.Ed trainees in pudukkottai district.*

Operational Definition of key terms used

1. Awareness

   Awareness is a favorable or unfavorable evaluation of something. Awareness are generally positive or negative views of a person, place, thing, or event – this is often referred to as the awareness object. People can also be conflicted or ambivalent toward an object, meaning that they simultaneously possess both positive and negative awareness towards the item in question.

2. Bachelor of Education (B.Ed) trainee teacher

   Bachelor of Education (B.Ed) trainee teacher is the trainee in pursuing the degree of bachelor in education course of the study in the college of education.

3. Leadership

   Leadership has been described as a process of social influence in which one person can enlist the aid and support of others in the accomplishment of a common task.

4. Leadership Qualities

   Leadership Qualities are based on the leadership behavior. Leadership Qualities are a valuable asset for someone looking to move up in n organization.

5. Pudukkottai District

   Pudukkottai District is a district of Tamil Nadu State in southern India. The city of Pudukkottai is the district headquarters.

Objectives of study

The study has the following objectives.

To study the awareness of Leadership Qualities among the B.Ed trainees in pudukkottai.

1. To find out whether there is significant difference in the Mean Score between male and female B.Ed trainees in the awareness of leadership qualities.
2. To find out to whether there is significant difference in the awareness Leadership Qualities Mean Score between Government College and Private College B.Ed trainees.
3. To find out if there is a significant difference in the awareness of Leadership Qualities Mean score between rural and urban area B.Ed trainees.
4. To find out if there is a significant difference in the awareness of Leadership Qualities Mean score between Hosteller and Day scholar area B.Ed trainees.
5. To find out if there is a significant difference in the awareness of Leadership Qualities Mean score between joint family and nuclear family area B.Ed trainees.
6. To find out if there is a significant differs in their awareness of Leadership Qualities on the basis of their parent's occupation.
7. To find out if there is a significant differs in their awareness of Leadership Qualities on the basis of their parent's educational qualification.
8. To find out if there is a significant differs in their awareness of Leadership Qualities on the basis of their parent's annual income.

Hypotheses of the study

The following research hypotheses have been formulated for the present study.

1. There is no significant difference in the Mean score of B.Ed trainees in the awareness of leadership qualities male and female trainees.

2. There is no significant difference in the awareness of Leadership qualities Mean score between Government College and Private College B.Ed trainees.
3. There is no significant difference in the Mean score of B.Ed trainees in the awareness of leadership qualities on the basis of rural area and urban area B.Ed trainees.
4. There is no significant difference in the awareness of Leadership qualities Mean score between hosteller and Day scholar B.Ed trainees.
5. There is no significant difference in the awareness of Leadership qualities Mean Score between joint family and nuclear family B.Ed trainees.
6. There is no significant difference in the awareness of B.Ed trainee awareness of Leadership qualities on the basis of their parent's educational qualification.
7. There is no significant difference in the Mean Score of B.Ed trainees in the awareness of leadership qualities on the basis of their parent's occupation.
8. There is no significant difference in the Mean Score of B.Ed trainees in the awareness of leadership qualities on the basis of their annual income.

Limitations of the study

1. The Present study is limited to the B.Ed trainees in Pudukkottai District and the samples of present study are 300.

2. The present study is limited only to eight of them viz. Gender, Locality, Type of College, residency, Type of family, Parent's Occupation Parent's Qualification, Parent's Annual Income.

Conclusion

The problem of the present study has been discussed briefly in this chapter out the need and significance objectives of the study. The terms operationally defined in this study have been reviewed theoretically from related literature has you a broader theoretical perceptive in the light of switch appropriate hypothesis to be framed and test a detailed discussion of the related literature having a bearing on the problem in hand follows in the next chapter.

Chapter-II

Review of Relative Literature

INTRODUCTION

Review of related literature pertaining to a problem marks the researcher familiar with the summary of previous research, the writings of recognized experts with what is already known, what is still unknown and untested and thus provides a background for the awareness of the present study. A review of related literature is an important pre- requisite for the planning and efficient execution of any investigation. The study of related literature gives the investigator an ides of the quantum of work done in the field makes him to scrutinize the methodology used and directs him to work along useful lines. This brings the researchers to the proximity of the solution.

Once a topic has been decided upon, it is essential to review all relevant materials which has bearing on the topic. It is necessary to show how the problem undcr investigation related literature is one of the first steps of the research process. It is valuable guide to defining the problem, recognizing it significance, suggestion promising data gathering devices, appropriate study design and source of data.

Purpose / Importance / Significance of Literature review

In the words of "the key to the vast store house of published literature may open doors to sources of significant problem and explanatory hypothesis and provide helpful orientation for definition of the problem, background for selection of procedure, and comparative date for interpretation of results". In order to be truly creative and original, one must read extensively and critically, one must read extensively and critically as a stimulus to think. "Besides enlarging the knowledge about the topic, writing a literature review will give the investigators to gain and demonstrate qualities in two areas.

1 Information seeking

The ability to scan the literature efficiently using manual or computerized methods, to identify a set of useful articles and books.

2 Critical appraisal

The ability to apply principles of analysis to identify unbiased and valid studies.

a. It enables the researcher to define his problem. The knowledge of related literature brings the researcher up to date on the work which others have done and thus to state the objective clearly used concisely.

b. It helps the researcher to avoid unfruitful and useless problem area.

c. It helps the researcher to avoid duplications of well established facts.

d. It helps the researcher to understand the research methodology which refers to the way; the study is to be conducted.

e. It helps the researcher to know about tool and instruments which proved to be useful in the previous studies.

f. The final and important specific reason for reviewing the related literature is to know about the recommendations of previous researchers listed in their studies for further research.

One of the essential aspects of research process is the review of related literature. It plays a crucial role in planning of the study.

Review of the related literature, besides, allowing the researcher to acquaint himself with current knowledge in the field or area in which he is going to conduct his research, serves the following specific purpose.

a. By reviewing the related literature the researcher can avoid unfruitful and useless problem areas. He can select those areas in which positive finding are very, likely to result and his endeavors would be likely to add to the knowledge in a meaningful way.

b. Through the review of related literature the researcher can avoid unintentional duplication of well established findings. It is no use to replicate a study when the stability and validity of its results have been clearly established.

c. The review of related literature gives the researcher an understanding of the research methodology which refers to the way the study is to be conducted. It helps the researcher to know about the tools and instruments which proved to be useful and promising the previous studies. The advantages of the useful and promising the previous studies. The advantages of the related literature are also to provide insight into the statistical methods through which validity of results is to be established.

d. The final and important specific reason for reviewing the related literature is to know about the recommendations of previous researchers listed in their studies for further research.

STUDIES CONDUCTED IN INDIA

Bskanth(2010) conducted research for the effectiveness of leadership qualities about contributing social modifies, acquiring independence for the country and constituting good administration. There are some who are born leadership like Adolf Hitler and Winston Churchill. But there are many who develop skills and powers to convert a leader and for some it is conditions that inspired them to take the leading. One of the bearing cases is the father of our nation, Mahatma Gandhi. He was neither a born leader nor gained leadership skills. For many of our freedom fighters it is the condition that incited them to take up the cause. But how did they come out as leaders? There are sure calibers that go into bringing in a leader.

They can either be acquired or is part of their personality. Be it a school leader or leader of a country or that of a terrorist organization these calibers are essential.

A good leader must be trusty, convinced, enthusiastic, broad, and amicable. It is very authoritative that thought, word and deed of conveyance concur to earn respect. Leaders call for to be a beginning of aspiration to learn form and a beginning of motivating to attain. Although he is a leader, he should take the team with him besides walk ahead or crusading from behind. Apart from setting goals, he should be a part of the team in realizing it. Disregarding however a position turns grave, a benevolent leader all of the time continues calm and composed resolute towards accomplishing the goal with a cool head.

A good leader always strives for excellence. He must never run out of words of boost and admiration. He must address every individual in the squad on par and acquit in a manner beseeming his personality.

Akslal (2010) classified the important qualities as follows:

1. Curiosity: A leader should be curious to know to discover or unravel the truths. This discovery should help in changing the environment/ situation for the better.
2. Creativity: A leader should have in him/her something called as the creative potential. An armchair/intellectual like leader will hardly liven up the environment.
3. Communication: A leader should be an effective communicator.
4. Character: the Character of a leader should be impeccable or flawless.
5. Courage: A leader should face even the worst of cases courageously, bravely!
6. Conviction: A leader should diligently hole on to his/her convictions. She cannot afford to be vulnerable.
7. Charisma: A leader should strive to perform make his/her team perform.
8. Competence: A leader should strive to perform, make his/ her team perform.
9. Common Sense: Although common sense is not so common, a leader should possess this quality in abudance.

Dwivedi R.S. (2006) Concluded that the visionary leadership has emerged as a key determinant of corporate survival, success and growth in today's turbulent environment. Successful leaders of 21st century have the capacity to create vision and also translate it into reality. Visionary leadership is transformative and based on the power of inspiration. It is characterized by the commitment to core spiritual values, with a clear vision, respect for empowering relationship, it is marked by an act of leading form the front, benevolence from within, respectful pluralism, continuous introspection and focus on legacy. It involves a dynamic and interactive process. As a visionary leader, A.S.J. Abdul Kalam substantially changed the organizational climate of DRDL prior to launching Integrated Guided Missile Awareness Program (IGMDP) using effective communication and providing clear direction to the various teams involved. Later on, a highly performing climate emerged, when he used further indigenous techniques to manage technology-oriented structure, search for capable project leaders, Science council, collaborative effort, transformation of organizational dynamics by empowering scientist's motivation, etc.

The outstanding success or DRDL is evidenced by the fact that country acquired the capability of mankind five state-of-the –art missile systems in record time. The visionary leadership style of Dr. Kalam is comparable to that of George Washington, the founding father of the USA, having far-reaching implications for guidance of new age leaders engaged in awareness tasks globally.

MasoodDani. B.(2006) Provided a new leadership alignment model incorporating various concepts focusing on leadership styles, Educational leadership, and situational strength. These concepts are brought together to introduce a leadership model, which looks not only at individual leadership and to effect of that on the organization but also at an organization as a system and how leadership behavior and culture in individual departments or sections in an organization can be explained. Based on the work or podskoff et al., a 23-item measure of transformational leadership questionnaire was student to evaluate transformational leaders. 339 followers from five colleges were asked to complete the questionnaire about their leaders and it was analyzed to identify transformational leaders.

SinhaParesha. N. (2005) conducted research tests for the effectiveness of leadership qualities training, using the full range leadership awareness program, upon organizational performance has been established. Quasi-field experiment research was conducted, resulting in an increase in the display of all five leadership skills factors and contingent reward behavior. There was a reduction in the display of passive leadership behavior as a found to be effective. Leadership training and awareness posited at the turn of the century that institution must adapt to unprecedented and accelerating speeds of change to survive in the global economy also recognized the strong leadership is an important key to organizational growth, change and renewal in these turbulent times, and that leadership is a resource in short supply. Partly as a result of these challenges, education appear to have turned their attention to leadership as a competitive advantage and the best way to cope with these changing times is to build high potential students through structured leadership awareness systems.

Vivekananda

Stand up, be bold, be strong. Take the whole responsibility on your own shoulders, and know that you are the creator of your own destiny. All the strength and succor you want is within yourself. Therefore make your own future.

Hold to the idea, "I am not the mind, I see that I am thinking, I am watching my mind act," and each day the identification of yourself with thoughts and feelings will grow less, until at last you can entirely separate yourself from the mind and actually know it to be apart from yourself.

All love is expansion, all selfishness is contraction. Love is therefore the only law of life. He who loves lives, he who is selfish is dying. Therefore love for love's sake, because it is law of life, just as you breathe to live.

Rao(2010) has classified the leadership styles, on the basis of the earlier research at the Indian Institute of Management, into the following:

A benevolent or paternalistic leadership style in which the top level manager believes that all his employees should be constantly guided treated with affection like a parent treats his children, is relationship oriented, assigns tasks on the basis of his own likes and dislikes, constantly guides them and protects them, understands their needs, salvages the situations of crisis by active involvement of himself, distributes rewards to those who are loyal and obedient, shares information with those who are close to him, etc

A critical leadership style is characterized as closer to Theory X belief pattern where the manager believes that employees should be closely and constantly goal oriented, cannot tolerate mistakes or conflicts among employees, personal power dominated, keeps all information to himself, works strictly according to norms and rules and regulations and is highly discipline oriented.

An Awareness of leadership style is characterized as an empowering style, where the top manager believes in developing the competencies of his staff, treats them as mature adults, leaves them on their own most of the times, is long term goal oriented, shares information with all to build their competencies, facilitates the resolution of conflicts and mistakes by the employees themselves with minimal involvement form him.

Awareness style by nature seems to be the most desired organization building style. However some individuals and some situations require at times benevolent and critical styles. Some managers are not aware of the predominant style they tend to use and the effects there style is producing on their employees.

This classification is based on the observations made by Stewart and Rao(1996) as a part of a collaborative study by the author and David McClelland of Harvard University using the Psychosocial Maturity Models of Stewart (Stewart and Rao, 1996). In this model when the TAT stories written by adult in response pictures that are supposed to arouse Achievement and other motives, were represented the Freudian awareness stages. Superimposing these observations and analyzing the styles of Indian Managers the author formulated the three leadership styles mentioned above.

Studies Conducted In Abroad

ChiokFoongLoke (2008) Examined the leadership behaviors on student outcomes in colleges. The Comparison of the results of the different types of setting and samples allow a better understanding of the relationship between leadership behaviors and students outcomes and thus help to determine if leadership worth the extra effort.

Nupponen(2006) also considered that effective leadership is vital to quality services for students. Effective leadership frameworks are needed as a starting point towards ensuring quality. Nupponen emphasizes the complex external social environment in which early childhood settings operate and the consequent need for self-reflection. As elsewhere she finds that there has been little Australian research that focuses on the leadership and management role of heads of center-based child care. She concludes that training and experience in college's management and leadership is needed in order to enhance the competence of center students.

Nelson Mandela(1990):*"I am fundamentally an optimist. Whether that comes from nature or nurture, I cannot say. Part of being an optimist is keeping one's head pointed toward the sun, one's feet moving forward."*

"No one is born hating another person because of the color of his skin, or his background, or his religion. People must learn to hate, and if they can learn to hate, they can be taught to love, for love comes more naturally to the human heart than its opposite."

Dalli(2005) reflected on professionalism in the early years highlights the importance of relationship and responsiveness in effective teacher practice. She asserts that the discourse of teacher professionals has changes from childcare workers to educators and that this is part of constructing a scholarly base of the teacher profession. She voices 'love' as a legitimate part of early teacher practice. In arguing for new concepts of leadership as well. She conducted a survey of ethics and professionalism(2003) which aimed to establish a grounds-up definition of professionalism, and found three key themes in teachers statements about what matters in professionalism in the teacher field in New Zealand: these were pedagogy, professional knowledge and skills, being able to articulate corners in a confident manner, demonstrating a knowledge of current educational research, and being aware of the educational research, and being aware of the educational political environment.

Kornor Hedge; NordvikHilmar(2004) determined the co relational analysis of the leadership traits measured by the revised NEO Personality Inventoryand three leadership styles, that is, change, personality, and integrity measured by Ekvall and Arvonen'sCPE common factors comprising leadership styles and personality domains were interpreted as "looking for new possibilities", "Hard working" and "dealing with people" Considering personality traits as behavioral tendencies in the leadership context, and due to the self-perceptions independent of context.

Ehrhart; Mark G; Kelin: Katherine J (2001) conducted a study in which particulars values and personality dimensions were used to predict participants preferences for charismatic leadership vs. two other leadership styles: relationship oriented and task-oriented leadership. The results showed that values and personality were useful in predicting leadership preferences.

Jack Welch(2001) expanded fundamental leadership principles in his book *Uack*: Straight from the Gut', There is only one way- the straightway. It sets the tone of the organization. Be open to the best of what everyone, everywhere, has to offer, transfer learning across you organization. Get the right people in the right jobs – it is more important than developing a strategy. An informal atmosphere is a competitive advantage. Make sure everybody counts and everybody knows they count. Legitimate self-confidence is a winner- the true test of self-confidence is the courage to be open. Business has to be fun- celebrations energize and organization. Never underestimate the other guy. Understand where real value is added and put your best people there. Know when to meddle and when to let go- this is pure instinct.

Stoker J.; Fisscher O.A.M; De Jong(2001) conducted a study that focused on the functioning of Research and Awareness(R&D) teams, the role of the team leader and characteristics of individual team members. After a brief overview of literature on leadership and innovation, some research results have a number of characteristics in common with R&D terms, such as dependent functioning of R&D terms, with a focus on the relations between leadership results of the study clearly suggest that leadership is important for the effectiveness of self-managing teams. For the two sets of teams studied, there are strong relations between leadership behavior and the outcome variables, and especially strong relations between charismatic and consultative leadership styles and the outcome variables.

Boatman.A.(2000) conducted research for the effectiveness of leadership qualities, leadership audit is a systematic, comprehensive, and objective process to identify all of the experiences by which students may develop leadership abilities. The results of the process create organizational awareness about leadership opportunities, form the basis for evaluation and planning, and provide date to determine the impact of new programs. Typically conducted by an auditor working with a steering committee, the leadership audit achieves its purpose through a verity of data collection techniques, including interviews, questionnaires and content analysis. If the campus community is well informed about and involved in the leadership audit, the process has significant potential to enhance student leadership qualities.

CONCLUSION

The survey of related literature has helped the investigator to have clear perspective if the problem chosen for the present investigation. The review related literature has enabled the investigator to formulate the relevant hypothesis for the present study based on this review, a suitable methodology and well planned procedure for present investigator is adopted and it is explained in further chapters.

Chapter III

Methodology

INTRODUCTION

"All the progress in born of enquiry. Doubt is often better than over confidence, for it leads to investigation" is a famous Hudson maxim in context of which the significance of research can be understood. Research includes scientific and inductive thinking and it promotes the qualities of logical habits of thanking and organization.

The success of any research depends upon suitable methodology with specific operational steps and well-constructed tools (K.Suchitha; 2010). The percent study which aims at finding out the awareness in pudukkottai district by using methodology as descriptive method.

Research Design

Before starting a research, the investigator will look for problem; he will read books, journals, research reports and other related literature. Based on this, he will finalize the topic for research. During this process, he will be in close contact with his guide.

As soon as the topic is decided, first task is to decide about design. Research design is conducted. It constitutes the blue print for the collection, measurement and analysis of data.

According to gay and Airasian (2000), a design is general strategy for conducting a research study. The nature of the hypothesis, the variables involved, and the constraints of the real world all contribute to selection of design.

Kothari (1988) says, Decisions regarding what? Where? When? How? Much? By What? Means concerning an inquiry or a research study constitute research design. Thus, it can be said that research design is an outline of what the researcher will do from writing of objectives, hypothesis and its operational implications to find analysis of data.

Thus according to nature and type of study the components of design will be decided. In short, efficient research design will help the researcher to carry out the study in a systematic way.

Purposes of research design

A research design helps the investigator to obtain answer to research problem and issues involved in their research, since it is the outline of entire research process

Design also tells us about how to collect data, what observation to be carry out, how to make them, how to analyse the data. Design also guides investigator about statistical techniques used to be used for analysis.Thus, design guides the investigator to carry out research step by step in an efficient way.

This chapter presents details regarding the following;

1. Selection of dependent variables and categorical variables.
2. Construction of tool to measure the "**Awareness of leadership qualities among B.Ed trainees**."
3. Reliability, validity of the tools illustrated
4. Explain the sampling procedure.
5. Scheduling the survey and collecting the data for Interpretation.

Statement of the Problem

The present investigation entitled "**Awareness of Leadership qualities among B.Ed trainees in Pudukkottai district.**

Objectives of study

The study has the following objectives.

To study the Awareness of Leadership Qualities among the B.Ed trainees in pudukkottai district.

1 To find out whether there is significant difference in the awareness Leadership Qualities Mean Score between male and female B.Ed trainees.

2 To find out to whether there is significant difference in the awareness Leadership Qualities Mean Score between Government College and Private College B.Ed trainees.

3 To find out if there is a significant difference in the awareness of Leadership Qualities Mean score between rural and urban area B.Ed trainees.

4 To find out if there is a significant difference in the awareness of Leadership Qualities Mean score between Hosteller and Day scholar area B.Ed trainees.

5 To find out if there is a significant difference in the awareness of Leadership Qualities Mean score between joint family and nuclear family B.Ed trainees.

6 To find out if there is a significant differs in their awareness of Leadership Qualities on the basis of their parent's occupation.

7 To find out if there is a significant differs in their awareness of Leadership Qualities on the basis of their parent's educational qualification.

8 To find out if there is a significant differs in their awareness of Leadership Qualities on the basis of their parent's annual income.

Hypotheses of the study

The following research hypotheses have been formulated for the present study.

1 There is no significant difference in the awareness of leadership qualities Mean score basis of male and female B.Ed trainees.

2 There is no significant difference in the awareness of Leadership qualities Mean score between Government College and Private College B.Ed trainees.

3 There is no significant difference in the Mean score of B.Ed trainees in the awareness of leadership qualities on the basis of rural and urban area B.Ed trainees.

4 There is no significant difference in the awareness of Leadership qualities Mean score between hosteller and Day scholar B.Ed trainees.

5 There is no significant difference in the awareness of Leadership qualities Mean Score between joint family and nuclear family B.Ed trainees.

6 There is no significant difference in the awareness of B.Ed trainee awareness of Leadership qualities on the basis of their parent's educational qualification.

7 There is no significant difference in the Mean Score of B.Ed trainees in the awareness of leadership qualities on the basis of their parent's occupation.

8 There is no significant difference in the Mean Score of B.Ed trainees in the awareness of leadership qualities on the basis of their annual income.

Limitations of the study

1. The Present study is limited to the B.Ed trainees in Pudukkottai District and the sample of present study is 300.

2. The present study is limited only to Eight of them viz. Gender, Locality, Type of institution, Residency, Types of Family, Parent's Occupation, Parent's Qualification, Parent's Annual Income.

Research Method

In the present study, "survey method" was employed for its suitability and accuracy. The normative survey methods a scientific method of describing and analyzing the present events conditions or relationship that exists; practices, the prevail views on awareness that are held; processes that are going on; effects that are being felt; or trends that are developing.

The normative survey research gives maximum contribution when it organizes from a problem existing within the framework of theory and when it is oriented towards the identification of factors and relationship worthy of investigations under controlled conditions.

Normative survey methods is concerned with the represent attempts to trace the status of phenomenon under investigation no category of education research is more widely used than the type known variously as the survey, the normative study and descriptive research. Surveys are oriented towards the isolation of factors. Survey and integrate these data and point to implications and interrelationships.

The survey approach to educational problems is one of the most commonly used approaches. It is followed in studying locals well as state, national and international aspects of education.

RESEARCH TOOL

In the present study the investigation selected questionnaire as the most important tool for collecting data because it is used increasingly to enquire into the current conditions, opinions and awareness of a group. The word tool is defined a means to collect evidence.

W.Best observes that the questionnaire is the most tools in collecting both quantitative and qualities information, for the present study questionnaire was occupied with view to gather information in details regarding on "Awareness of Leadership Qualities among the B.Ed trainees in Pudukkottai District".

CONSTRUCTION OF RESEARCH TOOL

In survey research, awareness of research tool occupies an important place for a prefect research the researchers. Visited the various B.Ed trainees at Pudukkottai districts and consulted with principal members regarding the research and the collection of data from trainees. First the researcher discussed with subject experts, faculty constructions of research tool, gathered some information and good their suggestions in this regard. As the step 40 items statements were given in the scale. The expert opinion were taken into account and on the basis of their remarks some items were modified and some reworded. Thus, a total of 30 items statements were given up and finalised.

Samples of the study

Sampling is the process of selecting a sample form the population. For this population 300 samples were observed from Pudukkottai district B.Ed colleges is divided into a number of parts called sampling units. In this study, the investigator used stratified **Random sampling** method to collect data on "Awareness of Leadership Qualities among B.Ed trainees in pudukkottai District".

The process of selecting the sample from specific population is called as sampling. In this study the Investigator has visited to 3 B.Ed colleges at Pudukkottai district. The scale was administrated to 300 students from 3 colleges and responses were collected. The response scores and tabulated to find out the awareness of leadership qualities.

A sample is composed of same fraction or part of the total number of elements or units in a defined population is known as sample. Only 300 students were selected as sample of the study by adopting Random sampling technique.

DESCRIPTION OF RESEARCH TOOL AND SCORING PROCEDURE

The research tool consist two parts, the part-A deals with general information about the respondents and the part-B deals with "Awareness of leadership qualities". The former part of this research tool was designed to seek information about the B.Ed trainees personal characteristics such as Gender, Residential locality, College Management, Type of college, college locality, Type of family, parents Educational Qualification, Parents Monthly Income, students Medium part of this tool was developed in order to study the B.Ed., trainees.

Awareness of leadership qualities Questionnaire consisted of 30 items, each item Statement the score was assigned to questionnaire is having both positive and negative statements. For the positive statements the weightages were given to of 5 of 1respectively for 'strongly agree', 'agree', 'no comments', 'disagree', 'Strongly disagree'.For the negative statements the reverse order was followed from 1 to 5.

Scoring procedure

Category	Positive Statement Scores	Negative Statement Scores
Strongly agree	5	1
Agree	4	2
No comments	3	3
Disagree	2	4
Strongly Disagree	1	5

This questionnaire has a maximum score of 160 and minimum score of 40. A High Score indicated a relatively high awareness of leadership qualities.

PILOT STUDY

The pilot stage is concerned with refining the items collected. The collected items were presented before the expert with a request to offer their considered opinion regarding the suitability objectivity clarity and relevancy of the statement collected from different sources.

The pilot study is an initial study which is conducted by the investigator to know more about the research problem in various aspects. Based on the pilot study, the main study was conducted by the investigator while administering the research in the pilot study, some doubts were raised by the higher secondary school students and the investigator clarified all of their doubts and difficulties. Based on that, the investigator modified the items.

VALIDITY OF THE TOOL

In validation process, the investigator used two measures in order to establish validation of tools. The first measure of validation is called reliability. The second measure of validation process is called validity. The investigator established content validity.

To find out the validity of research tool, the investigator discussed each and every item of the questionnaire with the experts in the relevant field of "Awareness of leadership qualities on B.Ed trainees in Pudukkottai district". Based on the opinion of the experts, the objectivity and worthiness of the items of the questionnaire were established.

In the validation process, the investigator used two measures in order to establish validation of the tools. The first measure of validation is called reliability. The second measure of validation process is called validity. The investigator established content validity. To find out the validity of research tool, the investigator discussed each and every item of the questionnaire with the experts in the relevant field to identify the "Awareness of Leadership Qualities among the B.Ed trainees in Pudukkottai District". Based on the opinion of the experts, the objectivity and worthiness of the items of the questionnaire were established. The investigator also modified some of the items in the questionnaire and some items in the questionnaire and some item were eliminated. This kind of scientific procedure helped the investigator to established sufficient content validity.

RELIABILITY OF TOOLS

The reliability of questionnaire on identifying the "Awareness of Leadership Qualities among the B.Ed Trainees of Pudukkottai District" was established by making a rational equivalence method. The reliability of the tool refers to the internal consistency observed in measurement of reliability. The reliability of questionnaire on identifying the "Awareness of Leadership Qualities among the B.Ed Trainees in Pudukkottai District" was established by making a rational equivalence method. The reliability of the tool refers to the internal consistency observed in measurement of reliability.

The investigator used the rational equivalence method to find the reliability of the tool. The reliability value is calculated as the reliability value is 0.87.

Since the reliability value is above the normal, the investigator concluded that the items given in the questionnaire are highly reliable.

SAMPLING TECHNIQUE USED

SI.NO	Category	Groups	No. of Samples	Total Number of Samples
1	Gender	Male	120	300
		Female	180	
2	Types of institutions	Government	100	300
		Private	200	
3	Locality	Rural	170	300
		Urban	130	
4	Residency	Hosteller	75	300
		Day Scholar	225	
5	Type of family	Joint family	161	300
		Nuclear family	139	
6	Parent's Occupation	Govt.job	219	300
		Private Job	81	
7	Parent's Qualification	Educated	71	300
		Uneducated	229	
8	Parent's annual income	Above 50,000	230	300
		Below 50,000	70	

COLLECTION OF DATA

The investigator herself met each and every trainee. Before going to administer the research tool, the investigator revealed the purpose of the present study to the B.Ed trainees and then asked them to give their responses for each and every item that are given in the questionnaires. The responses of the trainees were collected and recorded.

Analysis of data

The term analysis the refers to the combination of certain measure along with searching for part -10 and relationship that among groups for the present study the investigator collected the data from B.Ed study using the tool develop the find out questionnaire of sample with problems "Awareness of Leadership Qualities Among the B.Ed Trainees in Pudukkottai District" habits of B.Ed learners this reference to class room atmosphere.

Stastical Techniques used

The following statistical techniques have been proposed for the present study.

ARITHMATIC MEAN(X)

The mean of the distribution is commonly understood as the arithmetic average. The term guide-point averages familiar to students is a mean value.

It is computed by dividing the sum of all the scores by the number of scores. It is probably most useful of all statistical measures for in addition to the information that is provided. It is the base from which many other in important measures of computed.

M=Where
M= Mean
Fx= The sum of the scores of the distribution
N= Number of Scores

Arithmetic Mean from a frequency distribution:

We use statistical procedures to describe (or draw inferences about) groups of numerals (measurements). One way of describing a group of numerals is to organize them into a frequency table. The total of this frequency distribution. The total of this frequency distribution will be divided by the total of 'F' N to get Mean

$$x = A + \frac{fd}{n} xl$$

Where,

A= Assumed mean

N= Total number of frequency

D= Deviation from the assumed mean

i =Size of class interval

The standard Deviation

The standard deviation is the most common measure of variability, measuring the spread of the data set and the relationship of the mean to the rest of the data. If the data points are close to the mean, indicating that the responses are fairly uniform, then the standard deviation will be small. Conversely, if many data points are far from the mean, indicating that there is a wide variance in the responses, then the standard deviation will be large. If all the data values are equal, then the standard deviation will be zero.

't'-Test

't'test is based on "t' distribution and is a sample of mean judging the significance of difference between the Mean of sample in case of small samples when population variance in not known. In case of two samples paired t- test is used for judging the significance of the mean of difference between the two related. If judges the significance of the co-efficient of simple and partial correlation. The relevant test statistic is calculated from the sample data and then compared with its probable value based on t-distribution at a specific level of significance for concerning degree of freedom for accepting or rejecting the null hypothesis. This test applied only in case of small samples when population variance is not known.

t ='t' Value

M1= Mean of the first sample

M2= Mean of the Second Sample

1= Standard Deviation of the first

2= Standard Deviation of the Second sample

N1= Total Number of the first sample

N2=Total Number of the Second sample

CONCLUSION

The chapter III gives the details of research methodology and the procedure of varies aspects of data collection. The chapter also explains technique used for the study. It has also been clearly mentioned about tools of the study. Statistical inferences will be given in the next chapter IV.

Chapter-IV

Analysis and Interpretation of Data

Introduction

One of the important parts of any investigation is analysis and interpretation of data. The data collected in any field of activity becomes meaningful and useful only when there are subjected to statistical analysis and inference.

Analysis of data means studying the organized material in order to discover inherent facts. The data are studied from as many angles as possible explore the few facts. Once the research data have been collected data analysis has been made. Then the research interpreting is essentially needed to state whether the result shows the research data become meaningful after they are being analyzed and interpreted.

The analysis and interpretation of data involves the objective material in the possession of the research and his subjective reactions and desires to device from the data.

ANALYSIS OF DATA

Analysis of data mean studying the tabulated materials in orders to determine inherent fact of meaning. It involves the breaking down of the existing complex faders into simple parts and putting them together in a now arrangement for the purpose of interpretation.

According to Pearson, "Analysis is a research technique for objective, systematic and quantitative description of the manifest content of communication".

According to Prestly, "The discovery of order in the phenomena of nature, not withstanding their complexity and apparent confusion is rendered possible by process of analysis and synthesis which are foundation stone of all scientific methods".

After, collection the data from the respondents, the investigator gave frequencies for the correct responses and these frequencies were converted into scores and then investigator calculated the scores.

These scores were used to identify the level of "AWARNESS OF LEADERSHIP QUALITIES AMONG B.Ed TRAINEES IN PUDUKKOTTAI DISTRICT."

HYPOTHESES TESTING

Analysis is a technique of social research which presents qualitative data in an objective, systematic and quantitative.

The investigator also tests the significance to find out the significant difference between the various groups of demographic variables on "*Awareness of leadership qualities among B.Ed trainees in pudukkottai district*".

There is no significant difference in the Mean score of B.Ed trainees in the awareness of leadership qualities male and female trainees.

1. There is no significant difference in the awareness of Leadership qualities Mean score between Government College and Private College B.Ed trainees.
2. There is no significant difference in the Mean score of B.Ed trainees in the awareness of leadership qualities rural area and urban area B.Ed trainees.
3. There is no significant difference in the awareness of Leadership qualities Mean score between hosteller and Day scholarB.Ed trainees.
4. There is no significant difference in the awareness of Leadership qualities Mean Score between joint family and nuclear family B.Ed trainees.
5. There is no significant difference in the awareness of B.Ed trainee awareness of Leadership qualities on the basis of their parent's occupation.

6. There is no significant difference in the Mean Score of B.Ed trainees in the awareness of leadership qualities on the basis of their parent's educational qualification.
7. There is no significant difference in the Mean Score of B.Ed trainees in the awareness of leadership qualities on the basis of their annual income.

Hypothesis of the study

Null hypothesis; 1

The following research hypothesis has been formulated for the present study.

There is no significant difference in the awareness of leadership qualities Mean score between Male and female B.Ed trainees

Table 1

Gender	N	Mean	S.D	t-Value	Level of Significance 0.05 level
Male		120	73.58	18.50	
Female	180	74.89	19.17	0.59	Not Significant

Table value at 0.05 level for df=298

The above table reveals that the calculated t value (0.59) is lesser than the value 1.96 level of significance. It is found that there is no significant difference in the awareness of leadership qualities Mean scores between the Male and female trainees.

Therefore **Null hypothesis is Accepted.**

HYPOTHESIS: 2

There is no significant in the awareness of leadership qualities Mean Score between Government college and private Colleges B.Ed trainees.

Table 2

Type of institution	N	Mean	S.D	t-Value	Level of Significance 0.05 level
Government college	100	72.40	18.57		
Private college	200	76.42	19.67	1.73	Not Significant

Table value at 0.05 level for df=298

The above table reveals that the calculated t value (1.73) is lesser than the value 1.96 level of significance. It is found that there is no significant difference in the awareness of leadership qualities Mean scores between the Government colleges and private colleges.

Therefore **Null hypothesis is Accepted.**

HYPOTHESIS: 3

There is no significant in the awareness of leadership qualities mean Score Between Rural area and Urban area B.Ed trainees colleges.

Table 3

Locality	N	Mean	S.D	t-Value	Level of Significance at 0.05 level
Rural area	130	74.21	18.42	0.53	Not Significant
Urban area	170	75.31	17.12		

Table value at 0.05 level for df=298

The above table reveals that the calculated t value (0.53) is lesser than the value 1.96 level of significance. It is found that there is no significant difference in the awareness of leadership qualities Mean course between the Urban and Rural trainees. Therefore **Null hypothesis is accepted.**

HYPOTHESIS: 4

There is no significant in the awareness of leadership qualities Between Hosteller and Day scholar B.Ed trainees' colleges.

Table 4

Residency	N	Mean	S.D	t-Value	Level of Significance at 0.05 level
Hosteller	75	71.88	18.14		
Day scholar	225	73.21	19.97	0.53	Not Significant

Table value at 0.05 level for df=298

The above table reveals that the calculated t value (0.53) is lesser than the value 1.96 level of significance. It is found that there is no significant difference in the awareness of leadership qualities Mean Scores between the Hosteller and Days scholar trainees. Therefore **Null hypothesis is Accepted.**

HYPOTHESIS: 5

There is no significant in the awareness of leadership qualities Mean Score Between Nuclear family and joint family B.Ed trainees.

Table 5

Residency	N	Mean	S.D	t-Value	Level of Significance at 0.05 level
Nuclear family	139	75.82	18.57		
Joint family	161	73.62	17.82	1.05	Not Significant

Table value at 0.05 level for df=298

The above table reveals that the calculated t value (1.05) is lesser than the value 1.96 level of significance. It is found that there is no significant difference in the awareness of leadership qualities Mean score between the Nuclear family and joint family. Therefore **Null hypothesis is Accepted.**

HYPOTHESIS: 6

There is no significant in the awareness of leadership qualities Mean Score on the basis of their parent's occupation.

Table 6

Parent's occupation	N	Mean	S.D	t-Value	Level of Significance at 0.05 level
Government job	71	72.24	19.13		
Private job	229	74.32	17.72	0.82	Not Significant

Table value at 0.05 level for df=298

The above table reveals that the calculated 't' value (0.82) is lesser than the value 1.96 level of significance. It is found that there is no significant difference in the awareness of leadership qualities Mean score between the Government job and Private job. Therefore **Null hypothesis is Accepted.**

HYPOTHESIS: 7

There is no significant in the awareness of leadership qualities Mean Score Between Educated parents and Uneducated Parents B.Ed trainees colleges.

Table 7

Parent's occupation	N	Mean	S.D	t-Value	Level of Significance at 0.05 level
Parents education	N	Mean	S.D	t-Value	Level of Significance at 0.05 level
Educated parents	219	77.61	19.42		
Uneducated parents	81	75.22	18.12	0.99	Not Significant

Table value at 0.05 level for df=298

The above table reveals th*at* the calculated t value (0.99) is lesser than the value 1.96 level of significance. It is found that there is no significant difference in the awareness of leadership qualities Mean score between the Hosteller and Days scholar B.Ed trainees. Therefore **Null hypothesis is Accepted.**

HYPOTHESIS:8

There is no significant in the awareness of leadership qualities on the basis of their parent's income.

Table 8

Parent's income	N	Mean	S.D	t-Value at 0.05 level	Level of Significance
Above 50,000	70	76.77	18.87		
Below 50,000	230	78.25	20.14	0.56	Not Significant

Table value at 0.05 level for df=298

The above table reveals that the calculated t value (0.56) is lesser than the value 1.96 level of significance. It is found that there is no significant difference in the awareness of leadership qualities **on the basis of their parent's income.** Therefore **Null hypothesis is Accepted.**

CONCLUSION

In this chapter, the results of the statistical analysis and the interpretation have been presented. The summary of findings and suggestions are presented in the next chapter.

Chapter-V

Findings and Conclusion

Introduction

In the present investigation and attempt has been made to study the awareness of B.Ed trainees towards development of leadership qualities. This chapter details with findings of the statistical analysis and interpretation of the results. Suggestions further research also presented in this chapter.

Need for the study

The strength of educational system depends largely upon the quality of teachers. If the teacher is poor and ineffective, the entire edifice of education becomes shaky. The role of the teacher in the society is both significant and valuable. It has far-reaching influence on the society he lives in and no other personality can have an influence more profound than that of a teacher. Students are deeply affected by the teacher's love and affection, his character, his competence, and his moral commitment. A popular teacher becomes a model for his students. The students try to follow their teacher in his manners, costumes, etiquette, style of conversation and his get up.

Teacher's roles in the school

1. Mediator of learning.

2. Disciplinarian or controller of student's behavior.
3. Parent support.
4. Confidant to student.
5. Judge of achievement.
6. Organizer of curriculum.
7. Scholar and research specialist.
8. Member of teacher's organization

Teacher's roles in community

1. Public servant.
2. Expert in some areas of knowledge or skills.
3. Community leader.
4. Agent of social change.

Statement of the problem:

The present investigation entitled *"Awareness of Leadership qualities Among B.Ed trainees in pudukkottai district"*.

Objectives of the study

The study has the following objectives.

To study the awareness of Leadership Qualities among the B.Ed trainees in pudukkottai.

1. To find out whether there is significant difference in difference in the awareness of Mean Score between male and female B.Ed trainees.
2. To find out to whether there is significant difference in the awareness of Leadership Qualities Mean Score between Government College and Private College B.Ed trainees.
3. To find out if there is a significant difference in the awareness of Leadership Qualities Mean score between rural area and urban area B.Ed trainees.
4. To find out if there is a significant difference in the awareness of Leadership Qualities Mean score between Hosteller and Day scholar B.Ed trainees.

5. To find out if there is a significant difference in the awareness of Leadership Qualities Mean score between joint family and nuclear family B.Ed trainees.
6. To find out if there is a significant differs in their awareness of Leadership Qualities on the basis of their parent's occupation.
7. To find out if there is a significant differs in their awareness of Leadership Qualities on the basis of their parent's educational qualification.
8. To find out if there is a significant differs in their awareness of Leadership Qualities on the basis of their parent's annual income.

Findings of the study

From the results discussed in previous chapter the findings concerning the Awareness of leadership qualities among B.Ed trainees have been summarized as follows

I. Analysis of male and female trainees

The mean and deviation of the leadership qualities of Male and female B.Ed Trainees have shown that they are having high level of leadership Qualities.

II. Analysis of Government and private Institutions of B.Ed trainees.

The mean and deviation of the leadership qualities of Government and private Institutions B.Ed Trainees have shown that they are having high level of leadership Qualities.

III. Analysis of Rural area and urban area locality of B.Ed trainees.

The mean and deviation of the leadership qualities of Rural and Urban locality B.Ed Trainees have shown that they are having high level of leadership Qualities.

IV. Analysis of Hosteller and Days Scholar residency in B.Ed trainees.

The mean and deviation of the leadership qualities of Hosteller and Days Scholar Residency B.Ed Trainees have shown that they are having high level of leadership Qualities.

V. Analysis of Nuclear family and joint family type in B.Ed trainees.

The mean and deviation of the leadership qualities of Nuclear family and joint family type B.Ed Trainees have shown that they are having high level of leadership Qualities.

VI. Analysis of on the basis of parents occupation of B.Ed trainees.

The mean and deviation of the leadership qualities on the basis of their parent's occupation B.Ed Trainees have shown that they are having high level of leadership Qualities.

VII. Analysis of on the basis of parent's Educational qualification of B.Ed trainees.

The mean and deviation of the leadership qualities on the basis of parent's Educational qualification B.Ed Trainees have shown that they are having high level of leadership Qualities.

VIII. Analysis of on the basis of parent's annual income of B.Ed trainees.

The mean and deviation of the leadership qualities on the basis of parent's annual income B.Ed Trainees have shown that they are having high level of leadership Qualities.

SUGGESTIONS FOR FURTHER RESEACH

1. A study awareness of leadership qualities of D.T.Ed., students may be taken.
2. A study awareness of leadership qualities of B.E/ M.B.B.S students may be taken.
3. A study awareness of leadership qualities of School teachers may be taken.

Recommendation of the study

The function of leadership include stating basic values, announcing goals, organizing resources, reducing tensions between individuals, creating coalitions, coalescing workers and encouraging better performance.

Teacher trainees need a sense of how the organization works and how the actions of each individual affect organizational and strategic objectives. Qualities in determining the forces and factors that interface with organizations ability to accomplish its tasks can help the workers become a master problem solver, an innovator, and a team builder. So the teacher trainees must awareness of leadership qualities they can achieve high position in their life.

CONCLUSION

Learning to be effective must bring some behavioral changes in the student as she progress through Teacher education. Educators in the past where primarily interested in measuring the final achievements of students based on the result of test scores. But evaluation is not a quantitative aspect alone; it includes both quantitative and qualitative aspect of pupil's progress. Therefore, it should be a continuous process and it should concern more than the formal academic achievement of students.

BIBLIOGRAPHY

1. Aggarwal, J.C (1992). Teaching social studies a practical approach. New Delhi: Publishing Pvt. Ltd.
2. Aggarwal, J.c(2001). Basic Ideas in Education. New Delhi: Shipra Publications.
3. Bass, B.M. (1985). Leadership and Performance beyond Expectations. New York: Free Press.
4. Bernie Trilling, Charles Fadel.C.(2009). 21st century Skills. New York: John Willey & Sons Publisher.
5. Best, J.W. and Kahn, J.V(1999). Reserch in Education 7th ed. New Delhi: Prentice Hal of India.
6. Buch. M.B(Ed.) (1987). Third Survey of Research in Education 7th ed. New Delhi: NCERT.
7. Buch. M.B(Ed.) (1991) Fourth Survey of Research in Eduation 1978 – 83 New Delhi; NCERT.
8. Chemers. M. (1997). An Integrative theory of Leadership, Lawrence Erlbaum Associates Publishers.
9. Daniel, J.T.K (1990). Value Education Today. New Delhi: AIACHE.
10. Elahi,N. (1997). Teacher Education in India. New Delhi: Aph Publishing Corporation.
11. Good, C.V (1973). Dictionary of Education 3rd ed. New York: McGraw Hill Book Company.
12. Good, C.V (1973). The methodology of Educational Research. New York: D. Appletor Century co.
13. Lussier, R.N. & Achua, C.F (2010). Leadership Theory, Application, & skill Development (4th ed.), mason. OH.
14. Montana, Patrik, J., Bruce, H. (2008). Management, Hauppange, New York: Barron's Educational series, Inc.
15. National Council for Educational and Training(2000). Fifth Survey of Educational Research 1988-92 Abstracts Volume I&II, New Delhi: NCERT.

16. Page, G.T. et al. (1987). Effective Human Relations in Organizations 6th ed. Chennai: All India Publishers & Distributors Regd.

17. Spencer, Herbert. (1841). The Study of Sociology, New York: D.A Apploton.

18. Tittemore, James. A. (2003). Leadership at all levels. Canada: Boskwa Publishing.

6. Awareness on Moral Development

Chapter - I

INTRODUCTION

Education is the systematic training of the young children in schools; it is the inherent right of children early in their lives. Education is all forms of human learning; more specifically it is the process performed in specialized institutions called schools. It has often been thought, that people from different national, social, ethnic, religious and linguistic background can be encouraged to adopt a common outlook on life through a common schooling experience.

Education in general is expected to make people understand the values of life so that they can promote equality and social justice in a democracy. Education means both the acquisition of skills, habits and attitudes which help a person to lead a full and worthwhile life in this worldly. The work of education is to make the child become aware of its inner powers.

Education is the basic condition for the development of the whole man and vital instrument for accelerating the well being and prosperity of all in every direction.

Mahatma Gandhi says, “Education draws out the best in the child and man, body, mind and spirit”. Individual education helps in the building of the personality through his physical, intellectual and moral development.

Education instills in the child a sense of maturity and responsibility by bringing in him the desired changes according to his needs and demands of ever changing society of which he is an integral part. Education is a powerful and pervasive agent of change. It is the key that unlocks the door to development and modernization.

MEANING OF EDUCATION

The act or process of education and the result of education, as determined by the knowledge, skill or discipline of character is acquired and the process is unending. The act or process or training by prescribed or customary course of study or discipline-as, an education for the bar or the pulpit-has a finishing point and we say the student has finished his education.

The Destiny of India is now being shaped in her classrooms **(Kothari - 1966).** Education is the most essential human value. Knowledge is developed through literacy and education.

DEFINITION OF EDUCATION

J.C. AGGARWAL (1987), Education aims to seek and cultivate new knowledge, to engage vigorously and fearlessly in the pursuit of truth and to interpret old knowledge and benefits in the light of new needs and discoveries.

JOHN DEWEY writes the Education is the process of living through a continuous reconstruction of experience. It is the development of all these capacities in the individual, which will enable him to control his environment and fulfill his responsibilities.

THE VIRUS THAT CAUSES AIDS

HIV belongs to a family of viruses known as retroviruses. These viruses defy a general rule of biological systems whereby the genetic commandments flow from the master molecule deoxyribo nucleic acid (DNA) to ribonucleic acid (RNA) which results In the production of proteins that keeps the system working HIV, like all retroviruses, has an enzyme called reverse transcriptase, which actually reverses this emetic hierarchy and enables RNA to direct the synthesis of DNA first. Currently, it is best recognized as a family of closely related viruses, the commonest of them being HIV-I **a** distinctly form of HIV is common In West Africa It is called HIV-11.

BASIC INFORMATION ON HIV

AIDS is a condition that gradually destroys the body's immune defense system and makes the body vulnerable to opportunistic diseases. It is caused by infection with the Human Immunodeficiency Virus (HIV). The virus is spread when HIV infected fluids of one person pass into the body of another person. Infection can occur through unprotected sex (anal, vaginal, or oral) through use of contaminated needles, syringes and other piercing.

After HIV invades the body, it lives and multiplies in the white blood cells, which are the cells that protect the body from disease. As the virus multiplies, it damages or kills these and other cells, and the body becomes prey to a wide range of disease causing microbes. When HIV has destroyed enough white blood cells, the body is no longer able to fight off many infections, and a person begins to get sick. If the white blood cells don't die in HIV infected person, that person feels fine and looks fine. That person is asymptomatic (that is, has no symptoms of AIDS), but can still give the virus to someone else. People who are infected with HIV can be asymptomatic, looking and feeling well for ten years or even longer.

That is why the practice of safer sex is vitally important, even with people who seem to be well. As more and more white cells die, the HIV infected person begins to get sick and is then said to be symptomatic. When there are very few white cells left, particularly of the kind called CD4+ and one or more serious diseases start occurring, the HIV infected person has AIDS.

MODE OF TRANSMISSION OF HIV/AIDS

There are two primary ways a person can become infected. HIV/AIDS is most frequently passed through sexual intercourse with an infected person. Unfortunately, it is not the only disease passed in this manner. If a person has one of the other sexually transmitted diseases, they are at greater danger of contracting HIV. The HIV virus is present in some body fluids and can enter the body through contact with mucus membranes or cuts on the body.

Many people infected with the virus show no symptoms and often have not been tested. The most predominant reason for not being tested, in almost one-fourth of the population, is that they are afraid of a positive test. That's why it is so dangerous for people to have unsafe sex. The one and only way to be absolutely certain of avoiding infection via sexual contact is through abstinence from sex or sexual intercourse only with someone who has been tested and has not engaged in risky sexual behaviors in the past six months and is in a mutually committed relationship.

HIV/AIDS is also spread by sharing needles. Sharing needles with an infected person, even once, it is very risky. Many people have become infected with HIV and other germs this way. HIV from an infected person can remain in a needle or syringe and can then be directly injected into the body of the next person who uses it. Sharing any needles, including needles used for drugs, steroids, vitamins, ear piercing, or tattooing, is very dangerous.

One other mode of transmission is through blood or blood products. This mode of transmission is so rare these days that it is often not even counted as a possibility. Blood donors today are very carefully screened before they can even donate, and once they donate, all blood products are tested before they are used. One very important thing to remember is that one who is donating blood, is in no danger of contracting HIV/ AIDS because the needles are used only once, then they are destroyed.

CHARACTERISTICS OF HIV VIRUS THAT CAUSES AIDS

In the early stages, a mild flu and swollen glands are typical. But the symptoms are often unmistakable when full-blown AIDS develops. Loss of appetite, weight loss, constant fever, prolonged fatigue, diarrhea, constipation, changing bowel patterns, swollen glands, chills coupled with excessive sweating especially at nights, lesions in the mouth, sore throat, persistent cough, shortness of breath, tumors, skin rashes, headaches, memory lapses, swelling in the joints, pain in various parts of the body, vision problems and a regular feeling of lethargy and ill health make up the litany of symptoms. With immune systems out of kilter, HIV-positive persons are susceptible to several types of cancer, particularly Kaposi's Sarcoma (KS), an uncommon form that occurs under the skin and in the mucus membranes of the eyes, nose and mouth. Affected persons have lesions that appear as dark-colored raised blotches. Though the lesions are painless, once KS spreads to the lungs, lymph nodes and digestive tract, the victim experiences difficulty in breathing, gastrointestinal bleeding and painful swelling around the lymph nodes, especially in the legs.

PREVENTIVE MEASURES AND POST CARE OF HIV/AIDS

It can affect anyone male or female, married or single, young or old, rich or poor, in any community in the Nation, including those in smaller cities and towns. This makes HIV/AIDS a problem for all of us, heterosexual or homosexual.

AVOIDING HIV INFECTION

1. Delay sexual intercourse. Abstinence is the only sure protection.
2. Don't do drugs of any kind.
3. If sexual intercourse outside of a mutually exclusive relationship is chosen, use a latex condom and nonoxynol-9, according to package directions, each and every time, but remember that condoms are not fool proof.

PERINATAL (MOTHER-TO-CHILD) TRANSMISSION

Transmission of HIV from mother to baby during pregnancy, at birth or through breast-feeding. Also sometimes referred to as vertical transmission. Ninety percent of children reported with AIDS acquired HIV infection from their HIV-infected mothers. Sexually Transmitted Infection. It is also called venereal disease, an older public health term, or sexually transmitted diseases. Sexually transmitted infections are spread by the transfer of organisms from person to person during sexual contact. The complexity and scope of STIs have increased dramatically; more than 20 organisms and syndromes are now recognized as belonging to this category.

PREVENTION OF HIV VIRUS

No border can keep AIDS out, it cut across the entire time zones limit divide us. We owe ourselves and to others to develop the utmost commitment to act against AIDS on a global scale, and especially where the scourge is most prevalent. AIDS is a disorder characterized by severe suppression of the immune system of the body.

This immune deficiency renders the body susceptible to a variety of normally manageable Infections, cancers, and other diseases. HIV is spread through body fluids, such as blood and semen. The virus 15 most often spread through sexual contact It may also be spread through dirty syringes and needles such as those used by users of illegal drugs Social factors known to promote the rapid spread of the HIVIAIDS epidemic Include poverty, discrimination, sexual inequality, and inadequate health or social services. Although these conditions exist to varying degrees in every region of the globe, they are more prevalent in certain areas, resulting in increased numbers of HIV infections. As HIVIAIDS continues to spread, there has been an increasing impact on individuals, households, communities, and societies Both HIV infected and non-~infected people are affected, by the complicated social and economic consequences of the disease UNPA 1s supporting Lads prevention in most of its African family planning programs and also in some programs in Asia and the Caribbean. In addition, UNFPA supports separate AIDS communication programs in a number of African countries. Also, UNFPA 1s working closely with the WHOIGPA and within atonal AIDS committees to link AIDS prevention acclivities with family planning and maternal and child health activities.

No single strategy against AIDS can work everywhere; the approach In each country should reflect the epidemiological patterns of the infection." Nevertheless, because most HIV infections occurS adolescence, focusing on young people appears to be a crucial strategy. Another reason to focus prevention efforts on students that HIV-positive youth, because they were recently infected, is highly infectious. HIV is most Infectious when viral loads in the blood are high, resulting In HIV shedding in many body fluids normally, there are two such periods: the first period, the primary infection, occurs immediately after the HIV infection, and lasts only a few months the second period is at the end, when the HIV infection progresses to AIDS.

Preventing HIV infection among students also would help reduce the mounting cost of treatment, freeing resources that could help meet the other needs of young people For instance, in India the cost of tracing one AIDS patient for one year, even without expensive therapies, equals the annual cost of providing primary school students".

HUMAN IMMUNO VIRUS ANDS AIDS

HIV/AIDS presents major challenges to human survival, human rights and human development with implications far beyond the health sector. The social and economic consequences of the epidemic are perhaps one of the most serious threats to sustainable human development.

As on today, millions of Indians have been diagnosed with AIDS, millions have died. In less than 15 years, AIDS has become the principal killer of all Indians between the ages of 15 and 49. It has also been found recently that Indians do not have genetic protection against the AIDS virus compared to other groups, especially the southern population. This means that they get infected more easily compared to other groups. Since the epidemic began, an estimated 20 million people worldwide have been infected with HIV, the virus that causes AIDS.

People infected with HIV are our friends and neighbors, they are people in our offices and schools, temples, churches and mosques. They are our children, our parents, our brothers and sisters. They live in every state and Community in our Nation. Everyone needs to know about AIDS because it waits at everyone's door. Each of us must learn how to prevent infection with HIV, how to support the people around us who are HIV-infected, and how to make sure that our National, State, and Local Governments deal sensibly with this insidious disease. Hiding behind the veils of cultural superiority or karma is not an option. AIDS is a sexually transmitted disease and has to be tackled accordingly. HIV/AIDS is one of the fourteen major communicable diseases that affect the population in India.

The government has formulated the national aids prevention and control policy with the objectives and goals:

1. To prevent the spread of HIV infection and reduce any adverse economic and social impact.

2. To generate a feeling of ownership among all the participants at government and non-government levels to make it a national effort.

3. To create an active socio-economic environment for prevention of HIV/AIDS.

The policy also aims at providing care and support to people living with HIV/AIDS and to ensure protection/promotion of their human rights. Efforts are also being made at promoting better understanding of HIV infection among people, especially students, students and other sexually active sections to generate greater awareness about the nature of its transmission and to adopt safe behavioral practices for prevention. The probable mode of transmission among the reported number of AIDS cases has been observed to be sexual mode of transmission, transmission from mother to child, blood & blood products and Injecting drug users.

Vulnerability of Women/Girls: There are number of factors such as biological, socio-cultural and economic, which make women and young girls more vulnerable to HIV. The major source of infection is through heterosexual transmission and as compared to men. Women are at a biological disadvantage in controlling the infection. HIV is more easily transmitted from men to women than women to men. Infect, gender inequality and poverty are responsible for the spread as well as disproportionate impact of HIV/AIDS on women.

HIV/AIDS AWARENESS AND PREVENTION EDUCATION

HIV/AIDS awareness and prevention education means to promote health and prevent disease by providing the knowledge, the skills and the means to foster and sustain behavior that reduces risks, improves care and lessens the impact of illness (UNICEF, 2003). Keeping children HIV-negative is vital to future generations, but this is impossible unless they understand how the virus is transmitted and how to protect themselves. Children must be educated about HIV/AIDS and taught skills that translate this knowledge into action, negotiation, conflict resolution, critical thinking, decision-making and communication.

These skills improve children's self-confidence and ability to make informed choices such as postponing sex until they are mature enough to protect themselves from HIV. HIV/AIDS awareness and prevention education should be done during early adolescence (ages 10 to 14), because studies have shown that this is the best time to establish enduring patterns of healthy behavior. Increased HIV awareness and prevention could save 29 million people from infection by 2010 and bring down HIV infection rates among young people by a quarter (UNICEF, 2003).

HIV/AIDS EDUCATION

The expansion and improvement of HIV/AIDS education around the world is critical in preventing the spread of HIV. There are, an estimated

33.3 million people living with the virus, and each year millions more people becomes infected. Effective HIV/AIDS education can help, in preventing these new infections by providing people with information about HIV and how it is passed on, and in doing so equipping individuals with the knowledge to protect themselves from becoming infected with the virus.

HIV/AIDS education also plays a vital role in reducing stigma and discrimination. Around the world, it is caused to be a great deal of fear and stigmatization of people living with HIV, which is fuelled by misunderstanding and misinformation. This not only has a negative impact on people living with HIV, but can also fuel the spread of HIV by discouraging people from seeking test and treatment.

HIV/AIDS EDUCATION FOR YOUTH

Students are especially vulnerable to HIV and other sexually transmitted diseases (STDs). They are also vulnerable as regards drug use (and not just injected drugs). Even if they are not engaging in risk behaviors today, they may soon be exposed to situations that put them at risk. In many countries 60% of all new HIV infections are among 15- 24 years old. Also the highest rates of STDs are usually found in the age range 20-24 years, followed by 15-19 years.

It is commonly supposed that talking to young people about sex will make them do it. Such anxieties prevent many teachers, students and parents from talking about sexual matters. Alternatively, they may encourage an over-emphasis on the negative aspects of sex: unwanted pregnancy, sexually transmitted diseases, AIDS rather than positive aspects such as intimacy, sexual love and pleasure. Likewise when drugs are taken about the emphasis is often on the damage they can cause.

This kind of unbalanced approach is often seen through by young people. In consequence, they may reject all that adults have to say, seeking guidance and role models from peers and from the media. Contrary to what might popularly be believed, research looking at the effects of sex education on youth's sexual behavior offers little evidence that it hastens the onset of sexual experience, or increases sexual risk among those who are already sexually active. Indeed, several studies from different countries show that good quality of sex education can actually decrease the likelihood that young people will have sex and increase using condoms among those who are already sexually active. AIDS education for young people plays a vital role in global efforts to end the AIDS epidemic.

Despite the fact that HIV transmission can be prevented, every year hundreds of thousands of young people who infected with the virus. In 2009 alone, there were 8,90,000 new HIV infection amongst young people aged 15-24. Providing young people with the basic AIDS education enables them to protect themselves from becoming infected. Young people are often particularly vulnerable to sexually transmitted HIV, and to HIV infection as a result of drug usage. Acquiring knowledge and skills encourage young people to avoid or reduce behaviors that carry a risk of HIV infection. Even for young people who are not yet engaging in risky behaviors, AIDS education is important for ensuring that they are prepared for situations that will put them at risk as they grow older.

AIDS education also helps to reduce stigma and discrimination, by dispelling false information that can lead to fear and blame. This is crucial for prevention, as stigma often makes people reluctant, to be tested for HIV. Somebody who is not aware of his/her HIV infection is more likely to pass the virus to others. AIDS education can help to prevent this, halting stigma and discrimination before they have an opportunity to grow. Educating young people about HIV/AIDS is necessary to discuss about sensitive subjects such as sex and drug use. Many people believe that it is inappropriate to talk to young people about these subjects and fear that doing so will encourage young people to indulge in risky behaviors. Such attitudes are often based on moral or religious views rather than evidence, and severely limit AIDS education around the world. Substantial evidence shows that educating young people about safer sex and the importance of using condoms does not lead to increase in sexual activity.

In order to prevent becoming infected with HIV, young people need comprehensive information about how HIV is transmitted and what they can do to stop themselves from becoming infected. This information should be delivered without moral judgment.

IMPORTANCE OF HIV/AIDS EDUCATION IN PREVENTING HIV/AIDS

Each year there are many new HIV infections, which show that people either aren't learning the message about the dangers of HIV, or unable or unwilling to act on it. Many people are dangerously ignorant about the virus. Education has a key role to play both in preventing HIV/AIDS and in mitigating its effects on individuals, families, communities and society. As the disease has affected people from every nook and corner of the world without any age or gender parity, it is essential that HIV/AID education ought to be aimed at all parts of society, not only those groups who are seen as being particularly high-risk.

Even if education were completely successful, it would still have to be an ongoing process, to each generation, a new generation of people become adult and need to know how to protect themselves from infection. The older generations, who have hopefully already been educated, may need the message reinforced, and need to be kept informed, so that they are able to protect themselves and inform the younger.

There are three main reasons for AIDS education, the first of which is to prevent new infections from taking place. This can be seen as consisting of two processes. Giving people information about HIV, what HIV and AIDS are, how they are transmitted, and how people can protect themselves from infection. Teaching people how to put this information to use and act on it practically, how to get and use condoms, how to suggest and practice safer sex, how to prevent infection in a medical environment or when injecting drugs.

A second reason is that AIDS education is needed to improve quality of life for HIV positive people. Too often, AIDS education is seen as being something which should be targeted only at people who are not infected with HIV in order to prevent them from becoming infected. When AIDS education with HIV positive people is considered at all it is frequently seen only in terms of preventing new infections by teaching HIV positive people about the importance of not passing on the virus. An important and commonly neglected aspect of AIDS education with HIV positive people is enabling and empowering them to improve their quality of life. HIV positive people have varying educational needs, but among them are the need to be able to access medical services and drug provision and they need to be able to find appropriate emotional and practical support and help.

The third reason people need AIDS education to reduce stigma and discrimination. In many countries there is a great deal of fear and stigmatization of people who are HIV positive. This fear is too often accompanied by ignorance, resentment and ultimately anger. Sometimes the results of prejudice and fear can be extreme, with HIV positive people being burned to death in India, and many families being forced to leave their homes across the United States when neighbors discover a family member's positive status. Discrimination against positive people can help the AIDS epidemic to spread if people are fearful of being tested for HIV, then they are more likely to pass the infection to someone else without knowing.

HIV / AIDS EDUCATION IN SCHOOLS

Schools play a pivotal role in providing AIDS education for young people. Not only do schools have the capacity to reach a large number of young people, but school students are particularly receptive to learning new information. Therefore schools are a well established point of contact through which young people can receive AIDS education. The most common place for people to learn about HIV / AIDS is at school. Due to their capacity and universality, schools are a crucial setting for educating young people about AIDS. As young people are at a high risk of becoming infected with HIV, it is vital that they are educated about HIV transmission before they are exposed to situations that put them at risk of HIV infection. Schools play a major role in shaping the attitudes, opinions and behavior of young people and also ideal environments for teaching the social as well as the biological aspects of HIV/AIDS.

Members of the wider community can also increase their knowledge about HIV/AIDS through the school environment. Teachers who expand their understanding of the subject while planning lessons and receiving teacher training can pass this information on to adults as well as pupils, and the same can be said for children themselves, once informed about AIDS, they can tell their parents or their friends what they have learned.

At the same time, in many countries HIV/AIDS are significantly weakening the capacity of the education sector, and greater investment in education is vital for the provision of effective HIV prevention for young people.

A UNESCO study found that in Eastern and Southern Africa, children had 'low levels of knowledge' regarding HIV/AIDS which was attributed to, among other factors, lack of teacher training, lack of examination for students on the topic and unfruitful teaching the subject resulting from embarrassment.

It is widely recognized that the best approaches to sex and drug education in schools are broad based and have several components. These include the provision of factual information about biology, sexual development, and sexual and drug-related risks, a concern with personal relationships, feelings and values, an emphasis on the acquisition of relevant negotiation skills and a consideration of wider social pressures and cultural expectations. Successful sex education programmes have several key qualities.

These include the provision of information, exercises to encourage an appraisal of values, and role play rehearsal to teach sexual negotiation skills. Programmes that aim to reduce specific sexual risk-taking behaviours and which reinforce group norms against unprotected sex and discuss social pressures to have unprotected sexual activity have been shown to be particularly successful.

School curricula with these qualities have been shown significantly to reduce the likelihood that students who have not had sex prior to their exposure to the curriculum will have had unprotected sexual intercourse eighteen months later find out more information about sex education that works.

HIV/AIDS EDUCATION OUTSIDE OF SCHOOL

Although offering AIDS education at school is a principal method of reaching large numbers of young people, there are 75 million children around the world who are either unable to go to school or choose not to. In order to ensure that all young people are reached with basic AIDS education, programmes that target young people outside of schools are essential. Young people who are in school also benefit from receiving further information about HIV/AIDS from other sources, adding to and reinforcing what they learn in school. Families, friends, the wider community, mass media and popular culture all influence young people, and it is important that they convey accurate educational information about HIV/AIDS.

METHODS OF HIV/AIDS EDUCATION TO EDUCATE THE PUBLIC

There are a great variety of methods and materials that can be used to educate people about HIV/AIDS, including radio & television, booklets, billboards, street theatre, comic strips, and many more. The form in which HIV/AIDS education should be delivered, depends on the characteristics of those who are being educated. In order to reach the target group, it needs to be considered which environments, they will be most receptive in, and what media is most relevant to them. The Media Using the media is a powerful way of reaching large numbers of young people with HIV/AIDS information and prevention messages. Many countries have tried some forms of AIDS education advertisements, films, or announcements. The mass media has played a central role in many countries responses to AIDS since the very early days of the epidemic.

HIV/AIDS education can also have the detrimental effect of increasing stigma and discrimination towards people living with HIV. Some media messages try to change people's behavior by making the audience afraid of the consequences of becoming infected with HIV. This not only has the potential of making the target audience afraid of people infected with HIV but also carries the risk of portraying HIV positive people as at fault for becoming infected.

Media based HIV/AIDS education can be particularly harmful when targeted at specific risk groups, such as men who have sex with men or injecting drug users. Not only can this fuel stigmatization of these groups, but it can also hinder HIV prevention. By not representing the broad face of the epidemic, and instead focusing on risks to specific groups, the media encourages the attitude that AIDS is 'somebody else's problem' and that if you are not part of a risk group you don't need to worry about HIV/AIDS.

PEER EDUCATION

It is not just teachers who can provide education people's knowledge about HIV/AIDS can be influenced by a variety of different people, including family, friends, and the wider community. Peer education is education provided by somebody who is either directly part of the group receiving the information, or who is from a similar social background.

Peer education is a less formal method of educating, which can be more accessible to people who are not used to or dislike a formal classroom environment. At the same time, peer educators are trained on the subject, ensuring that the information they provide is accurate and reliable. This makes peer education a very effective way of reaching marginalized groups.

Peer education is the process by which a group is given information by someone who is a member of the same group or community, and who has already been trained in the subject. Peer education programmes are important for HIV prevention, as they are a cost-effective means of influencing the knowledge and attitudes of young people.

Young people are strongly influenced by the attitudes and actions of others in their age, and for many young people much of their existing knowledge of sex and HIV is based on information they have received from friends. This information can often be distorted. Peer education harnesses this method of sharing knowledge to convey accurate information about HIV/AIDS to young people.

In Asia, where the HIV epidemic is concentrated among high risk groups including sex workers, IDUs and MSM, more than nine out of ten young people infected with HIV are part of at least one of these groups. Yet, resources for HIV prevention amongst young people in this region have not been found to be targeted towards young people within high risk groups.

ACTIVE LEARNING

Active learning approaches are widely considered to be the most effective way for young people to learn health related and social skills. Furthermore, active learning offers an opportunity to make AIDS education lessons fun. AIDS education classes can be constructed to involve quizzes, games or drama.

CURRICULUM

When planning on AIDS education or curriculum, it is important to be aware of local guidelines, as many places have legislation that dictates what sex or AIDS education can or should be given. Local cultures also need to be taken into consideration, as views between cultures differ on issues that are a necessary part of AIDS education. The best place to start when planning AIDS education for young people is to talk to the young people themselves. Allowing learners to ask questions and encouraging their input will enable young people to express what they want from their AIDS education. Speaking to class also ensures that educators are aware of the current knowledge of the students. So that AIDS education can be more effectively targeted towards areas of informational need.

HIV/AIDS IN INDIA

There has been a rapid and uncontrolled expansion of HIV in the developing countries during the last two decades. HIV has become a serious problem for India with one of the highest rates of spread in the world. The picture in India today has a lot of similarities with the progress of HIV in Africa 15 years ago. Many features contribute to India's vulnerability concerning the transmission of HIV. India is a low income country with a large and young population, low educational and literacy rate and an increasing level of urbanization. Another contributory factor to the rapid spread of the HIV epidemic is lack of adequate knowledge about the disease among the people.

In 2006 UNAIDS estimated that there were 5.6 million people living with HIV in India, which indicated that there were more people with HIV in India than in any other country in the world. In 2007, following the first survey of HIV among the general population, UNAIDS and NACO agreed on a new estimate between 2 million and 3.1 million people living with HIV. In 2008 the figure was estimated to be 2.31 million. In 2009 it was estimated that 2.4 million people were living with HIV in India, which equates to a prevalence of 0.3%. While this may see low, because India's population is so large, it is third in the world in terms of greatest number of people living with HIV.

With a population of around a billion, a mere 0.1% increase in HIV prevalence would increase the estimated number of people living with HIV by over half a million. Though it is important to mention that there isn't one epidemic in India, rather there are many localized sub-epidemics due to the great variety on socio- cultural patterns and much vulnerability in India. Six states in India; Andhra Pradesh, Karnataka, Maharashtra, Manipur, Nagaland and Tamil Nadu have the highest incidence of HIV in the country (80% of the estimated HIV cases in India).

About 85% of the HIV infections in India are transmitted through heterosexual contacts and 15% through other ways such as injecting drugs (2.2%), blood transfusions (2.6%) and prenatal transmission (2.2%). In Manipur and Nagaland injecting drug use is the main mode of transmission. Young people are at high risk of getting infected by HIV. Consequently most of the HIV cases in India are found in the age group 15-24 years (35%). The main course of transmission among young people is through unprotected sexual contacts. Poor and unemployed students and street children are at a higher risk of getting infected due to low education and difficulties in getting access to prevention services. Many of them are exposed to HIV through sexual abuse or while selling sex for survival. In Andhra Pradesh, Karnataka, Maharashtra and Tamil Nadu more than 50% of the sex workers are infected with HIV. According to the latest report from UNAIDS, the HIV epidemic in high prevalence states is spreading from urban to rural areas and from high risk groups to the general population.

AIDS EDUCATION FOR STUDENTS IN INDIA

In India, where young people represent a large proportion of the country's population, an estimated 2.27 million people are living with HIV. In phase II of the country's National AIDS Control Programme, the Adolescent Education Programme (AEP) was launched. The programme aimed to train teachers and peer groups to educate the student community both in and out of school about life skills, HIV prevention and HIV related stigma and discrimination. Under the initiative 1,12,000 schools were covered and 2,88,000 teachers were trained. However, there is a discrepancy between the large amount of effort invested in HIV/AIDS curricula and training packages on a national level, and the lack of actual education being carried out in many schools. In the states of the country where there is a relatively low HIV prevalence, officials have been reluctant to encourage AIDS education, claiming that the problem is not significant enough in these areas to warrant a widespread educational response. In reality, it is crucial that young people learn about AIDS in areas with a low prevalence so that the prevalence stays low. In 2007 it was reported that a number of states had decided not to implement the Adolescence Education Programme in its present form, rejecting the material that had been supplied. Many young people cross India are still not receiving information about HIV.

AIDS CONTROL PROGRAMS IN INDIA

Soon after the first HIV/AIDS cases been reported in India in 1986, the Government of India initiated important measures to attack the epidemic. Pilot screening of high risk population started and a National AIDS Committee was immediately constituted by the Ministry of Health & family Welfare. In 987 a National AIDS Control Programmed was started. The National AIDS Committee was formed to bring together different ministries, private institutions and Non-Government organizations for effective collaboration in accomplishing the program. The Committee provides overall policy directions and controls the performance of the program.

To strengthen the AIDS programs at the state level, the state government has own organizations and committees. These take the policy decisions for implementation of the HIV/AIDS control program and make guidelines and plans in the respective states. NACO was established by the Government of India in 1992 and the organization is trying to reach the young people through different special programs. One of them is school

AIDS Education Programme which focuses on improving HIV awareness, helping young people to refrain from risk behaviors and instant develop a safe lifestyle. The program is running by the teachers in the school using the special module "Learning for life". Another program is The Universities talk AIDS Project for college students. This program is not only dealing with HIV/AIDS but also questions regarding relationships, marriage, sexuality and drugs. This programme is carried through with the help of seminars and workshops. It is estimated that this programme has reached over 7 million young people in India since the start in 1991. This is also a program meant for the out of school students in the rural areas called the villages Talk AIDS programme. This is a very important program since up to 100 million young people (10-25 years) are out of schools in India.

NEED OF THE STUDY

In the new millennium the world is undergoing many major transformations which may affect the lives of human beings. Almost daily, newspapers and magazines report about the impact of HIV and related problems.

The era of liberalization and globalization has been forcing people to confront many challenges. Though many studies have been done on this aspect, only a few studies have been undertaken on the aspect Awareness on the HIV Virus among the Higher Secondary Students.

According to WHO estimates, many people's had been Infected with HIV since the start of the epidemic Every day, more than 7000 adults and 500 babies are infected More than ***8*** million people have developed AIDS and the students In particular of the world are at ask due to the HIV.

This study aims at finding out whether in this Awareness on the HIV Virus among the Higher Secondary Students in particular. Therefore, this study was conducted to evaluate the Awareness on the HIV Virus among the Higher Secondary Students.

SCOPE OF THE STUDY

This study IS an earnest attempt to describe the awareness of the **HIV** virus, the way it enters the human immune system, ways to control it etc., A brief history of the origin, theory, preventive measures, ethical issues, economic and social Impacts etc. have been presented to provide a clear perception.

This study 1s a humble contribution in the direction of creating awareness towards the HIV Virus awareness, it attempts to examine the effects of awareness programmes on HIV, review the earlier studies made in this area, and to provide suggestions regarding the control measures.

STATEMENT OF THE PROBLEM

The purpose of the study is entitled as *"Awareness on the HIV Virus among the Higher Secondary Students in Pudukkottai District"*.

OBJECTIVES OF THE STUDY

The following are the general and specific objectives framed for the study;

1. To find the significant difference in the mean scores of awareness on the HIV virus among the higher secondary students in terms of their Gender.
2. To find the significant difference in the mean scores of awareness on the HIV virus among the higher secondary students in terms of their Locality.
3. To find the significant difference in the mean scores of awareness on the HIV virus among the higher secondary students in terms of their School management as Government and Aided.
4. To find the significant difference in the mean scores of awareness on the HIV virus among the higher secondary students in terms of their School management as Aided and Private.
5. There is no significant difference in the mean scores of awareness on the HIV virus among the higher secondary students in terms of their School management as Private and Government.
6. To find the significant difference in the mean scores of awareness on the HIV virus among the higher secondary students in terms of their School nature as Boy's and Girl's.
7. To find the significant difference in the mean scores of awareness on the HIV virus among the higher secondary students in terms of their School nature as Girl's and Co-education.
8. There is no significant difference in the mean scores of awareness on the HIV virus among the higher secondary students in terms of their School nature as Co-education and Boy's.
9. To find the significant difference in the mean scores of awareness on the HIV virus among the higher secondary students in terms of their Medium of study as Tamil and English.
10. To find the significant difference in the mean scores of awareness on the HIV virus among the higher secondary students in terms of their Family nature as Nuclear and Joint type.

11. To find the significant difference in the mean scores of awareness on the HIV virus among the higher secondary students in terms of their Parent education level as Schooling and Higher Education.
12. To find the significant difference in the mean scores of awareness on the HIV virus among the higher secondary students in terms of their Parent occupation as Government and Private Job.

HYPOTHESES OF THE STUDY

The following are the hypotheses constructed for the study

1. There is no significant difference in the mean scores of awareness on the HIV virus among the higher secondary students in terms of their Gender.
2. There is no significant difference in the mean scores of awareness on the HIV virus among the higher secondary students in terms of their Locality.
3. There is no significant difference in the mean scores of awareness on the HIV virus among the higher secondary students in terms of their School management as Government and Aided.
4. There is no significant difference in the mean scores of awareness on the HIV virus among the higher secondary students in terms of their School management as Aided and Private.
5. There is no significant difference in the mean scores of awareness on the HIV virus among the higher secondary students in terms of their School management as Private and Government.
6. There is no significant difference in the mean scores of awareness on the HIV virus among the higher secondary students in terms of their School nature as Boy's and Girl's.
7. There is no significant difference in the mean scores of awareness on the HIV virus among the higher secondary students in terms of their School nature as Girl's and Co-education.
8. There is no significant difference in the mean scores of awareness on the HIV virus among the higher secondary students in terms of their School nature as Co-education and Boy's.
9. There is no significant difference in the mean scores of awareness on the HIV virus among the higher secondary students in terms of their Medium of study as Tamil and English.
10. There is no significant difference in the mean scores of awareness

on the HIV virus among the higher secondary students in terms of their Family nature as Nuclear and Joint type.

11. There is no significant difference in the mean scores of awareness on the HIV virus among the higher secondary students in terms of their Parent education level as Schooling and Higher Education.
12. There is no significant difference in the mean scores of awareness on the HIV virus among the higher secondary students in terms of their Parent occupation as Government and Private Job.

DEFINITION OF THE KEY TERMS USED

HIV – Human Immuno Virus

VIRUS An organism visible only with an electron microscope viruses cause a wide variety of diseases in humans, including some cancers.

LIMITATIONS OF THE STUDY

The present study has the following limitations.

1. The sample is restricted to 250 samples.
2. Students of Higher Secondary school alone considered for the study.
3. The study is conducted in limited schools of Pudukkottai District.
4. The study was conducted in the year 2014-2015

CONCLUSION

In order to arrive at a convenient and appropriate conclusion, the present study has been arranged under five broad chapters:

Chapter I: "Conceptual Framework" introduces educational history and the research topic. It also spells out the aims and objectives of the study along with the hypothesis on which the investigation is based. It elaborated the scope of the study and its limitations as such.

Chapter II: Review of Related Literature is precisely drafted in this chapter.

Chapter III: Methodology, Universe and Sample, Tools for data collection, Method of Data Collection, along with factual position of sample is elaborated in this chapter.

Chapter IV: Under "Analysis and Interpretation of Data," the data has been analyzed and interpreted well.

Chapter V: “Findings and Conclusion” includes the major conclusions of the study derived from the analysis of data and provides few suggestions which are based on the findings. This chapter is followed by Bibliography and Appendices.

Chapter - II

Review of Related Literature

INTRODUCTION

Review of related literature implies locating, tracing and evaluating reports of research findings as well as reports of casual observations and opinions that are related to the individuals and planned research projects. The collection of available literature helps to uncover a number of studies related to the problem under study. Unless the areas of work that others have completed are ascertained and the areas left unexplored are identified to focus the light on those areas by the researchers.

Review of research is very essential for an investigator to know the area in which research work is needed for determining and describing the different dimensions of problems. This may provide scope for drawing a base of the conceptual frame work for the proposed study.

Keeping the above points in mind, the investigator has taken keen interest in the previous studies related to awareness on HIV and has gained valuable information from their procedures and finding which are of great aid in developing the present research work. A brief review of related literature and related studies are classified in Chronological order under different heads.

The review of related literature is presented in two sections. In the first section, the review of researches conducted in India and the second section, the review of researches conducted in Abroad was presented.

THE PURPOSE OF THE REVIEW OF LITERATURE

The purpose of this literature review was to convey to the reader what knowledge and ideas have been established on a topic. The literature review allowed the reader to be brought up to data regarding the state of research in the field and familiarizes the reader with any contrasting perspectives and viewpoints on the topic.

STUDIES CONDUCTED IN INDIA

Lal, SS., Vasan, RS., Sarma (2015), studied on "Knowledge and attitude of college students in Kerala towards HIV/AIDS, sexually transmitted diseases and sexuality". Knowledge about the spread of HIV and safe sexual practices has a critical impact on the prevention of the Acquired Immunodeficiency Syndrome (AIDS). We assessed the knowledge and attitude towards AIDS, Sexually Transmitted Diseases (STDs) and sexuality among college students in Thiruvananthapuram district, Kerala. The method of the study is performed a community-based, cross-sectional survey of 625 randomly selected under-graduate college students (164 boys, 461 girls, age 18-22 years). We administered a pre-tested, structured questionnaire to assess the knowledge and attitude of the students towards AIDS, STDs and sexuality. We generated knowledge and attitude scores from the student responses, and used multivariable linear regression to study the association of these scores with select predictor variables (notably gender and place of residence). The results of the study: 45% knew that AIDS is not curable at present. Only 34% were aware of the symptoms of STDs, and 47% knew that STDs are associated with an increased risk of AIDS. In multivariable analyses, male students ($p < 0.001$), and urban residents ($p = 0.006$) demonstrated a higher knowledge of AIDS and STDs. Students from urban areas ($p=0.014$) and those practising the Christian religion ($p = 0.042$) demonstrated more favourable attitudes towards AIDS. The conclusions: our study identified substantial lacunae in the knowledge and attitude towards AIDS, STDs and sexuality among college students in Kerala. The gap in knowledge between boys and girls, and between rural and urban students suggests the need for targeting girls and rural areas in the national AIDS education and awareness campaigns.

Payal Mishra, Shrotriya, V.P., and Iram Shaifali (2014), studied on "Adolescence Awareness: a better tool to combat HIV/AIDS". Adolescents are exposed to the risk of being victims of HIV/AIDS, mostly because of a low level of awareness of HIV/AIDS and inadequate access to HIV prevention and treatment services. School education has been described as a 'social vaccine', and it can serve as a powerful preventive tool. The objective is to assess, awareness of HIV/AIDS amongst adolescents of Bareilly District. The cross-sectional study involved 341 students, aged 11-19 years. A study instrument was used to assess study subjects' level of awareness regarding modes of transmission, preventive and curative measures of HIV/AIDS and the attitude towards PLWHA. Chi- square test was used to analyze data. The awareness regarding modes of transmission, methods of prevention and treatment was found to be significantly higher among boys as compared to girls (P < 001). There is a low level of awareness of HIV/AIDS amongst adolescents of Bareilly District. The challenge lies in developing programmes to spread awareness and to induce behavioral changes among them.

Ramesh Adhikari (2014), studied on "Are Nepali students at risk of HIV? A Cross – sectional study of condom use at first sexual inter course among college students in Kathmandu". Condoms offer the best protection against unintended pregnancies and Sexually Transmitted Infections. Little research has been conducted to determine the prevalence and investigate the influencing factors of condom use at first sexual intercourse among college students. The method of the study is a self-administered questionnaire was completed by 1137 school students (573 male and 564 female) in the Kathmandu Valley. Analyses were confined to 428 students who reported that they have ever had sexual intercourse. The association between condom use at first sexual intercourse and the explanatory variables was assessed in bivariate analysis using Chi-square tests. The associations were further explored using multivariate logistic analysis in order to identify the significant predictors after controlling for other variables. The results of the study are among the sexually active students, less than half (48%) had used condoms during first sexual intercourse. The results from the logistic regression analysis revealed that age, caste and/or ethnicity, age at first sexual intercourse, types of first sex partner, alcohol consumption and mass media exposure are significant predictors for condom use at first sexual intercourse among the school students. Students in the older age groups who had first sex, were about four times (16 to 19 years old) (OR = 3.5) more likely and nine times (20 or older) (OR = 8.9) more likely than the students who had sex before 16 years of age to use condoms at first sexual intercourse.

Lal, P., Anitha Nath, Badhan, S., and Gopal K Ingle (2013), reviewed on "A Study of Awareness about HIV/AIDS among Senior Secondary School Children of Delhi". The present study was undertaken by the Department of Community Medicine, Maulana Azad Schooland Harbans Kaur Memorial Trust (HKMC), a nongovernmental organization (NGO) and a partner of programme implementation by Delhi State AIDS Control Society (DSACS). Out of 1689 senior secondary schools in South Delhi area, 60 schools (3.5%) had been allotted to HKMC Trust by DSACS for carrying out school AIDS education programmes, in which there were 48 government schools (23 boys school, 23 girls and 2 co-educational) and 12 private co-educational schools. A total of 2592 students belonging to Classes IX to XI in these schools participated in the study. The response rate of students was 100%. The study was conducted over a period of 3 months from 1st August 2005 to 31st October 2005. The students were administered a pre-designed proforma, which included multiple choice questions. Written consent was obtained from the school principals after explaining the purpose of the study to them. Data were entered and analyzed using SPSS version 13.0 by means of simple comparison of proportions. Results and Discussion: With regard to the sources of information about HIV/AIDS, 79.6% of the students mentioned that television and radio were the main sources of information to them. Likewise, a majority (62.7%) of senior secondary students belonging to a government school in Chandigarh reported that they derived most of the information from TV and radio. In our study, only 9.5% of children had heard about HIV/AIDS through their respective school programmes. This finding suggests that school AIDS education should be strengthened further in schools. As much as 8.6% had obtained information from print media, whereas for 2.3%, friends remained the source of information.

Anurag Chaudhary, Mahesh Satija, Sarit Sharma, Singh, GPI., Soni, RK., and Sachar, RK., (2012), studied on "Awareness and perceptions of school children about female feticide in urban Ludhiana". Although the Indian girl child's position is precarious throughout the country, she remains the most vulnerable in Punjab. The objective of the study was to assess the awareness and perceptions of school children regarding female feticide. The design of the study was Cross-sectional study. The study involved collection of information regarding knowledge and perception of school students about female feticide using multiple choice questionnaires. A total of 527 students between the age group of 11-18 years of various schools of district Ludhiana, Punjab were the study subjects. They had come to participate in the poster competition on organ donation (SAARC Transplant games), organized by Department of Community Medicine, (D.M.C), Ludhiana. Out of total 527 students, 97.9% were aware of female feticide. Main source of information was TV (56%), followed by newspaper (33%). Majority of the students (65.2 %) felt that discrimination between boys and girls is prevalent in the society. Regarding perception of school students for curbing this social evil, 37.8% school students were of the view that awareness among the masses is the solution to stop this practice, while 25% of the students responded that equal status to girls will stop this practice of female feticide. The school students had optimum level of awareness about female feticide and almost all of them strongly felt that this harmful practice should be stopped altogether.

Bhatia, V., Swami, H., Puri, S., Mangat, C., and Gupta, A., (2012), studied on "An Intervention study to enhance AIDS awareness among underprivileged population in Chandigarh". It is estimated that worldwide, 33.2 million people were suffering, 2.1 million died and 2.5 million got newly infected from HIV/AIDS in the year 2007. Nearly 2.5 million people are suffering in India at present. Family Health Awareness Campaign (FHAC) has been implemented under National AIDS Control Programme (NACP) to scale up HIV/AIDS awareness in the vulnerable groups. Community based study was conducted in April 2001 to find out the impact of FHAC and IEC activities in 12 villages and slums in Chandigarh. Nearly 1-1.5 lac people are living in these areas. Information was collected from 323 subjects in pre-intervention phase and from 320 subjects in post-intervention phase in the age group of 15- 49 years. The awareness about AIDS increased from 58.2% to 70%. The major sources of information were mass media and friends. Knowledge regarding mode of spread also increased and the majority were aware about multiple sex partners and use of unhygienic / used syringes and needles, after the campaign. Knowledge regarding prevention of AIDS by using condom increased from 42% to 61.2%, having single partner from 59% to 72.3%, using safe blood from 14.9% to 29% and sterile needles/syringes from 18.1% to 33.9%. Over 90% of respondents consider AIDS as a dangerous disease. Community based intervention such as FHAC and IEC activities were successful in enhancing the awareness among underprivileged groups. Still a large section of the population remains unaware, thus regular efforts must be made to achieve universal awareness.

Sevanan Murugan, Sabarimuthu, and Chandran Gnana Desigan (2012), in their study on “Awareness about HIV/AIDS among adolescent boys in Tribal villages of Nilgiris District, South India”. An empirical study was conducted among the 300 adolescent boys in tribal villages of Nilgiris district, Tamil Nadu, South India during December 2007 - April 2008. A pre-tested proforma was used for conducting individual interviews to document pattern of sexual behaviours and awareness related to STD, HIV and AIDS. Among the 300 respondents, 67% belong to 15.19 years and 33% are 20-24 years old. Nearly 63% respondents are aware of STD’s and 93 % have the knowledge of HIV/AIDS. Only 1 respondent revealed to involve inhomosexual activity. Commercial Sex Workers (CSW) were the main reason for the transmission of HIV/AIDS and television play a major role in the dissemination of information about HIV/AIDS. Avoiding CSW, multiple sex workers, use of condoms can prevent the HIV/AIDS Education and correct scientific information are urgently needed to adolescent boys of tribal villages to avoid myths and misconceptions on HIV/ AIDS.

Chatterjee, C., Baur, B., Ram, R., Dhar, G., Sandhukhan, S., and Dan, A., (2011), reviewed on “A study on awareness of AIDS among school students and teachers of higher secondary schools in North Calcutta”. Higher Secondary School students and their teachers were studied to assess the knowledge about AIDS and attitude towards AIDS patients. Only 13.5% senior school students and 16.2% teachers had clear knowledge regarding AIDS its general aspects, transmission and prevention. Girls had higher and clear knowledge than boys. 45.8% of girls, 38.8% of boys and 20.3%

of teachers had positive attitudes towards nursing an AIDS case. It is suggested that schools have to device ways to open up more effective communication with students in relation to education in sex and AIDS. Training on AIDS should be emphasized on school teachers who on their turn can teach the students in a correct way about AIDS.

Rehana Kasur and Shabnam Bashir (2010), in their study on "Knowledge, attitude and belief on HIV/AIDS among the female senior secondary students in Srinagar District of Kashmir". Awareness on HIV/AIDS among adolescent female secondary school students, Srinagar district, Kashmir, was assessed through a study of their knowledge, attitude and belief about the disease. It was interesting to note, that approximately one fourth of the respondents have never heard of the disease. From those who were aware, 49.12 percent had no idea of the causative agent though the main source of information dissemination was electronic followed by print media, about 26 percent of the respondents had the perception that the disease is yet to reach the State. Ignorance of various risk groups within the society was also very much wide spread. A majority of the respondents (87.56 %) believed that the presence and spread of HIV/AIDS in the society were due to degradation of moral values among people many had expressed their reservations of discussing HIV/AIDS related issues with their parents. Hospitalization was preferred as a better way of managing AIDS patients by 48.44 percent of those interviewed. The above findings, in general, indicate a poor awareness of HIV/AIDS among educated adolescents in the capital city which indirectly reflects a much worse scenario of the illiterate rural counterparts who form bulk of the State's population.

J.V.Bhatnagar, M., Chopra, H. (2010), studied on "An Awareness Study about AIDS and Safe Blood among Higher Secondary Girl Students". Objective: To study the level of awareness regarding AIDS and safe blood among higher secondary girl students of Meerut city. Study design: Cross-sectional Setting: Four randomly selected higher secondary schools in Meerut city (two each from English and Hindi medium). Participants: Two hundred higher secondary girl students of Meerut city Hindi medium and 200 students from English medium. Statistical analysis: 'Z' test. Results: Overall awareness was 60.6% with mean score of 14.5#2.5. Statistically significant difference in awareness was observed in Hindi and English medium schools. Conclusions: Health education about AIDS and safe blood is the need of the hour for developing a healthy society.

Cheryl Koopman (2010), studied on "HIV / AIDS Stigma and Knowledge among Predominantly Middle-class high school Students in New Delhi, India". This study examined stigmatizing attitudes toward HIV/AIDS among predominantly middle class adolescents in New Delhi high schools. This study was specifically designed to: 1) Assess stigmatizing attitudes toward HIV/AIDS and sexuality, HIV/AIDS knowledge, and awareness of HIV related health resources, and 2) Examine whether HIV-related stigma and knowledge are related to one another and to gender,parents' education, an exposure to HIV / AIDS education in four high schools in New Delhi, 186 students completed a questionnaire assessing stigmatization of HIV/AIDS, stigmatization of sexuality, Knowledge of HIV/AIDS education and resources, and demographic characteristics. Adolescents varied in how much they stigmatized persons with HIV/AIDS. They generally lacked accurate knowledge about the disease and of related health resources. However, those with greater exposure to HIV/AIDS education demonstrated significantly greater HIV/ AIDS knowledge. Female adolescents demonstrated significantly less knowledge about HIV/AIDS compared with male adolescents, while the males reported significantly greater exposure to HIV /AIDS education compared with the females. These results suggest a need for greater HIV/ AIDS education and awareness of health resources, especially among female adolescents. Educator must directly address stigmatizing attitudes about HIV/AIDS, gaps in HIV/AIDS knowledge and awareness of HIV related health resources.

Chaudhuri Ramendra Narayan (2010), reviewed on "A study of awareness on HIV/AIDS among higher secondary school students in Central Kolkata". The study was undertaken in ward no. 40 of Kolkatta Municipal Corporation in January 2004. There were altogether four Government-run or Government-Aided Higher Secondary schools in that area. Our study was conducted in all the four schools of that ward. Prior permission was obtained from the school authorities and parents for conducting this study. All the students (258 in numbers) who were present on the days of data collection were included in the study. A pre-designed, pre-tested anonymous questionnaire was used for data collection. The questions were explained to them, and they were asked to write answers of the questions on their own. The responses were then analyzed using appropriate statistical methods. Awareness among boys was found to be significantly more than that among girls regarding communicability, modes of transmission and prevention of HIV/ AIDS. These findings were similar as observed by other researchers in different studies. Regarding history of sexual exposure, it was observed that 11.54% of boys and 1.56% of girls had premarital penetrative sexual exposure without using condoms, the difference being statistically significant. Awareness regarding vertical mode of transmission and necessity of sterilization of needle and screening of antenatal mothers for prevention of HIV/ AIDS was poor among both males and females. This was in conformity with a study by Abraham et al and by Kaur et al. It was observed in the present study that adolescents, especially girls, lacked awareness about HIV/ AIDS. A section of adolescents, though very small in number, also indulged in high-risk sexual behavior. IEC programs should be undertaken with regard to HIV/ AIDS, safe sex and avoidance of high-risk sexual behavior in schools to increase the awareness of adolescents. Scientific information regarding reproductive and sexual health should be included in the school curriculum to build up responsible sexual behavior among the students during adolescence as well as adulthood.

Suminder Kaur and Deepti, SS. (2009), studied on “Awareness of STDs and HIV/AIDS among the adolescent girls of classes IX-XII in Amritsar”. Adolescents are defined by the World Health Organization (WHO) as persons between 10 and 19 years of age (WHO 1998). Many adolescents around the world are sexually active because many sexual contacts among them are unprotected; they are at risk of contracting Sexually Transmitted Diseases (STDs). Another reason for their vulnerability to STDs is the lack of sex education, including education on STD prevention. Most parents do not discuss topics related to sexual issues and hence many teens turn to peers and to the media and get inaccurate information. The risk of becoming infected with Human Immunodeficiency Virus (HIV) during unprotected sex is two to four times greater for a woman (even higher in adolescent women) than for a man. Thus, this study was planned with the objective to study the knowledge about STDs, including HIV/Acquired Immunodeficiency Syndrome (AIDS) among school going adolescent girls (classes IX-XII) in a rural area and to assess the impact of health education on their knowledge.

Shankar, PR., Subish, P., Paudel, R., and Alam, K. (2008), studied on “Perception and Knowledge about HIV/AIDS among Students in a Schoolin Western Nepal”. Medical students are taught about HIV/AIDS throughout the curriculum. The objectives of the present study are: a) To study the perceptions and knowledge of medical students regarding HIV/ AIDS b) Obtain information on lacunae observed and. c) Compare the median scores among different sub-groups. The method of the study is the study was carried out among the first, third, (preclinical) and fifth and sixth semester (clinical) students at the Manipal College of Medical Sciences, Pokhara, Nepal. The students were explained the objective of to study and invited to participate. Written informed consent was obtained. Student perception regarding HIV/AIDS was studied by noting their degree of agreement with a set of 22 statements using a modified Likert-type scale. The median score was compared among different sub-groups. The results of the study are 163 students participated. The median score was 77 (maximum score 110). The median score was significantly higher among Nepalese students compared to other nationalities (p=0.000) and among the scholarship students compared to the self-financing (p=0.000). The free text comments stressed the importance of safe sex in controlling HIV/ AIDS. The conclusions of the study are the overall scores were high. The lacunae observed can be addressed through educational interventions.

The foreign and the self-financing students need greater training to tackle HIV/AIDS. The study had many limitations which may affect its generalizability and representativeness and more detailed studies are required.

STUDIES CONDUCTED IN ABROAD

An attempt has been made here to present the review of related literatures conducted in Abroad which can help to provide a sound background of the present study.

Lemessa Oljira, Yemane Berhane and Alemayehu Worku (2014), studied on "Assessment of comprehensive HIV/AIDS knowledge level among in-school adolescents in eastern Ethiopia" Journal of the International AIDS Society 2013. The dependent variable was comprehensive HIV/AIDS knowledge measured by correct answers to HIV/AIDS diagnosis and treatment, HIV transmission modes and HIV prevention methods; comprehensive knowledge was then redefined by the ability to identify correctly at least two major ways of preventing sexual transmission of HIV, to reject at least two most common local misconceptions about HIV transmission and by the correct knowledge of HIV diagnosis method. The independent variables were sex, age, area of residence, wealth index, parents' vital status, father's educational status, mother's educational status, major source of HIV/AIDS information, discussion on sexual topics with parents or other family members and ever having been taught HIV/AIDS and related issues at school. Results: Only about one in four, 677 (24.5%), in-school adolescents have comprehensive HIV/AIDS knowledge. The knowledge was better among in-school adolescents from families with a relatively middle or high wealth index (adjusted OR [95% CI]_1.39 [1.03_1.87] and 1.75 [1.24_2.48], respectively), who got HIV/AIDS information mainly from friends or mass media (adjusted OR [95% CI]_1.63 [1.17_2.27] and 1.55 [1.14_2.11], respectively) and who received education on HIV/AIDS and sexual matters at school (adjusted OR [95% CI]_1.59 [1.22_2.08]). The females were less likely to have comprehensive HIV/AIDS knowledge compared to males (adjusted for and [95% CI]_0.60 [0.49_0.75]). Conclusions: In general, only about a quarter of in-school adolescents had comprehensive HIV/AIDS knowledge. Although the female adolescents are highly vulnerable to HIV infection and its effects, they were by far less likely to have comprehensive HIV/AIDS knowledge. HIV/AIDS information, education and communication activities need to be intensified in high schools.

Charlotte Van Tuyckom (2014), in their study on "AIDS knowledge and sexual activity among Flemish secondary school students: a multilevel analysis of the effects of type of education". The behavior of adolescents puts them at an increased risk for HIV and other STIs, and their knowledge about HIV/AIDS is often inadequate. An understanding of how AIDS knowledge and sexual activity co-vary among Flemish secondary school students and of how education type, specifically, affects these students, is limited. This study addresses the question of whether the effects of education type on HIV/AIDS knowledge and sexual activity are independent of the socio-demographic characteristics of the students. Data from the Flemish Educational Assessment survey, which collected data from a large representative sample of third- and fifth-grade high school students (N = 11,872), were used. Data were analyzed using multilevel logistic and Poison regression techniques. There is an indication that type of education affects both an adolescent's sexual activity and his/her AIDS knowledge; these effects prove robust for differences in socio-economic backgrounds. Students in lower status education types are more likely to be sexually active and to have poorer AIDS knowledge. The relationship between AIDS knowledge and sexual activity is, however, more complex. Although students in education types with poorer AIDS knowledge are more sexually active, within each of these groups the sexually active have better AIDS knowledge than the non-sexually active. There is also evidence of active information seeking by sexually active students, which lead to improved AIDS knowledge. The findings are consistent with the literature on the role of the educational system in the reproduction of social inequalities. Students from lower status education types are at increased sexual risk compared to those from higher status types. There is also evidence of active information seeking by sexually active students, which leads to improved AIDS knowledge.

Visser, M.J., (2013) studied on "Life skills training as HIV/AIDS preventive strategy in secondary schools: evaluation of a large-scale implementation process". A life skills and HIV/AIDS education programme was implemented in secondary schools as a strategy to combat the spread of HIV/AIDS among school-going young people in South Africa. As part of a joint effort of the Departments of Health and Education, two teachers per school were trained to implement life skills training and HIV/AIDS education in schools as part of the school curriculum. The implementation of the intervention was evaluated in 24 schools in two educational districts in Gauteng province, using an action research approach. Data about the implementation were gathered through interviews and focus group discussions with school principals, teachers and learners. A repeated measurement research design was used to assess the impact of the intervention in terms of knowledge, attitudes and reported risk behaviour in a sample of 667 learners representing learners from grades 8 to 12 from different population groups. Results showed that the programme was not implemented as planned in schools due to organisational problems in the schools, lack of commitment of the teachers and the principal, non-trusting relationships between teachers and learners, lack of resources and conflicting goals in the educational system. In an outcome evaluation over the period of a year, it was found that learners' knowledge of HIV/AIDS increased and their attitudes were more positive although the changes may not be attributed to the programme alone. In the post-test more learners were sexually active, although preventive behaviour did not increase. The programme as implemented in the area did not succeed in changing high-risk behaviour patterns among school-going young people. From the evaluation of the intervention a few valuable lessons were learned about the content and implementation of HIV/AIDS preventive interventions, which could be useful in the implementation of various other HIV/AIDS preventive interventions in the community.

Singh, S.K., Manandhar, N., Prasai, M., Patowary and Krishna, G., (2013) reviewed on "An awareness study of HIV/AIDS among adolescent students of Chitwan district, Nepal". A cross sectional study was conducted among the adolescent students of 12 randomly selected higher secondary school of Chitwan district, Nepal with an objective to assess the awareness by studying their knowledge and attitude towards the disease. It is really very gratifying to note that 100.0% of the respondents had heard about the disease and majority of them (95.0%) had correct knowledge about the causative agents. Among the respondents quite large number of students (79.0%) knew about high risk age group and 81.0% were aware about safe sex as one of the major preventive measure. The attitude of respondents towards the AIDS patients was firmly positive. Among them 84.5% had no objection in treating AIDS patients in the general hospital with extra precaution. The main source of their information, education and communication were from electronic media. These observations were indicative of good awareness about the disease which will definitely help in bringing about behavioral change at the individual level and will go in a long way for prevention of transmission amongst the high risk groups and to contain its spread.

Angbo-Effi, O., Koffi, NM., and Diarra-Nam, AJ., (2013) in their studied on "Awareness, attitudes, and practices of secondary school students in relation to HIV/AIDS in Abidjan, Ivory Coast". In May 2001, we conducted a descriptive transversal survey with a single data collection phase in 13 schools in Abidjan, Ivory Coast. The purpose of the study was to evaluate the awareness, attitudes, and practices of teenagers with regard to HIV/AIDS. Most respondents (66.5%) were female. Mean age was 16.32 years (range, 13 to 19 years). Most respondents stated that they had heard about AIDS and demonstrated good factual knowledge. The most frequently mentioned method of prevention was condom use (89.2%). A total of 338 (56.1%) had already experienced sexual intercourse. However most sexually active respondents.

Etuk, S.J., (2013) reviewed on "Knowledge of HIV/AIDS among Secondary School Adolescents in Calabar, Nigeria". An observational study using structured questionnaire among secondary school students. About 181 (31.2%) of the adolescents did not know the aetiological agents of HIV/AIDS. Majority, 522 (90%) knew HIV/AIDS was transmitted through sexual intercourse. This level of knowledge was related to sex and class of study. Only 78 (13.4%) of them knew that HIV carriers might look normal. Majority, 519 (89.5%) did not know the features of AIDS. Only a few, 281 (48.4%) of the adolescents knew that avoidance of sex, keeping one sexual partner, 15 (2.6%), use of condom 101 (17.4%) and screening blood before transfusion, 31 (5.3%) could prevent HIV/AIDS transmission. Mass media was the main source of information on HIV/AIDS to these adolescents. About 191, (32.9%) of them believed HIV/AIDS cannot be prevented, 228 (39.3%) felt HIV/AIDS is common among the uneducated, 127 (21.9%) thought it is not common in Nigeria and 143 (24.7%) believed it is not common among the youths. Although awareness on HIV/AIDS is high among Secondary School adolescents in Calabar, the knowledge of the disease is still poor. Mass media as a source of information does not allow in-depth knowledge of the disease. Parents, teachers, as well as Health workers should be more involved in educating the youth on this dreaded disease.

Michelo, Charlesa, B., Sanday, Ingvild, FB., Fylkesnes and Knutb (2013),studied on "Marked HIV prevalence declines in higher educated young people: evidence from population-based surveys (1995-2003) in Zambia". Higher educational attainment has been associated with a greater risk of HIV infection in sub-Saharan Africa. We investigated change over time in HIV prevalence by educational attainment in the general population. The data stem from serial population-based HIV surveys conducted in selected urban and rural communities in 1995 (n=2989), 1999 (n = 3506) and 2003 (n = 4442). Analyses were stratified by residence, sex and age-group. Logistic regression was used to estimate age-adjusted odds ratio of HIV between low (Z 4 school years) and higher education ([8 years) for the rural population and between low (Z 7 school years) and higher education ([11 years) for the urban population. There was a universal shift towards reduced risk of HIV infection in groups with higher than lower education in both sexes among urban young people [odds ratio (or), 0.20; 95% confidence interval (CI), 0.05-0.73] in men and (or, 0.33; 95% CI, 0.15-0.72) in women. A similar pattern was observed in rural young men (or, 0.17; 95% CI, 0.05-0.59) but was less prominent and not statistically significant in rural women. In age 25-49 years, higher educated urban men had reduced risk in 2003 (or, 0.43; 95%CI, 0.26-0.72) but this was less prominent in women. The findings suggested a shift in the association between educational attainment and HIV infection between 1995 and 2003. The most convincing sign was the risk reduction among more educated younger groups where most infections can be assumed to be recent.

Abali, S.O., (2012) in their journal on "Assessment of HIV/AIDS awareness and changes in sexual practices among secondary school students in Nsukka environment". This study is aimed at assessing the awareness of HIV/AIDS and changes in sexual behaviour among the Nigerian teens. Two hundred and fifty secondary school students were interviewed. Only 5% of the respondents were able to state the full meaning of HIV / AIDS. A minority (28%) believed that HIV was real while the majority (72%) believed that HIV infects whites only. Fortyeight percent of them have changed their sexual practices owing to the AIDS menace. A small percentage (12%) believed that HIV/AIDS could kill. The study revealed low awareness of HIV/AIDS as well as misconception about the infection, especially in non-urbanized cities of Nigeria.

Maretha J Visser (2012) studied on "HIV/AIDS prevention through peer education and support in secondary schools in South Africa". The implementation and evaluation of a peer education and support programme in secondary schools to prevent and reduce high-risk sexual behaviour amongst adolescents is discussed. The aims of the programme were to provide accurate information about HIV/AIDS, discuss and reconsider peer group norms, and establish support for learners. In the programme that was implemented in 13 secondary schools in Tshwane, South Africa, peer educators were identified, trained and supported to implement the programme in their schools with the assistance of a teacher and post-graduate students as facilitators. Peer educators organised HIV awareness activities, facilitated class discussions on risk behaviour and gender relationships, and supported learners in solving personal problems. Process evaluation included weekly reports and focus group discussions with peer educators and teachers. A quasi-experimental design involving an experimental and control group, as well as pre and post-assessments, was used to evaluate the impact of the programme on psychological well-being, personal control, school climate and reported high-risk behaviour of learners aged between 13 and 20 years. The results showed that the percentage of learners in the experimental group who were sexually experienced, remained unchanged over the time period of 18 months. In contrast, a significantly increased percentage of learners in the control group were sexually experienced after the same time period. The control group also perceived more of their friends to be sexually experienced. No differences were reported in condom use in either of the groups. The findings of this study suggest that peer education can contribute to a delayed onset of sexual activity, and can therefore contribute to the prevention of HIV/AIDS amongst adolescents.

Meriamu and Ugiomoh Maria (2011) in their report on "Male gender roles and sexuality: implications for University girls' HIV/AIDS awareness in a Nigerian University". This study was conducted to examine the implications of male gender roles and sexuality for University girls' HIV/

AIDS awareness. Information was elicited from 2399 randomly selected undergraduate students, from the nine faculties of the University of Lagos, Nigeria. Results indicate moderate levels of HIV/AIDS awareness and that of the hypothesis testing showed a no significant difference at p> 0.05, as a result of male gender roles. The paper draws the conclusion that the prevalence rate of HIV/AIDS was on the increase, and that University undergraduate girls are more vulnerable because of high risks of sexual behaviour for monetary gains. The paper also concludes that intervention strategies cannot be achieved without addressing the issue of male gender roles and sexuality in the spread of HIV/AIDS infection.

Movahed, M., and Shoaa, S., (2010), studied on "The attitude towards HIV/AIDS among Iranian students (case study: high school students in Shiraz City)". Young people are of particular importance in state policies against AIDS. The present study investigated the attitude towards HIV/ AIDS and related socio-cultural factors among 600 high school students in Shiraz, Iran. The method of sampling is a stratified one and the instrument for collecting data is a self-administrated questionnaire. In this research, attitude has three dimensions knowledge, emotion and tendency to action. Descriptive statistics showed that students did not have enough knowledge about HIV/AIDS. The 44.3% of students had low knowledge, 36.9% moderate knowledge and only 18.8% had high knowledge. Also the results indicated that attitude for 69.8% of student has in middle level, 15.4% positive and 14.9% negative. Moreover, results suggested that loyalty to Islamic religious beliefs have an important role on attitude towards this disease. Major of study, sex, mother's occupation and use of some mass media such as books and newspapers were other main influencing factors in the students' attitude. Furthermore, this study showed that parent education, major of study, father's occupation and use of books and the internet are the most important variables affecting on the participants' knowledge. Age, sex, parents' education, religious beliefs, use of some mass media such as TV, the internet, newspapers, satellite and books affect emotion. Finally, there is a relationship between religious beliefs, sex and major of study, use of satellite, television, radio and books with tendency to action.

Ladatra, S., Taylor and Stephanie, N., (2010), studied on "Knowledge of Sexually Transmitted Infections among high school students." It has not been determined conclusively whether greater knowledge of Sexually Transmitted Infections (STIs) is associated with lower rates of STIs. This study sought to determine STI knowledge among high school students and factors associated with such knowledge, and to determine whether poor STI knowledge is associated with chlamydia or gonorrhea infection. Students in an urban United States school district serving a predominantly African American student population participated in a urine-based chlamydia and gonorrhea screening. Participants (N=3563) were surveyed about their knowledge of selected basic facts concerning STIs. Point-scores were assigned to knowledge items. Results: The mean knowledge score was 3.65 (range: 0 to 6; median: 4.00). In a multiple regression analysis, knowledge score was significantly associated with female gender (P <0.001), upper grade level (P<0.001) and a past infection with chlamydia or gonorrhea (P=0.001). In logistic regressions, knowledge score was not significantly associated with current infections with chlamydia (P=0.22) or gonorrhea (P=0.74). There was an insufficient basic knowledge of STIs among students and a lack of association between knowledge and current infections with chlamydia and gonorrhea. Translation to Health Education Practice: Health education curricula taught throughout the high school years should incorporate basic facts concerning STIs.

Peltzer, K., Cherian, L., and Cherian, VI., (2010), in their study on "AIDS awareness of secondary school pupils in the Northern province of South Africa". This study investigated AIDS awareness in secondary school pupils (mainly Northern Sotho and Xitsonga) in the Northern Province of South Africa. The randomly chosen sample included 622 Standard 9 pupils (254 boys and 368 girls) in the age range of 17 to 24 years (M of 19.3), who were administered a questionnaire on awareness of AIDS and socioeconomic status. Over 72% of the questions about AIDS were correctly answered, which suggests a fair amount of accurate information about AIDS; however, 18% were of the opinion that "AIDS does not exist" and 19% that "there is a cure for AIDS." Analysis of variance indicated no relationships for sex, age, ethnicity, or socioeconomic status with correct answers.

Alemayehu Bekelel and Ahmed Ale (2010), studied on "Effectiveness of IEC interventions in reducing HIV / AIDS related stigma among high school adolescents in Hawassa, Southern Ethiopia". Stigma and discrimination are among the major challenges in HIV / AIDS to disease prevention while IEC interventions are among the mechanisms to mitigate them. Objective: To determine the effectiveness of IEC interventions. Methods: interventional study was conducted from January to March 2007 among high school adolescents in Awassa Town using four different lEC interventions namely, interpersonal communication, pamphlets, educational video and the combination of the three interventions. Stigmatizing attitudes ranged from 0-65.2%. Multivariate logistic regression analyses showed grade, religion, beliefs in HIV transmission by witchcraft and HIV transmission by feeding on uncooked egg/meat of chicken that swallowed used condom were independent predictors of avoidant behavioral intentions. Residence, fathers' education, television ownership, witchcraft transmission, healthy looking person can have HIV, HIV prevention by having sex with virgin girls and PLWHA with multiple sexual partners were found to be the main determinants of coercive attitude. ANOVA (F-statistics) revealed that the interventions were effective with and statistical value of 17.484 (p-value<0.0001). Misconceptions on HIV transmission and prevention, stigmatizing and discriminatory attitudes were prevalent among the adolescents. Remarkable reduction in HIV related misconceptions, stigmatizing and discriminatory attitudes were observed. Hence, campaigns using combined IEC interventions on HIV/AIDS need to be intensified to dispel some of the prevailing misconceptions and associated stigma and discrimination among school adolescents.

Lawal, B.O., (2009) in his journal on "AIDS awareness among Secondary School Teachers in Kwara, Lagos & Ogun States of Nigeria". This study investigated HIV/AIDS awareness among secondary school teachers in Kwara, Lagos & Ogun States of Nigeria. Survey research method was used in carrying out the study. Questionnaires were used for data gathering after validation. Simple percentage as well as likert method of summated ratings was used for the data analysis. The study revealed that the level of awareness among secondary school teachers is very low. It was also revealed among others that the difference between single and married teachers in their awareness of HIV/AIDS is not significant. It was recommended among other things that individuals should avoid both premarital and extra-marital sex. That young people should be given awareness about HIV/AIDS. That government should provide adequate funding for HIV/AIDS research and that the pandemic should be discussed with other around you for the purpose of awareness.

Bimbola Kemi Odu and Florence Foluso Akanle (2008) studied on "Knowledge of HIV/AIDS and Sexual behaviour among the Youths in South West Nigeria". The study investigated the relationship between the sexual behaviour and knowledge of HIV/AIDS among the youths in South/West Nigeria. The study also investigated the different types of sexual behaviour and whether youths have the knowledge of key basic concept on HIV/AIDS. Using the descriptive research design, a total number of 1,420 undergraduates, who correctly filled the self constructed questionnaire in four different universities in four different states of South West geographical zone of Nigeria were sampled. A self constructed questionnaire which was validated using face, content and construct method of validation was used. The instrument had a construct and a test retest reliability of 0.76 and 0.85 respectively. Pearson Product Moment Correlation and t-test were used in the inferential analysis while frequency counts and percentages were used in describing the knowledge and sexual behaviour of youths. The result of the analysis revealed that most respondents were sexually active and were engaged in high risk sex such as casual, same sex, multiple sex and sex in exchange for money or favour. It was clear that youths have very high knowledge of key basic concept on HIV/AIDS but many youths have misconceptions about the cure of AIDS. The study recommended that policies and programmes that can transform the sexual life of youths or reduce their risk behaviours should be put in place while prevention message should be consistent, clear and effective to counteract other unreliable sources of information.

Clas Ahlm and Rune Andersson (2008) reviewed on "HIV/AIDS awareness and risk behavior among students in Semey, Kazakhstan: a cross-sectional survey". Until recently, young people in Kazakhstan have been only moderately affected by the global HIV epidemic. Today, however, the HIV epidemic in Central Asia is one of the most rapidly increasing epidemics in the world. It is mainly concentrated to vulnerable groups such as intravenous drug users, sex workers, the purchasers of sexual services and the financially marginalized. Young, sexually active people may however be the gateway for the epidemic to the general population, and knowledge about their attitudes and behavior is therefore important in planning preventive measures. The method of the study is to gather information about young students and their attitudes and knowledge about HIV/AIDS, we collected 600 structured questionnaires and made 23 semi-structured interviews among three groups of students. Response rate was 99%. The results of the study are almost 99% of the respondents had heard of HIV/AIDS, and 89% could identify ways to protect oneself against sexually transmitted HIV/AIDS. The main routes of transmission, sexual contact without condom and intravenous drug use, were both identified by 97% of the students. Twenty-five percent of the female students and 75% of the male students had had one or more sexual partners. More than 30% of the young men had purchased sex, and homosexuality was widely stigmatized. The conclusion of the study is risks for the spread of HIV/AIDS among young people in Kazakhstan include prostitution as well as stigmatization of the HIV positive and homosexuals. Protective factors are good knowledge about risks and protection, and opportunities to talk and gather information about sexuality and HIV/AIDS.

Jimoh, A. A. G. and Balogun O.R., (2007), studied on "Factors in the rate of acceptance of HIV/AIDS Voluntary Counselling and Testing (VCT) among Youths in Kwara State, Nigeria". HIV/AIDS has become a source of concern all over the world. The concern cannot be isolated from the devastating effects of HIV/AIDS on economic, social, political and technological development of any nation plagued by the virus. Nigeria is one of the countries with a high rate of HIV/AIDS prevalence. The current national rate is over 4%. Despite this challenge, the patronage of Voluntary Counselling and Testing is still very low. This study therefore examined the factors responsible for the rate of acceptance of Voluntary Counselling and Testing as expressed by youths in Kwara State. A total of 600 youths from the three Senatorial districts in the State were involved in the study. A survey instrument designed by the researchers was used to collect relevant information from the respondents. Among others, the study identified ignorance, poverty, inadequate number of VCT centers, stigma and discrimination as major factors responsible for the low patronage of

VCT centers in Kwara State. Gender and religion had no significant influence on the respondents views while place of residence had significant influence.

Hoque and Busi Ntuli-Ngcobo (2007), studied on "Knowledge regarding HIV/AIDS among home-based caregivers in Namibia". Lack of practical knowledge among home-based caregivers on Human Immunodeficiency Virus/ Acquired Immune Deficiency Syndrome (HIV/AIDS), Anti-Retroviral Therapy (ART) and poor individual adherence to treatment are among the root causes of ineffective ART service delivery in Namibia. The purpose of our study was to investigate the knowledge among home-based caregivers in Namibia regarding HIV/AIDS. The study was a descriptive, cross sectional one in which 89 participants completed a self-administered questionnaire to assess their knowledge of HIV/AIDS. Almost all (93%) of the respondents gave a correct definition of HIV. Over a tenth (11.3%) did not know that HIV decreases the body's ability to fight disease and 33.7% could not define AIDS. Almost all (98%) the home-based caregivers knew that HIV can be diagnosed only through a blood test and 91% mentioned that consistent and correct use of condoms during sexual intercourse protects one from HIV infection. Fewer than half (44%) of the respondents could indicate on-and-off fever as a symptom of AIDS and 16% mentioned that increased body weight is a sign of AIDS, which is incorrect. Although the knowledge of the caregivers on HIV/AIDS was above average in some aspects, there was still lack of knowledge on isolated issues such as AIDS definitions and signs and how HIV works. Training organisations in home-based care settings should emphasise the knowledge of AIDS definition and signs as well as of post-test counselling, consequence of poor adherence and facilities that issue anti-retroviral treatment.

Hmoud S Olimat and Salah H Al-Louzi (2006), reviewed on "A National Study on the knowledge and awareness of Jordanian high school students towards HIV/AIDS". The present study investigated Jordanian school students' knowledge of HIV/AIDS, its causes, symptoms, and their fears of contracting sexually transmitted infections (STIs) and HIV/AIDS. A cross-sectional design was used to collect data from a multistage representative sample of high school students, (N=6242) using a questionnaire designed specifically for the present study. Results showed that most respondents (97.6%) were aware of HIV/AIDS, with (57.9%) knew its symptoms, and (54.8%) belief that there was no effective cure to it, a high percentage (68.8%) expressed their fear of contracting (STIs), and 27.5% fear contracting HIV/AIDS due to their behavior or actions infected on them. Respondents showed erroneous knowledge on a number of means that in reality do not transmit HIV/AIDS such as casual mixing with infected people, sharing food and drinks with them or using public toilets. Comparisons between males and females and between those who fear AIDS and those who did not, showed significant differences in several issues concerning knowledge and means of transmission. A considerable gap in students' knowledge of HIV/AIDS transmission was found, with high level of fear of STIs and AIDS, accompanied with limited opportunities for education.

Danjin, M., and Onajole, A.T., (2006), reviewed on "HIV/AIDS risk behavioural tendencies among secondary school students in Gombe (Nigeria)". A cross sectional survey of HIV/AIDS risk behavioural tendencies among in-school youths, was conducted in Gombe metropolis, Nigeria. A total of 400 respondents were selected using multistage sampling technique, but only 395 of completed questionnaires were finally found usable. The subjects were in the ratio of 50.8% males to 49.2% females and their ages ranged between <13 and 24 years. Although, almost all of them (98.4%) ever heard of HIV/AIDS before and majority (88.9%) have heard of condom, sex related risky behaviours were still prevalent among them. This includes multiple sex partners in the last one year (10.5%), multiple life-time sex partners (14.1%), low rate of condom use in last sex (22.7%), sex in exchange for money or favour (9.8%), early sexual debut at less than 13 (18.8%), sex with female sex workers (12.2%) and diagnosed with STDs (6.8%). This scenario calls for urgent intervention measures such as HIV/AIDS school education programmes in the state and region.

CONCLUSION

The review has revealed the extent of contribution of educationalists in the area of the present study. From the review of the literature it is understood that only few studies have been undertaken to measure along with the title chosen.

Chapter - III

Methodology

NTRODUCTION

Research methodology involves systematic procedures starting from the initial identification of the problem to its final conclusions. Its role is to carry on the research work in a scientific and valid manner.

It provides the tools and techniques by which the research problem is attacked. It consists of procedures and techniques for conducting a study. It is of little value unless used properly. Proper use must be learnt by the researcher. It involves such general activities as identifying problems, review of the literature, formulating hypotheses, procedure for testing hypotheses, measurement, data collection and analysis of data, interpreting results and drawing conclusions.

Thus, it consists of all general and specific activities of research. Mastery in it enhances understanding of the research activities. Thus, research design and methodology have the identical meaning of mapping strategy of research.

RESEARCH DESIGN

The study was conducted to find out the Awareness on the HIV Virus among the Higher Secondary Students in Pudukkottai District. In this study, the descriptive design has been followed. Statistical tools such as "t" test have been employed in order to find out the significant difference in higher secondary school students.

RESEARCH PROCEDURE

This chapter presents details regarding the following:

1. Selection of Dependent variables and Categorical variables.
2. Construction of tools to measure the Awareness on the HIV Virus among the Higher Secondary Students in Pudukkottai District
3. Methods of establishing the reliability, validity of the tools constructed.
4. Sampling procedure adopted in this study.
5. Scheduling the survey and collecting the data.

STATEMENT OF THE PROBLEM

The purpose of the study is entitled as *"Awareness on the HIV Virus among the Higher Secondary Students in Pudukkottai District"*.

OBJECTIVES OF THE STUDY

The following are the general and specific objectives framed for the study

1. To find the significant difference in the mean scores of awareness on the HIV virus among the higher secondary students in terms of their Gender.
2. To find the significant difference in the mean scores of awareness on the HIV virus among the higher secondary students in terms of their Locality.
3. To find the significant difference in the mean scores of awareness on the HIV virus among the higher secondary students in terms of their School management as Government and Aided.
4. To find the significant difference in the mean scores of awareness on the HIV virus among the higher secondary students in terms of their School management as Aided and Private.
5. There is no significant difference in the mean scores of awareness on the HIV virus among the higher secondary students in terms of their School management as Private and Government.
6. To find the significant difference in the mean scores of awareness

on the HIV virus among the higher secondary students in terms of their School nature as Boy's and Girl's.

7. To find the significant difference in the mean scores of awareness on the HIV virus among the higher secondary students in terms of their School nature as Girl's and Co-education.
8. There is no significant difference in the mean scores of awareness on the HIV virus among the higher secondary students in terms of their School nature as Co-education and Boy's.
9. To find the significant difference in the mean scores of awareness on the HIV virus among the higher secondary students in terms of their Medium of study as Tamil and English.
10. To find the significant difference in the mean scores of awareness on the HIV virus among the higher secondary students in terms of their Family nature as Nuclear and Joint type.
11. To find the significant difference in the mean scores of awareness on the HIV virus among the higher secondary students in terms of their Parent education level as Schooling and Higher Education.
12. To find the significant difference in the mean scores of awareness on the HIV virus among the higher secondary students in terms of their Parent occupation as Government and Private Job.

HYPOTHESES OF THE STUDY

The following are the Hypotheses framed for the study

1. There is no significant difference in the mean scores of awareness on the HIV virus among the higher secondary students in terms of their Gender.
2. There is no significant difference in the mean scores of awareness on the HIV virus among the higher secondary students in terms of their Locality.
3. There is no significant difference in the mean scores of awareness on the HIV virus among the higher secondary students in terms of their School management as Government and Aided.
4. There is no significant difference in the mean scores of awareness on the HIV virus among the higher secondary students in terms of their School management as Aided and Private.
5. There is no significant difference in the mean scores of awareness on the HIV virus among the higher secondary students in terms of their School management as Private and Government.

6. There is no significant difference in the mean scores of awareness on the HIV virus among the higher secondary students in terms of their School nature as Boy's and Girl's.
7. There is no significant difference in the mean scores of awareness on the HIV virus among the higher secondary students in terms of their School nature as Girl's and Co-education.
8. There is no significant difference in the mean scores of awareness on the HIV virus among the higher secondary students in terms of their School nature as Co-education and Boy's.
9. There is no significant difference in the mean scores of awareness on the HIV virus among the higher secondary students in terms of their Medium of study as Tamil and English.
10. There is no significant difference in the mean scores of awareness on the HIV virus among the higher secondary students in terms of their Family nature as Nuclear and Joint type.
11. There is no significant difference in the mean scores of awareness on the HIV virus among the higher secondary students in terms of their Parent education level as Schooling and Higher Education.
12. There is no significant difference in the mean scores of awareness on the HIV virus among the higher secondary students in terms of their Parent occupation as Government and Private Job.

LIMITATIONS OF THE STUDY

The present study has the following limitations.

1. The sample is restricted to 250 samples.
2. Students of Higher Secondary school alone considered for the study.
3. The study is conducted in limited schools of Pudukkottai District.
4. The study was conducted in the year 2014-2015

RESEARCH METHOD

The investigator preferred **survey method** for the present study. In this study, the investigator used survey method to collect data and to identify the "Awareness on the HIV Virus among the Higher Secondary Students in Pudukkottai District".

RESEARCH TOOLS

In the present study the investigation selected standardized questionnaire as tool for the most important collecting data because it is used increasingly to enquire the current conditions, opinions and attitude of a groups.

W. Best observes that the questionnaire is the most tools in collecting both quantitative and quantitative information, for the present study questionnaire was prepared with view to gather information in details regarding on *Awareness on the HIV Virus among the Higher Secondary Students in Pudukkottai District.*

CONSTRUCTION OF RESEARCH TOOLS

The research tool on "Awareness on the HIV Virus among the Higher Secondary Students in Pudukkottai District" was standardized by researcher with 40 numbers of Questions framed as Questions and the personal data sheet was constructed by the investigator in the present study. The respondents who respond the correct answers were given scores and these score were considered for data analysis.

SAMPLES OF THE STUDY

After finalizing the variables of present study, consideration was given to whether the entire population is to be made the subject for data collection or a particular group is to be selected as representative of the whole population. The entire population here refers to the higher secondary school students studying in Pudukkottai District.

DESCRIPTION OF RESEARCH TOOL AND SCORING PROCEDURE

Before administering the test necessary instruction and directions were given to the students. No time limit is given to the students were asked to complete the inventory as early as possible. It is a five point scale of opinion types of tool.

PILOT STUDY

The pilot stage is concerned with refining the items collected. The collected items were presented before the expert with a request to offer their considered opinion regarding the suitability objectivity clarity and relevancy of the statement collected from different sources.

The opinion of the experts was taken into consideration. The pilot study is an initial study which is conducted by the investigator to know more about the research problem in various aspects.

Based on the pilot study, the main study was conducted by the investigator while administering the research in the pilot study, some doubts were raised by the school students and the investigator clarified all of their doubts and difficulties.

Based on that, the investigator gave the instructions. Further, the investigator obtained some ideas from the experts and modified the irrelevant Item that is coming in the present study. After getting response from the respondents, the investigator gave frequencies for the correct response and these frequencies were converted into scores and those scores were used to Analysis and interpretation of data.

SCORING AND CONSOLIDATION OF DATA

Scoring was done as per the scoring scheme. The scores obtained in all questionnaires along with the personal data are consolidated and tabulated on consolidation sheet for the purpose of analysis. Each subject was given a specific number, the concerned with specific line, following a specific order as 5, 4, 3, 2 & 1 respectively for Positive type of Questions. And 1, 2, 3, 4 & 5 marks were allotted for the Negative type of Question respectively.

The Negative Questions were numbered as 2, 7, 8, 17, 18, 19, 20, 21, 22, 23, 24, 33, 34, 35 and the other of the Forty numbers are Positive aspect Questions.

VALIDITY OF THE TOOL

In validation process, the investigator used two measures in order to establish validation of tools. The first measure of validation is called reliability. The second measure of validation process is called validity. The investigator established content validity. To find out the validity of research tool, the investigator discussed each and every item of the questionnaire with the experts in the relevant field respectively. Based on the opinion of the experts, the objectivity and worthiness of the items of the questionnaire were arranged.

RELIABILITY OF THE TOOL

The reliability of questionnaire on indentifying Awareness on the HIV virus among the Higher Secondary Students was established by making a rational equivalence method. The reliability of the tool refers to the internal consistency observed in measurement of reliability. And the tool has the sufficient reliability value as **'r'** is equals to **0.89** consistencies.

SAMPLING TECHNIQUE USED

Random sampling method was adopted for this purpose. In this method random sampling every individual in the population has an equal and independent chance of being chosen for the samples.

After finalizing the variables of present study, consideration was given to whether the entire population is to be made the subject for data collection or a particular group is to be selected as representative of the whole population. The entire population here refers to all the under higher school students studying in Pudukkottai District.

Of the above two techniques, the selection of a group as a representative of the whole population was found to be more convenient and suitable. This technique leads to a considerable save of time, effort and finance. The number of students selected will be small, and so it is possible to make a detailed and intensive study. This generally leads to more accurate and reliable results. As this sampling technique has many advantages, it was selected for the collection of data.

In any behavioral research, various methods are utilized for selection and drawing of samples. After a detailed study of all these methods and considering the variables selected for the research work, the Random sampling method was found to be most suitable.

In the Random sampling method, the entire population will be divided into smaller homogenous groups or strata, and then a sample is selected within each group. Every sampling unit in the population is placed in one of the strata prior to the selection of the sample so that the sum of the strata is identical with the population. Random sampling method has certain merits as a technique of sampling.

In this Random sampling method, the investigator has greater control over the selection of the sample when compared with simple random sampling. In simple random sampling, although every group has a chance of being selected and included in the sample, there is every possibility, and sometimes it does not happen, that certain important groups are left unrepresentative. But, in Random sampling methods no important group is likely to be left out.

In Random sampling method, much depends on stratification process. The following precaution were taken while stratifying the population: the variables involved in the study were taken note of; care was taken to see that each stratum in the universe was large enough in size so that selection of items could be done on random basis; the strata formed were definite and clear cut; each stratum was free from influence of the other; and there was no overlapping.

COLLECTION OF DATA

The data required for the present study has been broadly divided into two categories via primary and secondary sources. The primary data were collected through an interview schedule. The secondary data were collected from articles, newspapers, magazines, published and unpublished records of Government organizations, etc.

The investigator herself met each and every school students who are studying in various high schools located at Pudukkottai District.

Before going to administer the research tool, the investigator revealed the purpose of the present study to the higher secondary school students and then asked them to give their responses for each and every item that are given in the questionnaire. The responses of the school students were recorded.

ANALISIS OF DATA

The collected data were coded and converted into percentage values. The data have been represented by way of tables and graphs. The data collected through the interview schedule have been processed.

The term analysis refers to the compilation of certain measures along with searching for pattern and relationship that among groups. For the present study the investigator collected the data from higher secondary school students using the tool developed to find out questionnaire of sample with the Awareness on the HIV Virus.

This involves computing measures of central tendency like Mean and the measures of variability like Standard deviation. The computed values are used to describe the property of the particular sample and description of data to manageable size.

STATISTICAL TECHNIQUES USED

Statistical Techniques serves the fundamental purpose of the description and inferential analysis. It is concerned with numerical description of a particular group observed. Any similarity to those outside the group cannot be taken for granted. The data describe one group only. Simple educational research involves descriptive statistics and provides valuable information about the nature of a particular group or class.

Data collected from tests have little meaning or significance until they have been classified or rearranged in a systematic way.

The following Statistical Techniques were used in this study.

1. Mean (M)
2. Standard Deviation (S.D.)
3. 't' – test for determine the significance of difference between means of two sub-groups.

ARITHMETIC MEAN

The mean of a distribution is commonly understood as the arithmetic average. It is computed by dividing the sum of all scores by the number of scores.

STANDARD DEVIATION (S.D)

Standard Deviation is the square-root of the mean of the squares of the deviations of all the items from the arithmetic mean. It is represented by the letter 'ó'.

CONCLUSION

In this chapter the methodology of the study was explained clearly. Each and every step was carefully planned and executed. The research strategies and the collection procedures have been explained. The next chapter deals with the analysis and interpretation of data.

Chapter - IV

Analysis and Interpretation of Data

INTRODUCTION

The research work in any field is said to be more meaningful and purposeful when the collected data is carefully processed and systematically analyzed. On the basis of this analysis and interpretation, the researcher will be able to arrive at meaningful conclusions and draw proper inferences. Analysis of data involves studying the tabulated material, in order to determine the inherent facts or meanings. It involves breaking down existing complex factors into simpler parts and putting the parts together in new arrangements for the purpose of interpretation.

ANALYSIS OF DATA

According to Carter, V. Good, A. S. Barr Douglas and E. Scates, "Analysis is a process, which enters research in one form or the other form in the very beginning. It may be fair to say in general that, research consists of two larger steps the gathering of data and the analysis of the data". In the process of analysis, no similarities, differences, trends and outstanding factors should go unnoticed and the data should be studied from as many angles as possible to find out the facts.

Interpretation is the application of deductive and inductive logic to the research process. Interpretation is purely subjective and there is scope for committing many errors at this stage. An adequate knowledge of the process and a capacity of critical thinking are very essential to safeguard against misinterpretation of collected data. In fact, analysis and interpretation of data determine the worth of the research.

TESTING OF HYPOTHESES

HYPOTHESIS: 1

There is no significant difference in the mean scores of awareness on the HIV virus among the higher secondary students in terms of their Gender.

TABLE: 1

The following table shows the mean scores, standard deviation and 't' value of awareness on the HIV virus among the higher secondary students in terms of their Gender.

Gender	N	M	SD	df	't' value	Level of Significance at 0.05
Male	123	163.76	11.82			
Female	127	164.18	11.63	248	0.28	Not Significant

INTERPRETATION:

Since the calculated 't' value **0.28** is smaller than the table value 1.96 at 0.05 level of significance. It is inferred that, there is no significant difference between the mean scores of awareness on the HIV virus among the higher secondary students in terms of their **Gender**.

RESULT:

Hence the null hypothesis is accepted.

HYPOTHESIS: 2

There is no significant difference in the mean scores of awareness on the HIV virus among the higher secondary students in terms of their Locality.

TABLE: 2

The following table shows the mean scores, standard deviation and 't' value of awareness on the HIV virus among the higher secondary students in terms of their Locality.

School Locality	N	M	SD	df	't' value	Level of Significance at 0.05
Rural	142	164.23	9.9*8			
Urban	108	163.64	13.69	248	0.56	Not Significant

INTERPRETATION :

Since the calculated 't' value **0.56** is smaller than the table value 1.96 at 0.05 level of significance. It is inferred that, there is no significant difference between the mean scores of awareness on the HIV virus among the higher secondary students in terms of their **Locality.**

RESULT :

Hence the null hypothesis is Accepted.

HYPOTHESIS : 3

There is no significant difference in the mean scores of awareness on the HIV virus among the higher secondary students in terms of their School management as Government and Aided.

TABLE: 3

The following table shows the mean scores, standard deviation and 't' value of awareness on the HIV virus among the higher secondary students in terms of their School management as Government and Aided.

School Type	N	M	SD	df	't' value	Level of Significance at 0.05
Government	80	165.64	8.60			
Aided	120	164.19	10.94	198	1.04	Not Significant

INTERPRETATION:

Since the calculated 't' value **1.04** is smaller than the table value 1.96 at 0.05 level of significance. It is inferred that, there is no significant difference between the mean scores of awareness on the HIV virus among the higher secondary students in terms of their **School management as Government and Aided**.

RESULT:

Hence the null hypothesis is accepted.

HYPOTHESIS: 4

There is no significant difference in the mean scores of awareness on the HIV virus among the higher secondary students in terms of their School management as Aided and Private.

TABLE: 4

The following table shows the mean scores, standard deviation and 't' value of awareness on the HIV virus among the higher secondary students in terms of their School management as Aided and Private.

School Type	N	M	SD	df	't' value	Level of Significance at 0.05
Aided	120	164.19	10.94			
Private	50	160.8	16.46	168	1.33	Not Significant

INTERPRETATION:

Since the calculated 't' value **1.33** is smaller than the table value 1.96 at 0.05 level of significance. It is inferred that, there is no significant difference between the mean scores of awareness on the HIV virus among the higher secondary students in terms of their **School management as Aided and Private**.

RESULT:

Hence the null hypothesis is accepted.

HYPOTHESIS: 5

There is no significant difference in the mean scores of awareness on the HIV virus among the higher secondary students in terms of their School management as Private and Government.

TABLE: 5

The following table shows the mean scores, standard deviation and 't' value of awareness on the HIV virus among the higher secondary students in terms of their School management as Private and Government.

School Type	N	M	SD	df	't' value	Level of Significance at 0.05
Private	50	160.8	16.46			
Government	80	165.64	8.60	128	1.92	Not Significant

INTERPRETATION:

Since the calculated 't' value **1.92** is smaller than the table value 1.96 at 0.05 level of significance. It is inferred that, there is no significant difference between the mean scores of awareness on the HIV virus among the higher secondary students in terms of their **School management as Private and Government**.

RESULT:

Hence the null hypothesis is accepted.

HYPOTHESIS: 6

There is no significant difference in the mean scores of awareness on the HIV virus among the higher secondary students in terms of their School nature as Boy's and Girl's.

TABLE: 6

The following table shows the mean scores, standard deviation and 't' value of awareness on the HIV virus among the higher secondary students in terms of their School nature as Boy's and Girl's..

School Nature	N	M	SD	df	't' value	Level of Significance at 0.05
Boy's	119	164.27	10.76			
Girl's	45	164.76	9.67	162	0.28	Not Significant

INTERPRETATION:

Since the calculated 't' value **0.28** is smaller than the table value 1.96 at 0.05 level of significance. It is inferred that, there is no significant difference between the mean scores of awareness on the HIV virus among the higher secondary students in terms of their **School nature as Boy's and Girl's**.

RESULT:

Hence the null hypothesis is **accepted.**

HYPOTHESIS: 7

There is no significant difference in the mean scores of awareness on the HIV virus among the higher secondary students in terms of their School nature as Girl's and Co-education.

TABLE: 7

The following table shows the mean scores, standard deviation and 't' value of awareness on the HIV virus among the higher secondary students in terms of their School nature as Girl's and Co-education.

School Nature	N	M	SD	df	't' value	Level of Significance at 0.05
Girl's	45	164.76	9.67			
Co-Education	86	163.16	13.82	129	0.77	Not Significant

INTERPRETATION:

Since the calculated 't' value **0.77** is smaller than the table value 1.96 at 0.05 level of significance. It is inferred that, there is no significant difference between the mean scores of awareness on the HIV virus among the higher secondary students in terms of their **School nature as Girl's and Co-education**.

RESULT:

Hence the null hypothesis is accepted.

HYPOTHESIS: 8

There is no significant difference in the mean scores of awareness on the HIV virus among the higher secondary students in terms of their School nature as Co-education and Boy's.

TABLE: 8

The following table shows the mean scores, standard deviation and 't' value of awareness on the HIV virus among the higher secondary students in terms of their School nature as Co-education and Boy's.

School Nature	N	M	SD	df	't' value	Level of Significance at 0.05
Co-Education	86	163.16	13.82			
Boy's	119	164.27	10.76	203	0.62	Not Significant

INTERPRETATION:

Since the calculated 't' value **0.62** is smaller than the table value 1.96 at 0.05 level of significance. It is inferred that, there is no significant difference between the mean scores of awareness on the HIV virus among the higher secondary students in terms of their **School nature as Co-education and Boy's**.

RESULT:

Hence the null hypothesis is Accepted.

HYPOTHESIS: 9

There is no significant difference in the mean scores of awareness on the HIV virus among the higher secondary students in terms of their Medium of study as Tamil and English.

TABLE: 9

The following table shows the mean scores, standard deviation and 't' value of awareness on the HIV virus among the higher secondary students in terms of their Medium of study as Tamil and English.

Medium of Study	N	M	SD	df	't' value	Level of Significance at 0.05
Tamil	170	164.56	10.32			
English	80	162.74	14.20	248	1.02	Not Significant

INTERPRETATION:

Since the calculated 't' value **1.02** is smaller than the table value 1.96 at 0.05 level of significance. It is inferred that, there is no significant difference between the mean scores of awareness on the HIV virus among the higher secondary students in terms of their **Medium of study as Tamil and English**.

RESULT:

Hence the null hypothesis is accepted.

HYPOTHESIS: 10

There is no significant difference in the mean scores of awareness on the HIV virus among the higher secondary students in terms of their Family nature as Nuclear and Joint type.

TABLE: 10

The following table shows the mean scores, standard deviation and 't' value of awareness on the HIV virus among the higher secondary students in terms of their Family nature as Nuclear and Joint type.

Family Nature	N	M	SD	df	't' value	Level of Significance at 0.05
Nuclear	112	161.91	13.53			
Joint	138	165.65	9.71	248	2.45	Significant

INTERPRETATION:

Since the calculated 't' value **2.45** is greater than the table value 1.96 at 0.05 level of significance. It is inferred that, there is significant difference between the mean scores of awareness on the HIV virus among the higher secondary students in terms of their **Family nature as Nuclear and Joint type**.

RESULT:

Hence the null hypothesis is rejected.

HYPOTHESIS: 11

There is no significant difference in the mean scores of awareness on the HIV virus among the higher secondary students in terms of their Parent education level as Schooling and Higher Education.

TABLE: 11

The following table shows the mean scores, standard deviation and 't' value of awareness on the HIV virus among the higher secondary students in terms of their Parent education level as Schooling and Higher Education.

Parent Education Qualification	N	M	SD	df	't' value	Level of Significance at 0.05
Schooling	155	164.53	12.21			
Higher Education	95	163.07	10.82	248	0.98	Not Significant

INTERPRETATION:

Since the calculated 't' value **0.98** is smaller than the table value 1.96 at 0.05 level of significance. It is inferred that, there is no significant difference between the mean scores of awareness on the HIV virus among the higher secondary students in terms of their **Parent education level as Schooling and Higher Education**.

RESULT:

Hence the null hypothesis is accepted.

HYPOTHESIS: 12

There is no significant difference in the mean scores of awareness on the HIV virus among the higher secondary students in terms of their Parent occupation as Government and Private Job.

TABLE: 12

The following table shows the mean scores, standard deviation and 't' value of awareness on the HIV virus among the higher secondary students in terms of their Parent occupation as Government and Private Job.

Parents Occupation	N	M	SD	df	't' value	Level of Significance at 0.05
Government Job	83	164.90	11.03			
Non-Government Job	167	163.52	12.03	248	0.90	Not Significant

INTERPRETATION:

Since the calculated 't' value **0.90** is smaller than the table value 1.96 at 0.05 level of significance. It is inferred that, there is no significant difference between the mean scores of awareness on the HIV virus among the higher secondary students in terms of their **Parent occupation as Government and Private Job**.

RESULT:

Hence the null hypothesis is accepted.

CONCLUSION

In this chapter the collections of data were tabulated, analyzed and interpreted. The next chapter deals with the summary findings and conclusion of the investigation.

Chapter - V

Findings and Conclusion

INTRODUCTION

Knowledge is power and half-knowledge is always dangerous. All the members of a society irrespective of their proper health care procedures in general and preventive steps for HIV Virus in particular. Knowledge is the best capital for investment since it always brings one return and not losses. Hence, better knowledge leads to better way of life especially among the higher secondary school students.

Today all the developing nations have so many social problems and right now HIV is &e one of the worst and the most challenging of the problems which confronts the administrators and policy makers of these countries. Moreover, the AIDS epidemic is threatening the very fabric of existence of young people of our mankind. Hence, if the times do have a better and correct knowledge of HIV then they can wage war against the AIDS epidemic and work for an HIV free tomorrow and lead a healthy life

STATEMENT OF THE PROBLEM

The purpose of the study is entitled as *Awareness on the HIV Virus among the Higher Secondary Students in Pudukkottai District".*

OBJECTIVES OF THE STUDY

The following are the objectives constructed for the study

1. To find the significant difference in the mean scores of awareness on the HIV virus among the higher secondary students in terms of their **Gender**.
2. To find the significant difference in the mean scores of awareness on the HIV virus among the higher secondary students in terms of their **Locality**.
3. To find the significant difference in the mean scores of awareness on the HIV virus among the higher secondary students in terms of their **School management as Government and Aided**.
4. To find the significant difference in the mean scores of awareness on the HIV virus among the higher secondary students in terms of their **School management as Aided and Private**.
5. There is no significant difference in the mean scores of awareness on the HIV virus among the higher secondary students in terms of their **School management as Private and Government**.
6. To find the significant difference in the mean scores of awareness on the HIV virus among the higher secondary students in terms of their **School nature as Boy's and Girl's**.
7. To find the significant difference in the mean scores of awareness on the HIV virus among the higher secondary students in terms of their **School nature as Girl's and Co-education**.
8. There is no significant difference in the mean scores of awareness on the HIV virus among the higher secondary students in terms of their **School nature as Co-education and Boy's.**
9. To find the significant difference in the mean scores of awareness on the HIV virus among the higher secondary students in terms of their **Medium of study as Tamil and English.**
10. To find the significant difference in the mean scores of awareness on the HIV virus among the higher secondary students in terms of their **Family nature as Nuclear and Joint type**.
11. To find the significant difference in the mean scores of awareness on the HIV virus among the higher secondary students in terms of their **Parent education level as Schooling and Higher Education**.
12. To find the significant difference in the mean scores of awareness on the HIV virus among the higher secondary students in terms of their **Parent occupation as Government and Private Job**

HYPOTHESES OF THE STUDY

The following are the hypotheses constructed for the study;

1. There is no significant difference in the mean scores of awareness on the HIV virus among the higher secondary students in terms of their **Gender**.
2. There is no significant difference in the mean scores of awareness on the HIV virus among the higher secondary students in terms of their **Locality**.
3. There is no significant difference in the mean scores of awareness on the HIV virus among the higher secondary students in terms of their **School management as Government and Aided**.
4. There is no significant difference in the mean scores of awareness on the HIV virus among the higher secondary students in terms of their **School management as Aided and Private**.
5. There is no significant difference in the mean scores of awareness on the HIV virus among the higher secondary students in terms of their **School management as Private and Government**.
6. There is no significant difference in the mean scores of awareness on the HIV virus among the higher secondary students in terms of their **School nature as Boy's and Girl's**.
7. There is no significant difference in the mean scores of awareness on the HIV virus among the higher secondary students in terms of their **School nature as Girl's and Co-education**.
8. There is no significant difference in the mean scores of awareness on the HIV virus among the higher secondary students in terms of their **School nature as Co-education and Boy's.**
9. There is no significant difference in the mean scores of awareness on the HIV virus among the higher secondary students in terms of their **Medium of study as Tamil and English.**
10. There is no significant difference in the mean scores of awareness on the HIV virus among the higher secondary students in terms of their **Family nature as Nuclear and Joint type**.
11. There is no significant difference in the mean scores of awareness on the HIV virus among the higher secondary students in terms of their **Parent education level as Schooling and Higher Education**.
12. There is no significant difference in the mean scores of awareness on the HIV virus among the higher secondary students in terms of their **Parent occupation as Government and Private Job**

FINDINGS OF THE RESEARCH

The findings of the study are as follows

1. There is no significant difference between the mean scores of awareness on the HIV virus among the higher secondary students in terms of their **Gender**.
2. There is no significant difference between the mean scores of awareness on the HIV virus among the higher secondary students in terms of their **Locality.**
3. There is no significant difference between the mean scores of awareness on the HIV virus among the higher secondary students in terms of their **School management as Government and Aided**.
4. There is no significant difference between the mean scores of awareness on the HIV virus among the higher secondary students in terms of their **School management as Aided and Private**.
5. There is no significant difference between the mean scores of awareness on the HIV virus among the higher secondary students in terms of their **School management as Private and Government**.
6. There is no significant difference between the mean scores of awareness on the HIV virus among the higher secondary students in terms of their **School nature as Boy's and Girl's**.
7. There is no significant difference between the mean scores of awareness on the HIV virus among the higher secondary students in terms of their **School nature as Girl's and Co-education**.
8. There is no significant difference between the mean scores of awareness on the HIV virus among the higher secondary students in terms of their **School nature as Co-education and Boy's**.
9. There is no significant difference between the mean scores of awareness on the HIV virus among the higher secondary students in terms of their **Medium of study as Tamil and English**.
10. There is significant difference between the mean scores of awareness on the HIV virus among the higher secondary students in terms of their **Family nature as Nuclear and Joint type**. It was because of the Family environment.
11. There is no significant difference between the mean scores of awareness on the HIV virus among the higher secondary students in terms of their **Parent education level as Schooling and Higher Education**.

12. There is no significant difference between the mean scores of awareness on the HIV virus among the higher secondary students in terms of their **Parent occupation as Government and Private Job**.

SUGGESTIONS FOR THE FURTHER RESEARCH

The following studies in awareness on HIV Virus may be undertaken for further research.

1. A comparative study of awareness on HIV Virus among secondary and higher secondary school students.
2. A study of awareness on HIV Virus among high school students.
3. A comparative study of awareness on HIV/AIDS education among secondary school students.
4. A comparative study of awareness on HIV/AIDS education among high secondary school students.

RECOMMENDATIONS OF THE STUDY

In view of the findings of this survey, I wish to make the following recommendations:

1. School HIV education programme should be reinforced with well designed with messages targeted at sensitizing secondary school students in the potential risks of HIV infection at their age.
2. Voluntary Counseling and Testing (VCT) services should be extended or reinforced in all secondary schools.
3. Similar risk behavioral surveys should be carried out among out of- school adolescents.
4. HIV awareness Education should be planned, executed and evaluated in the context of Indian Values and culture.
5. Teacher's awareness on HIV/AIDS and their role in providing HIV awareness in schools should be evaluated in the light of school programmes offered to the students.
6. Effective policies, proper investment in awareness on HIV would create healthy environment.

CONCLUSION

Formulation of strategies and the present research on HIV virus for the higher secondary students in future is one of the objectives of this research work. The following have emerged as a result of the present study. Counseling services for suspected cases of the HIV awareness should be expanded to increase their reach to all those who need them and that too, in time.

Adequate awareness testing facilities should be made available for the higher secondary students. in this the findings examines there is no significant difference between the mean scores of awareness on the HIV virus among the higher secondary students in terms of their Gender, Locality, School management as Government and Aided, School management as Aided and Private, School management as Private and Government, School nature as Boy's and Girl's, School nature as Girl's and Co-education, School nature as Co-education and Boy's, Medium of study as Tamil and English, Parent education level as Schooling and Higher Education, Parent occupation as Government and Private Job. But there is significant difference founded in the mean scores of awareness on the HIV virus among the higher secondary students in terms of their Family nature as Nuclear and Joint type. It was because of the Family environment.

Bibliography

1. Akande, A. (2014). AIDS-related beliefs and behaviours of students: Evidence from two countries (Zimbabwe and Nigeria). *International Journal of Adolescence and Youth.* 4(3/4), 285-303.

2. Bandawe, C.R. & Foster, D. AIDS-related beliefs, attitudes and intentions among Malawian students in three secondary schools. AIDS Care, 8(2), 223-232.

3. Carael, M., Clelard, J. Deheneffe, J.C., Ferry, B. & Ingham, R. Sexual behaviour in developing countries: Implications for HIV control, 9, 1171- 1175.

4. Chitsulo, L. *AIDS cases surveillance update: Half year report, 1996.* Lilongwe: Ministry of Health and Population, National AIDS Control Programme.

5. Elkind, D. Egocentrim redux. Development Review, 5, 218-226.

6. Flisher, A.J., Ziervogel, C.F., Chalton, D.O., Leger, P.H. & Robertson, B.A. Risk-taking behaviour of Cape Peninsula high school students: Part VIII- Behaviour. *South African Medical Journal,* 83, 495-497.

7. Kalichman, S.C. Understanding AIDS: A guide for mental health professionals. Washington, D.C: American Psychological Association.

8. Kapiga, S.H., Nachtigal, G. & Hunter, D.J. Knowledge of Aids among secondary school pupils in Bugamoyo and Dar-Es-Salaam, Tanzania. AIDS, 5(3), 325-328.

9. Levine, C. Commentary: AIDS prevention and education: Reframing the message. AIDS Education and Prevention, 3(2), 147-163.

10. Logoe, W.L. Klepp, K.I. & Skutle, A. Sexual debut and predictors among secondary school students in Arusha, Tanzania. AIDS Care, 8(4), 443-452.

11. MacLaclan, M. Chimombo, M. & Mpemba, N. AIDS education for youth through active learning: A school-based approach for Malawi. *International Journal of Educational Development*, 17(1), 41-50.

12. Maluwa-Banda, D.W. *Adolescent sexuality and HIV/AIDS in Malawi: Knowledge, attitudes and bevaviour of secondary school students.* Unpublished Ph.D. Thesis: University of Alberta, Canada.

13. NACP. *AIDS cases surveillance report.* Lilongwe: NACP. National Control Programme (NACP) AIDS cases surveillance report. Lilongwe: NACP.

14. Pilllai, V.K., Barton, T. & Benefo, K. Sexual activities among junior secondary school girls in Zambia, *Journal of Biosocial Science*, 29(3) 297- 301.

15. Puja, G.K. & Kassimoto, T. Girls in education ad pregnancy at school. In Z.T. Masabo & R. Liljestrom (Eds), *Chelewa, chelewa: The dilemma of teenage girls* (pp. 54-75). Stockholm: Scandivavian Institute of African Studies.

16. Puttallo, A.L.S., Malonza, M., Kimani, G.G., Muthee, A. Otieno, P.A.O., Odhiambo.

17. K., Moses, S & Plummer, F.A. Survey of knowledge, behaviour and attitudes relating to HIV infection and AIDS among Kenyan secondary school students. AIDS Care, 6(2), 173-181.

18. Schopper, D. Research on AIDS interventions in helping countries: State of art. *Social Science and Medicine*, 30, 1265-1272.

19. Stout, J.W. & Rivara, F.P. Schools and sex education. Does it work? Pediatrics, 83, 375-379.

20. The Strategic Planning Unit *Malawi National HIV/AIDS Strategic Framework 2000-2004*. Lilongwe: Ministry of Health and Population, National AIDS Control Programme.

21. UNAIDS (*Emerging issues and challenges for women, young people and HIV/AIDS (Second Edition)*. Geneva: Author (Published on internet at Wilson, D. & Lavelle, S. Psychosocial predictors of intended condom use among Zimbabwean adolescents. *Health Education Research: Theory & Practice*, 7(1), 55-68.